ABSOLUTISM AND ITS CONSEQUENTIALIST CRITICS

ABSOLUTISM AND ITS CONSEQUENTIALIST CRITICS

Edited by
Joram Graf Haber

Rowman & Littlefield Publishers, Inc.

ROWMAN & LITTLEFIELD PUBLISHERS, INC.

Published in the United States of America
by Rowman & Littlefield Publishers, Inc.
4720 Boston Way, Lanham, Maryland 20706

Library of Congress Cataloging-in-Publication Data

Absolutism and its consequentialist critics / [edited] by Joram Graf Haber.
p. cm.
Includes bibliographical references.
1. Ethical absolutism. 2. Consequentialism (Ethics) I. Haber, Joram Graf.
BJ1031.A27 1993 171—dc20 93–10218 CIP

ISBN 0–8476–7839–3 (cloth : alk. paper)
ISBN 0–8476–7840–7 (paper : alk. paper)

Printed in the United States of America

∞™ The paper used in this publication meets the minimum requirements of American National Standard for Information Sciences—Permanence of Paper for Printed Library Materials, ANSI Z39.48–1984.

For Joshua

Contents

Introduction

I

Moral absolutism is a theory ordinarily regarded as opposed to consequentialism.[1] By "consequentialism" is meant the theory according to which the rightness of an action is uniquely determined by the value of the consequences resulting therefrom.[2] By "moral absolutism" is meant the theory according to which there are certain kinds of actions that are absolutely wrong; actions that could never be right whatever the consequences. So construed, absolutism and consequentialism are rivals of each other; for if the morality of conduct is *uniquely* determined by the value of the consequences resulting therefrom, then there cannot be conduct that is absolutely wrong, or wrong no matter what the consequences.[3]

---

[1] Moral absolutism is also regarded as a theory opposed to "ethical relativism." In the sense in which it is opposed to the latter, it is a theory according to which there are universal truths transcending provincial conceptions of right and wrong.

[2] More specifically, consequentialism is the theory according to which the rightness of an action is wholly determined by the value of its consequences as compared with the values of the consequences of competing ways of acting.

[3] I should add that absolutism and consequentialism need not be construed as rival moral theories. The principle that it is always wrong to act in a manner that does not maximize consequences is a species of absolutism, but not one that rivals moral absolutism. There is also a sense in which every moralist (including the consequentialist) is an absolutist since it cannot be denied that every instance of an immoral action-type is itself immoral. However, these versions of absolutism are excluded since the concern of this volume is with the kinds of absolutism that conflict with consequentialism.

I should also add that the manner in which the two theories conflict is not exactly clear. Consequentialism, as ordinarily understood, is the theory according to which the rightness of an act is wholly determined by the value of its consequences as compared with the consequences of alternative ways of acting. Absolutism does not merely say that other factors are also relevant; it says that they are relevant in

The appeal of absolutism lies in the value of the convictions we intuitively hold and our obstinate unwillingness to give them up. Thus, the absolutist finds consequentialism unacceptable because, in principle at least, its acceptance forces us to abandon our most sacred intuitions. This is because if consequences alone uniquely determine right and wrong conduct, then anything in principle is morally permissible, even the most chilling of immoral conduct.

Consider, for instance, the torturing of children. On consequentialist grounds, it is permissible to torture a child to prevent the deaths of more numerous people. Consider as well the judicial execution of the innocent. On consequentialist grounds, it is permissible to execute the innocent where doing so serves as a deterrent to crime. However, since actions such as these violate our most cherished beliefs about what we may not do, absolutists insist that consequentialism is false.

Several points are in order here. First, torturing children and executing the innocent are only two of the action-types typically regarded by absolutists as forbidden. Traditionally, the list has included lying, adultery, sodomy, etc.[4] Strictly speaking, however, absolutism is a purely formal theory—one is absolutist who subscribes to a principle of the form "For some values of ϕ (where ϕ ranges over an action-type), in no situation could it be right to ϕ." Thus, while torturing children and executing innocents are the kinds of actions characteristically put forward as absolutely forbidden, one can be absolutist about any kind of action.

A second point is that one need not be an absolutist to deny the permissibility of the action-types in question—*deontologists* deny their permissibility as do a host of theorists from other traditions. What distinguishes the absolutist from the (nonabsolutist) deontologist, however, is not the position on the prohibitions in question, but the considerations put forward as needed to override them. Typically, for instance, the deontologist will deny that it is permissible to execute

---

such a way that some kinds of acts would be wrong no matter what the comparison of consequences was like. So construed, consequentialism and absolutism are *contraries* of each other. However, as Anscombe understands "consequentialism," it and absolutism are *contradictories* of each other. She says that if one rejects absolutism and allows that any kind of action could be made permissible if the consequences of not performing it are desperate enough, then it "is of no importance" whether one holds that the rightness of actions is determined in whole or in part by comparative facts about the value of their consequences (Elizabeth Anscombe, "Modern Moral Philosophy," *Philosophy* 33 (1958), pp. 1–10, @ p. 9n).

But however we interpret absolutism, that is, as contraries or contradictories, it is clear that it does not depend on consequentialism for its coherence and unity. I mention this because a reviewer of this text falsely remarked that absolutism lacks coherent unity.

[4] Jewish law puts idolatry on its list of actions Jews are absolutely prohibited to do (Sanhedrin, 74).

the innocent even where doing so is cost-effective. What is admitted, however, is that if the consequences of not doing so are desperate enough, then killing the innocent is morally permissible. The absolutist, by contrast, denies that there is any situation desperate enough to override the prohibited conduct. Thus, it is not as if absolutists and deontologists disagree over whether it is permissible to torture young children (or execute the innocent); what they disagree about is whether anything can override the prohibited conduct.

Similarly, it would be misleading to suggest that absolutists and *consequentialists* disagree over whether it is permissible to torture young children. Consequentialists hardly suggest that such conduct is permissible. In fact, they for the most part share the intuitions held by absolutists and deontologists alike. However, not unlike the deontologist, the consequentialist contends that if the consequences of not torturing children are desperate enough (e.g., a terrorist will detonate a bomb in a crowded arena unless you torture an innocent child), then torturing a child is morally permissible. Indeed, for the consequentialist, it would be wrong *not* to torture the child in the situation described. By contrast, the absolutist contends that no situation is desperate enough to override the forbidden conduct, not even the circumstances in the aforementioned case.

In the light of the above, it is possible to further refine our understanding of absolutism. We can call absolutist one who denies that there is a possible world in which ϕing is permissible for whatever value of ϕ is at issue. In essence, this is what distinguishes the absolutist on the one hand from the deontologist and consequentialist on the other. For each of the latter contends that there is a possible world in which ϕing is permissible with the difference between the latter being that the deontologist sees right and wrong as not wholly determined by the value of the consequences, while the consequentialist sees right and wrong as exactly so determined.

II

On the above interpretation of moral absolutism, it turns out that few philosophers merit the appellation. Kant is an obvious exception. In his well-known essay "On a Supposed Right to Lie from Altruistic Motives" (Selection I), Kant argues against the permissibility of lying even to a would-be murderer inquiring about his chosen victim's whereabouts. He says that "to be truthful (honest) in all deliberations . . . is a sacred and absolutely commanding decree of reason, limited by no expediency."[5] Taking the last clause literally, Kant is absolutist,

[5] See p. 17 this volume.

for he would presumably argue against lying under any conditions. And it would be *this* position that would make him absolutist; for the test is not whether for some value of ϕ ϕing is forbidden, it is whether ϕing is forbidden in every situation. As Scheffler puts it in speaking of torture:

> in order to be an absolutist . . . one must hold that it would be impermissible to torture one child to death even if that were the only way to prevent, say, everyone else in the world's being tortured to death.[6]

Germain Grisez and Russell Shaw are philosophers whom it is also safe to call absolutist. In "Persons, Means, and Ends" (Selection II), they argue that basic moral goods are incommensurable—they cannot be traded off one against the other. This being so, one cannot, say, lie to prevent a murder from taking place without implying that truth-telling and life-saving *can* be so measured. But if there is no measure by which competing goods can be compared, and we cannot trade off one good for another, then, for whatever value of ϕ is at stake, there is no good more than that which would constitute a reason to override it. Otherwise put, there is nothing that could make it right to ϕ.[7]

But while Kant and Grisez and Shaw can safely be called absolutists, there are other philosophers who cannot be so called though they fancy themselves to be friends of the thesis. Consider, for instance, Elizabeth Anscombe, whom many regard as a champion of absolutism. In her "War and Murder" (Selection III), Anscombe takes pains to argue that it is absolutely wrong to intentionally kill an innocent human being. However, after pointing out how it is possible that obedience to absolute moral prohibitions can have dire consequences, she is quick to point out that there is a limit to how dire they can be. Writing for her fellow Catholics, Anscombe suggests that it will never happen that doing something absolutely forbidden will be the only way to save the Church from extinction. And the reason she gives is her "faith in the divine promises that make us believe that the Church cannot fail."[8] But in speaking of a "limit" to how dreadful the consequences of not performing a forbidden action can be, Anscombe is implying that the limit is contingent and not logically impossible. (Is there no state of affairs so dreadful that it is logically impossible for God to bring it about?) But if that is so, then Anscombe is admitting a possible world in which killing is permissible if the consequences of not doing so are desperate enough.[9]

---

[6] Samuel Scheffler, *The Rejection of Consequentialism* (Oxford: Clarendon Press, 1988), p. 86.

[7] But see p. 25 where Grisez and Shaw seem to defend a different position.

[8] See p. 40 this volume.

[9] I'm not entirely comfortable with this. In the introduction to her collected

Now it would be tempting to say that Anscombe is not an absolutist were it not for the fact that she is widely regarded as a champion of the thesis and there are other philosophers who take similar positions. Take Alan Donagan for instance (Selection IV). After arguing that Hebrew-Christian morality is largely absolutist and that the precepts within it are rationally defensible, Donagan writes:

> In laying down that its precepts are to be observed no matter what the consequences, traditional morality does not imply that they are to be observed, let us say, if the consequences should be the death of everybody on earth.[10]

Clearly, Donagan is allowing a point at which the prohibitions of morality break down implying that there is a possible world in which moral prohibitions are not absolutely forbidden after all. At the same time he is quick to point out that "strict adherence to traditional common morality will never, except by unforeseeable accident, have calamitous consequences. . . ."

Apparently, both Donagan and Anscombe are saying that it can never be right to ϕ with certain exceptions which, for one reason or another, do not count. For Anscombe, the relevant exception is the failure of the Catholic Church which she discounts as a matter of faith. For Donagan, the relevant exception is some calamitous event which he discounts since we could never be sure that adherence to morality will lead to a calamity.[11] That this latter is the case is evidenced by Donagan's thinking that "it is probable that much of what is done on the ground of such escape clauses will be mistaken . . . The examples commonly offered in support of such escape clauses . . . impute to agents a knowledge they cannot possess."[12] Compare Donagan on this score to Peter Geach (Selection V) who argues that knowledge of God is needed to see that we must not do evil so that good may come of it, and the reason he gives is that God alone has the foresight to see that one ought not to make an exception to absolute moral prohibitions.

Generalizing from these cases, we can say that Anscombe, Donagan,

---

philosophical papers, Anscombe remarks that "War and Murder" was expressly written for a Catholic audience and to that end relied upon a common set of religious beliefs. (See *The Collected Works of G. E. M. Anscombe*, Vol. III, Minneapolis: University of Minnesota Press, 1981.) This being so, it may be unfair to interpret the Anscombe of "War and Murder" as offering an analysis of moral absolutism proper. Still, she does admit to a possible world in which murder is permissible.

[10] See p. 59 this volume.

[11] To be a strong absolutist, Donagan would have to say that we could never be sure that calamities will never happen, not that we can never predict with certainty.

[12] See p. 60 this volume.

and Geach are committed to the view according to which for some values of ϕ, it could never be right to ϕ except in some cases which, for one reason or another, do not count. If we call this attenuated version of absolutism "weak absolutism" (despite the infelicity of the term) and call "strong absolutism" the view previously referred to as absolutism *simpliciter*, then Anscombe, Donagan, and Geach are absolutists notwithstanding the problems cited.

Furthermore, not only are Anscombe, Donagan, and Geach absolutists (in the weak sense of the term), but so are Charles Fried and Bernard Williams. After defending what *he* calls absolutism (Selection VI), Fried observes:

> We can imagine extreme cases where killing an innocent person may save a whole nation. In such cases it seems fanatical to maintain the absoluteness of the judgment, to do right even if the heavens will in fact fall. And so the catastrophic may cause the absoluteness of right and wrong to yield. . . .[13]

And again:

> The concept of the catastrophic is a distinct concept just because it identifies the extreme situations in which the usual categories of judgments (including the category of right and wrong) no longer apply.[14]

In passages like these, Fried shows himself an advocate of "weak absolutism" by saying that catastrophic cases produce conceptual anarchy. As Fried says later on,

> I do not know . . . whether I would be willing to kill an innocent person to save the whole of humanity from excruciating suffering and death. There are boundaries to each of these concepts themselves, and the concepts themselves often become blurred, indeterminate, subject to judgments of prudence at those boundaries.[15]

Thus, Fried is committed to the view that "In no situation could it be right to ϕ" except when a catastrophe occurs, but that doesn't count since in that situation the concepts of right and wrong no longer apply. Bernard Williams suggests though does not exactly endorse a similar view when he intimates that in extreme situations (when the consequences of not ϕing would be disastrous), "it cannot matter any more what happens."[16]

---

[13] See p. 76 this volume.

[14] Ibid.

[15] Charles Fried, *Right and Wrong* (Cambridge, Mass.: Harvard University Press, 1978), p. 31.

[16] See p. 100 this volume.

There is, then, both a strong and a weak version of absolutism according to which for some values of ϕ, with some modifications, it is never right to ϕ whatever the consequences. These positions should not be confused with the view according to which "For some values of ϕ, it is never right to even think about performing them." Anscombe holds this view when, in a well-known passage, she remarks that "If someone really thinks, *in advance*, that it is open to question whether such an action as procuring the judicial execution of the innocent should be quite excluded from consideration—I do not want to argue with him; he shows a corrupt mind."[17] So, too, Bernard Williams intimates this position when he suggests that "It could be a feature of a man's moral outlook that he regarded certain courses of action as unthinkable, in the sense that he would not entertain the idea of doing them. . . ."[18]

Still another form of absolutism that R. G. Frey identifies (Selection VIII) and which he attributes to James Cargile is the view that there are some values of ϕ which, even if there are instances that are not immoral, are nonetheless such that a person of good character could not bring himself to do. In connection with this, Frey mentions torturing a baby to save twenty people from dying, and amputating (with a hacksaw and no anesthesia) the gangrenous leg of a dying person in order to save that person's life. An absolutist of this variety holds that no one of good character can perform such acts and still be considered good. Against this view, Frey argues that if one were to perform these actions for the right reasons (to save twenty people in the one case, the dying man in the other), then that motive alone would enable us to call the person who performed them good. Otherwise put, a person is not bad if what motivates that person is the welfare of others and so we cannot say that there are some acts a good person cannot bring himself to do.

III

Thus far, we have defined absolutism, identified various versions of it, but have said nothing about its theoretical underpinnings and little about what consequentialists think are its weaknesses. With respect to the former, Kant grounded absolutism in reason's capacity to give itself the moral law. He argued that respect for the moral law prohibits us from acting from subjective principles that one cannot will as universal laws. Anscombe grounds absolutism in Scripture as does

---

[17] Anscombe, "Modern Moral Philosophy," *Philosophy* 23 (January 1957), pp. 16–17.

[18] See p. 100 this volume.

Geach, at least in part. (Geach does not think that we need God to know what it is forbidden to do, though we do need God to have knowledge of the absolute prohibitiveness of the prohibitions we identify.)

Fried grounds absolutism in deontological norms. He argues that if what we choose has value, then the process of choice must be such that what comes out of it has value. For Fried, then, the concepts of right and wrong which are predicated on actions (as opposed to consequences of actions) have overriding moral status because they establish our position as freely choosing beings. Donagan grounds absolutism in a Kantian analysis of what it means to have respect for persons while Williams grounds it in the value of personal integrity. Finally, Stuart Hampshire (Selection IX) grounds absolutism in virtue, that is, in what it means to live a desirable life, while Alan Gewirth in Selection X grounds it in what he calls the Principle of Generic Consistency, a principle requiring of every agent that she respect her recipients' necessary conditions of action.

With respect to its critics, consequentialists typically argue that absolutism is irrational—it commits us to the view that we should produce less good than we are in a position to produce and prevent less evil than we are in a position to prevent. Often, the controversy centers around hypothetical cases (such as the ones discussed by Philippa Foot in Selection XI) where an agent is faced with performing an absolutely forbidden action or allowing a disastrous state of affairs to obtain.[19] In cases like "the fat man in the cave,"[20] for example, the consequentialist argues (against the absolutist) that it is simply irrational not to kill him if the alternative is to allow the others to perish. (For a different view on a related theme, see Anscombe's "Who Is Wronged?"—Selection XII.)

Kai Nielsen (Selection XIII), for one, takes issue with the absolutist's intuition that it is never permissible to kill an innocent person. Speaking of the "fat man in the cave," Nielsen contends that it is no less counter-intuitive to kill the fat man than it is not to, and that this implies there is a possible world in which killing is permissible. (He also makes the point that if this is so, then *thinking* of killing the fat man is hardly indicative of a corrupt mind.) Having argued, then, that refusing to kill the fat man is at least as problematic as not killing him,

[19] Anscombe, for one, has denounced the use of "fantastic" examples in moral philosophy. See Anscombe, "Does Oxford Moral Philosophy Corrupt the Youth?" *The Listener* 57 (1957), p. 267.

[20] A "fat" man leading a group of potholers out of a cave is stuck in its mouth. In a very short time, the tide will be upon them and they will all drown unless the man is promptly unstuck. The potholers have with them a stick of dynamite and can blast him out. The dilemma is this: either they blast out the innocent man or they all drown.

Nielsen makes two other points that are characteristic of consequentialist critics. The first is that consequentialists typically share the same intuitions as absolutists while insisting that they can account for them in a way that absolutists cannot. (In speaking of "the magistrate and the threatening mob,"[21] for instance, Nielsen is skeptical that consequentialism requires that the magistrate execute the innocent derelict.) The second point is that there is nothing sacred about our moral intuitions. If, for instance, we have the intuition that it is always wrong to kill but the intuition generates problematic counterexamples, then that is a reason to give up our intuition. Conservativism for conservatism's sake is an irrational dogma.

Cases like the fat man in the cave and the magistrate and the threatening mob are favorites of consequentialists since they are devised in such a way that the agent must choose between ϕing (acting in a way that is absolutely forbidden) and not ϕing while allowing ψ (a foreseen and bad though unintended outcome). The claim here is that where the alternative to ϕing is letting ψ, it is preposterous not to ϕ. Absolutists, on the other hand, insist that there is a morally relevant difference between ϕing on the one hand and letting ψ on the other; between what one does and what one allows. As absolutists see it, it is the *intent* to ϕ that is primarily responsible for the wrongness of ϕing. Conversely, when one refuses to ϕ while allowing ψ, the agent is not responsible for letting ψ no matter how bad an outcome ψ may be. For this reason, the absolutist insists that there is a morally relevant difference between killing the fat man and letting the potholers die; between lynching the derelict and letting the mob wreak its havoc.

The distinction between ϕing and letting ψ has traditionally led absolutists to embrace the doctrine of double effect (D.D.E.). This doctrine allows for a difference between what an agent intends and what an agent foresees though does not intend. This doctrine, discussed in detail by Philippa Foot, traditionally tells us that we may never intend bad so that good may come of it, but we may do what is not bad in itself notwithstanding the bad side effect, if the good we seek is greater than the bad.[22]

It is easy to see why the D.D.E. appeals to absolutists. Given the many cases where an act has both good and bad consequences, the

---

[21] An uncontrollable mob threatens to take bloody revenge on a provincial town unless a culprit is produced for a crime that has been committed. The magistrate does not know who the culprit is but is aware of a derelict who, though innocent, could be framed and promptly executed so as to satisfy the mob's thirst. The dilemma is this: either frame the derelict or risk the wrath of the threatening mob.

[22] More specifically, an act that has both good and bad foreseen consequences is permissible provided: (1) the act itself is not impermissible; (2) the good and not the bad consequences are intended; (3) the bad consequences are not the means to the good; and (4) the good consequences are commensurate with the bad.

doctrine preserves the absolute prohibitiveness of the act while at the same time provides that we may perform those acts having forseeably bad effects provided we don't intend the bad effects that ensue. Accordingly, the doctrine tells us what we may not do and at the same time tells us what we may do.

Typically, one finds absolutists employing the D.D.E. to resolve the so-called obstetrical dilemmas. The doctrine is used, for example, to explain why excising the fatally cancerous uterus of a pregnant woman is morally permissible while the performing of an abortion is not even though carrying of the pregnancy to term will be fatal to the mother. Under the terms of the doctrine, a hysterectomy turns out to be a case of indirect causation of death, while the loss of the fetus is a foreseen but unintended consequence of the surgery. This is not the case, however, for the standard abortion procedure, even when used to save a woman's life. In that case, the death of the fetus is understood to be intended and thus its causation prohibited. Indeed, direct causation of fetal death is prohibited even if both the woman and the fetus will otherwise die. (Traditional casuists were fond of saying "Better two deaths than one murder.") A similar analysis is employed in the so-called craniotomy cases discussed by Jonathan Bennett at the outset of his essay (Selection XIV).

Of course, consequentialists hardly think kindly of the D.D.E. convinced as they are that consequences alone determine right conduct. Thus, one of the objectives that Bennett has is to show that the difference between ϕing and letting ψ cannot be made the way absolutists think it can. After examining several possible interpretations of the ϕing/letting ψ distinction, Bennett concludes that one who accepts it either fails to see what it involves or is dogmatically committed to obeying a higher authority. (But see Anscombe again, Selection XV, for another point of view.) In a similar vein, James Rachels (Selection XVI) argues against the ϕing/letting ψ distinction and goes even further in concluding that absolutists suffer not only from "a muddled intellect" but from "an unfeeling heart" as well.

Aside from the craniotomy cases, absolutists and consequentialists often lock horns on the question of what actions are permissible in times of war. In her influential paper "Mr. Truman's Degree,"[23] Anscombe takes Truman to task for bombing Japan in an effort to bring the war to an end. There, she arduously defends the D.D.E. and argues that Truman behaved unethically in directly intending to kill innocent persons notwithstanding the good that was to come of it. And the reason she gives is that the intentional killing of noncombatants is absolutely prohibited and is precluded by the D.D.E.

---

[23] Elizabeth Anscombe, *The Collected Philosophical Papers of G. E. M. Anscombe*, Vol. III (Minneapolis: University of Minnesota Press, 1981), pp. 62–71.

Thomas Nagel's "War and Massacre" (Selection XVII), R. B. Brandt's "Utilitarianism and the Rules of War" (Selection XVIII), and R. M. Hare's "Rules of War and Moral Reasoning" (Selection XIX) form a trilogy of readings wherein consequentialists Brandt and Hare argue against Nagel's absolutism. Here, one sees the absolutist and the consequentialist debate the moral implications of atomic and saturation bombings as well as the ethical implications of unintentionally but foreseeably killing noncombatants in the process of targeting munitions supplies for destruction (what the United States referred to euphemistically as "collateral damage" during its air raids on Iraq). Brandt, for instance, argues that the rules of war that are morally justifiable are consequentialist ones since they are just those rules that a rational, impartial spectator would choose to put oneself under a contract to obey. Nagel, on the other hand, thinks it objectionable that a rational, impartial spectator would choose rules that are optimific in this way.

Two points that Nagel makes are particularly interesting. The first is his claim that a rational, impartial spectator would not choose rules that are optimific. This is interesting given the consequentialist claim that what is wrong with absolutism is its insistence that we not ϕ even when ϕing results in a better outcome than would result if we did not ϕ. As the consequentialist sees it, it is *irrational* not to do that which has the best outcome.

The view of rationality to which the consequentialist appeals links rationality with optimizing. Presumably, the absolutist would object to this interpretation. And while it is not entirely clear how the argument might procede, he would presumably argue that there is an interpretation of "rationality" according to which it is possible for one's values to be rational and that the absolutist's values are rational while the consequentialist's ones are not.

A second point Nagel makes that is worth addressing is that consequentialist considerations *should* be respected when they're overwhelmingly powerful and extremely certain. Now this is uninteresting given our distinction between "strong" and "weak" absolutism. We could simply call Nagel a "weak" absolutist and there would be nothing remarkable about the matter. However, in his book *The View from Nowhere*, Nagel suggests that his absolutism is grounded in the perspective of the agent rather than in a more impersonal perspective (or "perspective of the universe") to which consequentialists typically appeal.[24] Otherwise put, consequentialists maintain that an action is right if, *from an impersonal standpoint*, the action is the one that will produce the best state of affairs that is open to the agent at the time of

[24] Bernard Williams also has this view. I thank Hilary Putnam for calling this to my attention.

acting. Nagel, on the other hand, is suggesting that such a perspective is chimerical; there is no perspective other than of the agent. (There is no "view from nowhere.")

The view that there is no "God's eye perspective" from which to determine if an action is right is closely linked with John Taurek's thesis which, if not outright absolutist, does have implications for absolutist thought. In his "Should the Numbers Count?"[25] Taurek argues that there are no value-comparative truths about various states of affairs that obtain as a result of an agent's conduct. He maintains that if faced with the choice of giving a lifesaving drug to five people who could all be saved by it or to one who could be saved by it but only if she got it all, Taurek says we should flip a coin. He rejects the view that, "from an impartial standpoint," five dead and one alive is a worse scenario than one dead and five alive. For Taurek, there is only the standpoints of the parties involved. And since, from each party's standpoint, it is a worse thing that that party should die rather than the other, it follows that no one party's loss is greater than another from some alleged but fanciful impartial point of view.

Grisez and Shaw defend a similar view. They write,

> Human life [should be] regarded not as a concrete, specific, essentially quantifiable object but as a good in which each person participates but which none exhausts or sums up in himself. In such a view of reality it is simply not possible to make the sort of calculation which weighs lives against each other . . . and thus determine whose life shall be respected and whose sacrificed. The value of life, each human life, is incalculable, not in any merely poetic sense but simply because it is something not susceptible to calculation, measurement, weighing, and balancing.[26]

Suppose then that this thesis is true; the implications for absolutism are obvious. Faced with the choice of ϕing or letting ψ, an agent still ought not to ϕ since, ex hypothesi, there is no way to compare ψ with the states of affairs that obtain if the agent ϕs. And this will hold true for whatever value of ψ is at issue.

But why think that there is no value-comparative truth about various states of affairs? One reason that suggests itself has to do with the Kantian claim that rational beings are valuing agents who themselves are the locus of all that has value. But if rational beings are beings *for whom* mere "things" have value, then rational beings are beings that

---

[25] John M. Taurek, "Should the Numbers Count?" *Philosophy and Public Affairs* 6, no. 4 (Summer 1977), pp. 293–310.

[26] Germain Grisez and Russell Shaw, *Beyond the New Morality* (Notre Dame, Ind.: University of Notre Dame Press, 1974), p. 131. Grisez and Shaw are inconsistent. In a passage cited above, they defend the view that basic moral goods are incommensurable. In saying here, however, that human life is infinitely valuable as compared to other moral goods, they imply that basic moral goods *are* commensurable.

have value in a way that is incomparable with the way anything else has value. (As Kant put it, rational beings are "above all price.") In other words, rational beings cannot have value the way, say, works of art have value, since what value works of art have they have because of the value placed on them by rational beings. (Consider: Rational beings cannot have value any more than scales can have weight.) This Kantian move has merit at least where ϕ stands for "killing the innocent" and ψ represents "letting n number of people die" where n >1. But since absolutist prohibitions often include the prohibition against killing, it is easy to see how absolutism may be grounded in the subjective viewpoint of the moral agent.

A related view that I defend elsewhere[27] is the view that there *is* a value-comparative truth about the states of affairs that result if the agent ϕs rather than lets ψ, but they are not what the consequentialist thinks. (At least this is true where "killing the materially innocent" stands as a value of ϕ.) Starting with the premise that the value of a human life *is* measurable, I argue that that value is infinitely large. This being so, when an agent commits a murder, the agent has deprived the world of an infinite value.[28] The same result obtains if the agent refuses to ϕ and lets ψ instead. (Once you have infinity, you cannot add to it.) Thus, whether the agent ϕs or lets ψ, the disvalue that obtains is the same. But if that is the case—or so I argue—then there cannot be circumstances so dire as to make ϕing a permissible action.

[27] Joram Graf Haber, "The Value of Human Life: An Absolutist Strategy for Attacking Consequentialism." In *Explorations of Value*, edited by Thomas Magnell (The Netherlands and Atlanta: Rodopi Press, Forthcoming).

[28] I use "murder" by means of illustration. My own absolutism is a purely formal one according to which the worst action that can be committed against a single individual is the worst action that can be committed at all. This analysis is neutral on the value that gets ascribed to ϕ.

I

On a Supposed Right to Lie from Altruistic Motives

Immanuel Kant

In the journal *France*[1] for 1797 Part VI, No. I, page 123, in an article entitled "On Political Reactions"[2] by Benjamin Constant,[3] there appears the following passage:

> The moral principle, "It is a duty to tell the truth," would make any society impossible if it were taken singly and unconditionally. We have proof of this in the very direct consequences which a German philosopher has drawn from this principle. This philosopher goes so far as to assert that it would be a crime to lie to a murderer who asked whether our friend who is pursued by him had taken refuge in our house.*

[1] [The journal *Frankreich im Jahre 1797. Aus den Briefen deutscher Männer in Paris*, published in Altona.]

[2] [*Des réactions politiques* had appeared in 1796 and was translated in this journal.]

[3] [Henri Benjamin Constant de Rebecque (1767–1830), the French writer, statesman, and orator.]

* "J. D. Michaelis[4] of Göttingen expressed this extraordinary opinion earlier than Kant. But the author of this essay has informed me that Kant is the philosopher spoken of in this passage."—K. F. CRAMER.†[5]

† That this was really said by me somewhere I hereby admit, though I cannot now remember the place.[6]—I. KANT.

[4] [Johann David Michaelis (1717–91), biblical scholar, professor in Göttingen.]

[5] [Karl Friedrich Cramer (1752–1807), the editor of *Frankreich* . . . , formerly professor of Greek and oriental languages and homiletics at Kiel, had been dismissed in 1794 because of his open sympathy for the Revolution.]

[6] ["Such a place is not to be found in Kant's previous works."—HEINRICH MAIER (editor of the Academy edition of this work).]

The French philosopher on page 124 refutes this principle in the following manner:

> It is a duty to tell the truth. The concept of duty is inseparable from the concept of right. A duty is that which in one being corresponds to the rights of another. Where there are no rights, there are no duties. To tell the truth is thus a duty; but it is a duty only in respect to one who has a right to the truth. But no one has a right to a truth which injures others.

The πρῶτον ψεῦδος in this argument lies in the sentence: "To tell the truth is a duty, but it is a duty only toward one who has a right to the truth."

It must first be noted that the expression, "to have a right to truth" is without meaning. One must rather say, "Man has a right to his own truthfulness (*veracitas*)," i.e., to the subjective truth in his own person. For to have objectively a right to truth would mean that it is a question of one's will (as in questions of what belongs to individuals generally) whether a given sentence is to be true or false. This would certainly produce an extraordinary logic.

Now the first question is: Does a man, in cases where he cannot avoid answering "Yes" or "No," have a right to be untruthful? The second question is: Is he not in fact bound to tell an untruth, when he is unjustly compelled to make a statement, in order to protect himself or another from a threatened misdeed?

Truthfulness in statements which cannot be avoided is the formal duty of an individual to everyone,* however great may be the disadvantage accruing to himself or to another. If, by telling an untruth, I do not wrong him who unjustly compels me to make a statement, nevertheless by this falsification, which must be called a lie (though not in a legal sense), I commit a wrong against duty generally in a most essential point. That is, so far as in me lies I cause that declarations should in general find no credence, and hence that all rights based on contracts should be void and lose their force, and this is a wrong done to mankind generally.

Thus the definition of a lie as merely an intentional untruthful declaration to another person does not require the additional condition that it must harm another, as jurists think proper in their definition (*mendacium est falsiloquium in praeiudicium alterius*). For a lie always harms another; if not some other particular man, still it harms mankind generally, for it vitiates the source of law itself.

---

* I should not like to sharpen this principle to the point of saying, "Untruthfulness is a violation of duty to one's self." This principle belongs to ethics, but here we are concerned with a legal duty. [Ethics as a] theory of virtue sees in this transgression only worthlessness, which is the reproach the liar draws upon himself.

This benevolent lie, however, can become punishable under civil law through an accident (*casus*), and that which escapes liability to punishment only by accident can also be condemned as wrong even by external laws. For instance, if by telling a lie you have prevented murder, you have made yourself legally responsible for all the consequences; but if you have held rigorously to the truth, public justice can lay no hand on you, whatever the unforeseen consequences may be. After you have honestly answered the murderer's question as to whether his intended victim is at home, it may be that he has slipped out so that he does not come in the way of the murderer, and thus that the murder may not be committed. But if you had lied and said he was not at home when he had really gone out without your knowing it, and if the murderer had then met him as he went away and murdered him, you might justly be accused as the cause of his death. For if you had told the truth as far as you knew it, perhaps the murderer might have been apprehended by the neighbors while he searched the house and thus the deed might have been prevented. Therefore, whoever tells a lie, however well intentioned he might be, must answer for the consequences, however unforseeable they were, and pay the penalty for them even in a civil tribunal. This is because truthfulness is a duty which must be regarded as the ground of all duties based on contract, and the laws of these duties would be rendered uncertain and useless if even the least exception to them were admitted.

To be truthful (honest) in all declarations, therefore, is a sacred and absolutely commanding decree of reason, limited by no expediency.

Mr. Constant makes a thoughtful and correct remark on decrying principles so strict that they are alleged to lose themselves in such impracticable ideas that they are to be rejected. He says, on page 23, "In every case where a principle which has been proved to be true appears to be inapplicable, the reason is that we do not know the middle principle which contains the means of its application." He adduces (p. 121) the doctrine of equality as the first link of the social chain, saying (p. 122):

> No man can be bound by any laws except those to the formulation of which he has contributed. In a very limited society this principle can be applied directly and needs no mediating principle in order to become a common principle. But in a society consisting of very many persons, another principle must be added to this one we have stated. This mediating principle is: the individuals can participate in the formulation of laws either in their own person or through their representatives. Whoever wished to apply the former principle to a large society without making use of the mediating principle would invariably bring about the destruction of the society. But this circumstance, which would only show the ignorance or the incompetence of the legislator, proves nothing against the principle.

He concludes (p. 125) that "a principle acknowledged to be true must never be abandoned, however obviously danger seems to be involved in it." (And yet the good man himself abandoned the unconditional principle of truthfulness on account of the danger which it involved for society. He did so because he could find no mediating principle which could serve to prevent this danger; and, in fact, there is no principle to be interpolated here.)

If we wish to preserve the names of the persons as they have been cited here, the "French philosopher" confuses the action by which someone does harm (*nocet*) to another in telling the truth when he cannot avoid making a statement, with the action whereby he does the other a wrong (*laedit*). It was only an accident (*casus*) that the truth of the statement harmed the occupant of the house; it was not a free act (in a juristic sense). For to demand of another that he should lie to one's own advantage would be a claim opposed to all lawfulness. Each man has not only a right but even the strict duty to be truthful in statements he cannot avoid making, whether they harm himself or others. In so doing, he does not do harm to him who suffers as a consequence; accident causes this harm. For one is not at all free to choose in such a case, since truthfulness (if he must speak) is an unconditional duty.

The "German philosopher" will not take as one of his principles the proposition (p. 124): "To tell the truth is a duty, but only to him who has a right to the truth." He will not do so, first, because of the ambiguous formulation of this proposition, for truth is not a possession the right to which can be granted to one and denied to another. But he will not do so chiefly because the duty of truthfulness (which is the only thing in question here) makes no distinction between persons to whom one has this duty and to whom one can exempt himself from this duty; rather, it is an unconditional duty which holds in all circumstances.

Now in order to proceed from a metaphysics of law (which abstracts from all empirical conditions) to a principle of politics (which applies these concepts to cases met with in experience), and by means of this to achieve the solution of a problem of politics in accord with the universal principle of law, the philosopher will enunciate three notions. The first is an axiom, i.e., an apodictically certain proposition which springs directly from the definition of external law (the harmony of the freedom of each with the freedom of all others according to a universal law). The second is a postulate of external public law (the will of all united according to the principle of equality, without which no one would have any freedom). Third, there is the problem of how it is to be arranged that, in a society however large, harmony may be maintained in accordance with principles of freedom and equality (namely, by means of a representative system). The latter will then become a principle of politics, the organization and establishment of which will entail decrees drawn from the practical knowledge of men, which will have in view only the mechanism of the administration of justice and how this may be suitably carried out. Law must never be accommodated to politics but politics always accommodated to law.

The author says, "A principle recognized as true (I add, recognized as an a priori and hence apodictic principle) must never be abandoned, however obviously danger seems to be involved in it." But one must only understand the danger not as a danger of accidentally doing a harm but only as a danger of doing a wrong. This would happen if I made the duty of being truthful, which is unconditional and the supreme juridical condition in testimony, into a conditional duty subordinate to other considerations. Although in telling a certain lie I do not actually do anyone a wrong, I formally but not materially violate the principle of right with respect to all unavoidably necessary utterances. And this is much worse than to do injustice to any particular person, because such a deed against an individual does not always presuppose the existence of a principle in the subject which produces such an act.

If one is asked whether he intends to speak truthfully in a statement that he is about to make and does not receive the question with indignation at the suspicion it expressed that he might be a liar, but rather asks permissions to consider possible exceptions, that person is already potentially a liar. That is because he shows that he does not acknowledge truthfulness as an intrinsic duty but makes reservations with respect to a rule which does not permit any exception, inasmuch as any exception would directly contradict itself.

All practical principles of right must contain rigorous truth, and the so-called "mediating principles" can contain only the more accurate definition of their application to actual cases (according to rules of policy), but they can never contain exceptions from the former. Such exceptions would nullify their universality, and that is precisely the reason that they are called principles.

II

Persons, Means, and Ends

Germain Grisez and Russell Shaw

Are there ethical absolutes? Are there moral norms which should never be violated and therefore things which should never be done regardless of the circumstances and the consequences? In other words, is there anything about which it is true to say "It is *always* wrong to do *that*, no matter what"?

Almost instinctively most people would answer Yes, and then would go on to cite some action which they feel should never be performed: purposely to torture a small child, for instance. Yet for many ethical theorists the answer is No. For them there are no ethical absolutes and therefore no actions which can flatly be ruled out as beyond the pale of acceptable human behavior.

This is not to suggest that such theorists are themselves vicious or immoral. People who do not believe in ethical absolutes may indeed be high-minded and right-living, in particular cases more so perhaps than those who hold that there are some actions which ought never to be performed.

The issue here, however, is not whose private life and personal conduct are more upstanding and blameless. The question is, rather, Whose ethical position is true? Is any action whatsoever allowable, at least in certain circumstances? Or are there actions which it is never morally right to perform?

What is at issue here is far removed from idle speculation. This is one of the most burning ethical questions of our times, a matter of far-reaching practical ramifications for individual and social life.

Most, and perhaps all, of the modes of responsibility yield ethical absolutes, and people generally have no difficulty accepting them as true. Few, for example, would suggest that revenge, as contrary to the mode which excludes acting against an instance of human good in order to vent one's wrath, sometimes is morally acceptable behavior. While destructive feelings are not within our direct control, we nevertheless have a responsibility to control such impulses in indirect ways and to refrain from harming ourselves or others to satisfy hostility. No matter how difficult it is to fulfill, no decent person doubts that this is a serious responsibility. Decent people do of course differ in their views of what constitutes "revenge," and some would argue—wrongly in our view—that some acts of a retaliatory nature are permitted or even required by, say, justice. The point, though, is that, even if they consider certain retaliatory acts acceptable, decent people always consider it wrong to harm anyone simply to satisfy hostility.

The case, however, is often very different with regard to ethical absolutes generated by . . . [a] . . . mode of responsibility . . . [that] . . . can be expressed this way: *Do not let the attraction exercised by one instance of a basic human good lead you, in pursuing it, to act against another instance of a basic human good.* It is never right to act directly against some instance of a human good for the sake of another—to treat one as a mere means, as if it were not an aspect of the person, and the other as the end. To do so is clearly contrary to the first principle of morality and the ideal of integral human fulfillment, which enjoins consistent openness to the whole spectrum of human goods.

"To act directly against an instance of a human good" means to make and carry out a choice to destroy, damage, or impede that good in one or more instances. Critics of our position have sometimes seized on such expressions to undermine it. How is it possible to destroy, damage, or impede a basic human good? But notice that we are speaking of particular instances of a human good, the good as it is realized or realizable in some human being or human beings. Obviously, one cannot literally destroy, damage, or impede a basic human good as a reason for acting, but one can do enormous harm to human beings. Even the Nazis could not destroy the basic good of human life in itself, but they did kill millions of people.

A. Respecting Human Goods

Openness to human goods is the basis of a right moral attitude. In acting directly against an instance of any basic good for the sake of another instance (either of the same or a different good) we treat that against which we act as if it were nothing but a means to an end. But the goods that comprise the elements of our personhood are themselves the reasons and the ends of human action; as such they cannot reasonably be treated as mere means. The minimum requirement for a morally correct attitude—simultaneous respect for all the basic goods—in practice means refusing to do injury to one instance as a means of achieving another.

What does this notion of acting directly against one instance of the fundamental goods for the sake of some other really entail? In practice something like the following. A person who is about to violate this mode of responsibility is about to adopt a proposal which involves detriment or injury to a human good in a particular instance. He or she is inclined to do this because it contributes to the realization of another instance of a good. Clearly, such an individual already has made or is about to make a determination that the good which will be realized in the second instance outweighs the good which will suffer injury in the first. In adopting such a proposal an individual simply cannot remain open to the good which will suffer detriment, for this good is being violated. In adopting the proposal he or she also necessarily wills this violation and in doing so adopts, at least implicitly, a narrowed and restricted view of the purposes which go to make up human personhood, that is, of personhood itself.

But, the objection goes, the way of proceeding which we have just described is reasonable—indeed, it is the morally right way to act in many cases—if the quantity of good in the instance preferred outweighs the quantity in the instance treated as a means to the end. Is it not rational and ethically correct to choose the way of acting which promises to bring about the greater good?

This is the line of reasoning recommended by those who subscribe to the ethical system known as "consequentialism" or "proportionalism." But their recommendation is mistaken. Instances of basic human goods are incommensurable: they cannot be measured against one another as the proportionalist calculus requires.

There is a twofold incommensurability. First, it is impossible to measure different categories of human good against one another, since the basic human goods are not reducible to one another or to some ultrabasic category of good underlying all the rest. Comparing categories of good is rather like dividing apples by oranges. Choices, though, are not between or among categories of goods, but instances of goods, so this incommensurability is not precisely what renders the calculus impossible. . . .

Second, however, it is no less impossible to measure different instances of the same good against one another and determine that one instance outweighs the others. Each instance, each real possibility for choice, has some appeal not found in its competitors. Where shall I go on vacation, the mountains or the seashore? I find both possibilities appealing, but in somewhat different ways, and that is precisely why I must *choose* between them; if the seashore had all the appeal of the mountains and its own besides, there would be no choice to make—I would simply tumble spontaneously and without choice for the clearly superior alternative.

Consequentialism would work if choices were between possibilities which differed from one another *only* in the quantity of good they promised. If, for instance, one had a pure case of bringing about the deaths of more people or fewer people, and nothing else of human importance were involved, one would surely prefer to kill fewer. The greater good/lesser evil would be so clear that no choice would be required or even possible.

An example helps make this clearer. You are at the controls of a runaway trolley car approaching an intersection where the tracks divide. To the right a crowd of people is crossing the street, to the left only two or three. You clang the bell and steer left. But where one does hesitate and deliberate it is because the problem is more complicated than bringing about the deaths of more or fewer people. Something else is involved. Suppose that, as you careen down the hill on your trolley, you actually know something about the people in the two intersections: the crowd to the right is made up of a gang of toughs crossing against the traffic light because they habitually ignore the rules of society; the handful of people to the left are decent citizens—a mother with a baby in a stroller, an elderly rabbi—crossing the street on a green light. And you ask yourself: Shouldn't I avoid killing those few people who have the right of way, even though that will mean killing those many people who are not respecting others' right of way?

Artificial as the example is, it makes the crucial point that whenever we have a real choice to make, it is because we are confronted with various possibilities, each embodying a diverse mix of human goods. Consequentialism or proportionalism requires that one weigh and measure the good as represented in the various possibilities and opt for the instance promising more good. But each of the several possibilities comprises, not merely so much (on an imaginary scale) of a certain human good, but a unique "package" of instances of various goods whose very uniqueness makes it impossible to measure it against other, similarly unique "packages" competing to be chosen.

Many proportionalists recognize the difficulty with their system and have tried to correct it. However, it cannot be corrected. Their system requires that two incompatible conditions be met: first, that a morally significant choice be made; second, that the option offering the greater quantity of good be known. Now, where a morally significant choice is made, one has the option of choosing the morally wrong alternative while knowing the morally right one. But if one alternative really did embody the greater good and if that were known, it would be impossible in such a case to choose the inferior alternative, for people are incapable of preferring less good to more. All that proportionalists or consequentialists really are saying is that it is wrong to choose that which practical judgment, according to their understanding of it, makes it impossible to choose. Their approach is not just false but utterly unworkable, and thus it is meaningless as practical guidance.

B. Are There Inalienable Rights?

It is essential to bear in mind that human goods are what human life and action are all about. The language we use here is unavoidably abstract. But the goods themselves are not abstractions, existing "out there" beyond us and other people. Rather, they are aspects of human beings, ourselves or others—aspects which either already exist in actuality or have the potential of being realized. To act directly against one of the fundamental goods is therefore to violate an actual or possible aspect of the personhood of a real person or persons: to violate "life" means violating *somebody's* life—for instance, means killing or mutilating someone. This amounts to using a human person as a mere means to an end.

Critics of the view that there are ethical absolutes nevertheless sometimes refer to them disparagingly as "legalistic absolutes." Rhetoric aside, the implication is that this position exalts law (legalism) at the expense of the person. But the defense of ethical absolutes, properly understood, does not mean assigning primacy to bloodless law over flesh and blood persons. On the contrary, it constitutes a defense of persons and their inalienable rights.

If there are no absolute responsibilities, there are no inalienable rights. If it were true that any action, no matter what, is permitted in certain circumstances, then no good intrinsic to the person would be safe from invasion and suppression, provided the justifying circumstances existed. This is true even in regard to ethical theories which propose the existence of virtual absolutes: norms which proponents of such theories say they can hardly conceive as being in practice subject to violation and actions whose justifying circumstances they can scarcely envision as ever arising. While the proponents of such theories may not be able to envision such circumstances, others less idealistic are quite able to imagine, and find, just the circumstances in which people can be sacrificed to the attainment of ulterior ends.

If there are no ethical absolutes, human persons, rather than being the norm and source from which other things receive their value, become simply items or commodities with a relative value—inviolable only up to the point at which it is expedient to violate them in order to achieve an objective. It would then make no sense at all to speak of the immeasurable value of the human person. Far from being immeasurable—that is, beyond calculation—the value of a person would be quite specific and quantifiable, something to be weighed in the balance against other values.

As a matter of fact, it is often assumed that just this sort of weighing of human goods and human persons is possible. The assumption enters in, tacitly in many instances, as a result of confusion between fundamental goods constitutive of the person, each of which shares in the immeasurability of the still unfolding mystery of the person, and a specific objective which is never completely identical with the person.

Typically, an individual with such an attitude will think along the following lines: Two lives are better than one; therefore, if two innocent lives can be saved by sacrificing one innocent life, it is entirely right to sacrifice the one life in order to save the two.

An example dramatizes this attitude. In wartime a military commander is confronted with a group of prisoners who possess important information about the enemy's plans. He needs the information in order to prevent loss of life among his own troops, but the prisoners will not tell him what he wants to know. In order to compel the prisoners to talk, he has one of them executed as an example to the others and thereby frightens the survivors into divulging the desired information. By taking one life he has saved other lives, and according to the principle that two lives are better than one (or twenty better than two, or two thousand better than twenty, and so on) his action seems not only expedient but morally right.

As we have seen, this way of reasoning would make good sense if the only issue were whether to cause more deaths or fewer. But that is not so. For example: the military commander *chooses* to kill the prisoner, whereas the deaths he hopes to prevent are not ones which he would choose but—if he were to act differently—would only accept; moreover, he breaks faith with the prisoner, since it is commonly understood that military prisoners who behave themselves will not be executed; furthermore, he leads the other prisoners to betray their comrades, something repugnant to soldiers which the commander would not wish to happen to his own men. A *lot* more than causing more deaths or fewer is at stake.

One arrives at a different judgment of how one ought to proceed in such circumstances if human life is regarded, not as one of the things of relative value which a person *has*, but as an intrinsic component of the person, and so as a value which shares in the *dignity* of the person. In denying that we can choose to kill one person for the sake of two, we really are denying that two persons are "worth" twice as much as some other real person. On this view it is simply not possible to make the sort of calculation which weighs persons against each other (my life is more valuable than John's life, John's life is more valuable than Mary's and Tom's combined, or vice versa) and thus to determine whose life shall be respected and whose sacrificed. The value of each human person is incalculable, not in any merely poetic sense, but simply because it is not susceptible to calculation, measurement, weighing, and balancing.

Traditionally this point has been expressed by the statement that the end does not justify the means. This is a way of saying that the direct violation of any good intrinsic to the person cannot be justified by the good result which such a violation may bring about. What is extrinsic to human persons may be used for the good of persons, but what is intrinsic to persons has a kind of sacredness and may not be violated.

C. Ethical Absolutes and Consequentialist Solutions

Ultimately, of course, the conviction that the end does justify the means and that, in consequence, there is no action which could not in some circumstances, however remote, be morally justifiable represents a consequentialist/proportionalist approach to the entire question of ethics and action. . . . It may be worth speculating on why this attitude has become so common in our times and society, and, in particular, why it is so evident in regard to the fundamental human good of life. There are, it seems, several reasons.

First, of course, people naturally tend to think in second-level, means-ends terms; children learn this kind of action first. At this level the reasonableness of what one does depends on its effectiveness in getting what one wants. And whenever anyone, child or adult, disregards moral requirements in order to get what he or she wants, the behavior has at least this much reasonableness—it makes sense in that narrow frame of reference. Hence those doing what is morally wrong can console themselves with the thought "I'm acting reasonably." From this it is only a short step to saying that moral goodness means acting efficiently to get what one wants, especially when one's objective is morally acceptable and the only question concerns the means of getting it.

Second, as we have seen, there is a legitimate place for calculating the costs and benefits of various means and choosing one over another on that basis. We do this whenever we have a second-level objective in view, and the differences among the various means of reaching it appear morally insignificant.

In modern times, however, this way of thinking has come to bulk larger and larger because of the rise of technology, accounting, cost analysis, and similar techniques. Because this approach is so reasonable and effective in its place, there is a tendency to extend it to areas where it does not belong—specifically, to the settling of moral issues. The situation is exacerbated when, as commonly happens, in wartime or war-related circumstances leaders adopt this approach, disregarding moral constraints and considering alternatives simply for their effectiveness in forcing the enemy to surrender.

This points to yet another possible element to explain the prevalence of the attitude we are describing: the nuclear deterrent strategy of the United States and other countries.

It is a central element of this strategy that, if pressed to the wall in war, the United States and other nuclear nations would rain down nuclear bombs on enemy cities. Leaving aside the question whether such a course of action would make sense (although it would in fact be senseless), the strategy is built on the presumption that the United States and the other nations involved would really do what they say they are prepared to do. Otherwise the deterrent would not be credible.

For years then, Americans and the people of other nations which have nuclear deterrents have been living with the knowledge and intention that this is how their countries would, in certain circumstances, act. In subtle but real ways this fact—of nuclear deterrent strategy and all it implies—has helped to undermine the foundations of moral perception and moral thought in our society. This is a broad statement, and one whose truth it is impossible to demonstrate. Yet it stands to reason that this appalling fact has, like a sort of moral disease, infected national life, deadened ethical sensitivity, and poisoned many aspects of our society. It has accustomed us to the idea that it is morally right to will evil for the sake of good.

We do not propose a solution. We only suggest that the nuclear deterrent strategy represents a frighteningly logical application of the principle that the end *does* justify the means. Having willingly although regretfully accepted this principle in one critical area of national life, we can hardly expect to be immune from its influence in many others.

It is of course true that acceptance of the principle that there are ethical absolutes—that the end does not justify the means—implies willingness to accept or tolerate some finite damage rather than act directly against an instance of fundamental human good. A nation unwilling to act unjustly in war, for example, may have to accept defeat; an individual unwilling to act dishonestly in a competitive situation may have to accept some financial or other loss.

Those who argue that the end justifies the means will frequently argue as well that this readiness to suffer damage is unreasonable. But to one who is determined not to limit the meaning of human life to the quantifiable, who is determined instead to preserve the inviolability of the person against threats and infringements, it will be the most reasonable thing in the world.

III

War and Murder

G. E. M. Anscombe

1. The Use of Violence by Rulers

Since there are always thieves and frauds and men who commit violent attacks on their neighbours and murderers, and since without law backed by adequate force there are usually gangs of bandits; and since there are in most places laws administered by people who command violence to enforce the laws against lawbreakers; the question arises: what is a just attitude to this exercise of violent coercive power on the part of rulers and their subordinate officers?

Two attitudes are possible: one, that the world is an absolute jungle and that the exercise of coercive power by rulers is only a manifestation of this; and the other, that it is both necessary and right that there should be this exercise of power, that through it the world is much less of a jungle than it could possibly be without it, so that one should in principle be glad of the existence of such power, and only take exception to its unjust exercise.

It is so clear that the world is less of a jungle because of rulers and laws, and that the exercise of coercive power is essential to these institutions as they are now—all this is so obvious, that probably only Tennysonian conceptions of progress enable people who do not wish to separate themselves from the world to think that nevertheless such violence is objectionable, that some day, in this present dispensation, we shall do without it, and that the pacifist is the man who sees and tries to follow the ideal course, which future civilization must one day pursue. It is an illusion, which would be fantastic if it were not so familiar.

In a peaceful and law abiding country such as England, it may not be immediately obvious that the rulers need to command violence to the point of fighting to the death those that would oppose it; but brief reflection shews that this is so. For those who oppose the force that backs law will not always stop short of fighting to the death and cannot always be put down short of fighting to the death.

Then only if it is in itself evil violently to coerce resistant wills, can the exercise of coercive power by rulers be bad as such. Against such a conception, if it were true, the necessity and advantage of the exercise of such power would indeed be a useless plea. But that conception is one that makes no sense unless it is accompanied by a theory of withdrawal from the world as man's only salvation; and it is in any case a false one. We are taught that God retains the evil will of the devil within limits by violence: we are not given a picture of God permitting to the devil all that he is capable of. There is current a conception of Christianity as having revealed that the defeat of evil must always be by pure love without coercion; this at least is shewn to be false by the foregoing consideration. And without the alleged revelation there could be no reason to believe such a thing.

To think that society's coercive authority is evil is akin to thinking the flesh evil and family life evil. These things belong to the present constitution of mankind; and if the exercise of coercive power is a manifestation of evil, and not the just means of restraining it, then human nature is totally depraved in a manner never taught by Christianity. For society is essential to human good; and society without coercive power is generally impossible.

The same authority which puts down internal dissension, which promulgates laws and restrains those who break them if it can, must equally oppose external enemies. These do not merely comprise those who attack the borders of the people ruled by the authority; but also, for example, pirates and desert bandits, and, generally, those beyond the confines of the country ruled whose activities are viciously harmful to it. The Romans, once their rule in Gaul was established, were eminently justified in attacking Britain, where were nurtured the Druids whose pupils infested northern Gaul and whose practices struck the Romans themselves as "dira immanitas." Further, there being such a thing as the common good of mankind, and visible criminality against it, how can we doubt the excellence of such a proceeding as that violent suppression of the man-stealing business[1] which the British government took it into its head to engage in under Palmerston? The present-day conception of "aggression," like so many strongly influential conceptions, is a bad one. Why *must* it be wrong to strike the first blow in a struggle? The only question is, who is in the right.

[1] It is ignorance to suppose that it takes modern liberalism to hate and condemn this. It is cursed and subject to the death penalty in the Mosiac law. Under that code, too, runaway slaves of all nations had asylum in Israel.

Here, however, human pride, malice and cruelty are so usual that it is true to say that wars have mostly been mere wickedness on both sides. Just as an individual will constantly think himself in the right, whatever he does, and yet there is still such a thing as being in the right, so nations will constantly wrongly think themselves to be in the right—and yet there is still such a thing as their being in the right. Palmerston doubtless had no doubts in prosecuting the opium war against China, which was diabolical; just as he exulted in putting down the slavers. But there is no question but that he was a monster in the one thing, and a just man in the other.

The probability is that warfare is injustice, that a life of military service is a bad life "militia or rather malitia," as St. Anselm called it. This probability is greater than the probability (which also exists) that membership of a police force will involve malice, because of the character of warfare: the extraordinary occasions it offers for viciously unjust proceedings on the part of military commanders and warring governments, which at the time attract praise and not blame from their people. It is equally the case that the life of a ruler is usually a vicious life: but that does not shew that ruling is as such a vicious activity.

The principal wickedness which is a temptation to those engaged in warfare is the killing of the innocent, which may often be done with impunity and even to the glory of those who do it. In many places and times it has been taken for granted as a natural part of waging war: the commander, and especially the conqueror, massacres people by the thousand, either because this is part of his glory, or as a terrorizing measure, or as part of his tactics.

2. Innocence and the Right to Kill Intentionally

It is necessary to dwell on the notion of non-innocence here employed. Innocence is a legal notion; but here, the accused is not pronounced guilty under an existing code of law, under which he has been tried by an impartial judge, and therefore made the target of attack. There is hardly a possibility of this; for the administration of justice is something that takes place under the aegis of a sovereign authority; but in warfare—or the putting down by violence of civil disturbance—the sovereign authority is itself engaged as a party to the dispute and is not subject to a further earthly and temporal authority which can judge the issue and pronounce against the accused. The stabler the society, the rarer it will be for the sovereign authority to have to do anything but apprehend its internal enemy and have him tried; but even in the stablest society there are occasions when the authority has to fight its internal enemy to the point of killing, as happens in the struggle with external belligerent forces in international warfare; and then the characterization of its enemy as non-innocent has not been ratified by legal process.

This, however, does not mean that the notion of innocence fails in this situation. What is required, for the people attacked to be non-innocent in the relevant sense, is that they should themselves be engaged in an objectively unjust proceeding which the attacker has the right to make his concern; or—the commonest case—should be unjustly attacking him. Then he can attack them with a view to stopping them; and also their supply lines and armament factories. But people whose mere existence and activity supporting existence by growing crops, making clothes, etc. constitute an impediment to him—such people are innocent and it is murderous to attack them, or make them a target for an attack which he judges will help him towards victory. For murder is the deliberate killing of the innocent, whether for its own sake or as a means to some further end.

The right to attack with a view to killing is something that belongs only to rulers and those whom they command to do it. I have argued that it does belong to rulers precisely because of that threat of violent coercion exercised by those in authority which is essential to the existence of human societies. It ought not to be pretended that rulers and their subordinates do not choose[2] the killing of their enemies as a means, when it has come to fighting in which they are determined to win and their enemies resist to the point of killing: this holds even in internal disturbances.

When a private man struggles with an enemy he has no right to aim to kill him, unless in the circumstances of the attack on him he can be considered as endowed with the authority of the law and the struggle comes to that point. By a "private" man, I mean a man in a society; I am not speaking of men on their own, without government, in remote places; for such men are neither public servants nor "private." The plea of self-defence (or the defence of someone else) made by a private man who has killed someone else must in conscience—even if not in law—be a plea that the death of the other was not intended, but was a side effect of the measures taken to ward off the attack. To shoot to kill, to set lethal man-traps, or, say, to lay poison for someone from whom one's life is in danger, are forbidden. The deliberate choice of inflicting death in a struggle is the right only of ruling authorities and their subordinates.

In saying that a private man may not choose to kill, we are touching on the principle of "double effect." The denial of this has been the

[2] The idea that they may lawfully do what they do, but should not intend the death of those they attack, has been put forward and, when suitably expressed, may seem high-minded. But someone who can fool himself into this twist of thought will fool himself into justifying anything, however atrocious, by means of it.

corruption of non-Catholic thought, and its abuse the corruption of Catholic thought. Both have disastrous consequences which we shall see. This principle is not accepted in English law: the law is said to allow no distinction between the foreseen and the intended consequences of an action. Thus, if I push a man over a cliff when he is menacing my life, his death is considered as intended by me, but the intention to be justifiable for the sake of self-defence. Yet the lawyers would hardly find the laying of poison tolerable as an act of self-defence, but only killing by a violent action in a moment of violence. Christian moral theologians have taught that even here one may not seek the death of the assailant, but may in default of other ways of self-defence use such violence as will in fact result in his death. The distinction is evidently a fine one in some cases: what, it may be asked, can the intention be, if it can be said to be absent in this case, except a mere wish or desire?

And yet in other cases the distinction is very clear. If I go to prison rather than perform some action, no reasonable person will call the incidental consequences of my refusal—the loss of my job, for example—intentional just because I knew they must happen. And in the case of the administration of a pain-relieving drug in mortal illness, where the doctor knows the drug may very well kill the patient if the illness does not do so first, the distinction is evident; the lack of it has led an English judge to talk nonsense about the administration of the drug's not having *really* been the cause of death in such a case, even though a post mortem shews it was. For everyone understands that it is a very different thing so to administer a drug, and to administer it with the intention of killing. However, the principle of double effect has more important applications in warfare, and I shall return to it later.

3. The Influence of Pacifism

Pacifism has existed as a considerable movement in English speaking countries ever since the first world war. I take the doctrine of pacifism to be that it is *eo ipso* wrong to fight in wars, not the doctrine that it is wrong to be compelled to, or that any man, or some men, may refuse; and I think it false for the reasons that I have given. But I now want to consider the very remarkable effects it has had: for I believe its influence to have been enormous, far exceeding its influence on its own adherents.

We should note first that pacifism has as its background conscription and enforced military service for all men. Without conscription, pacifism is a private opinion that will keep those who hold it out of armies, which they are in any case not obliged to join. Now universal conscription, except for the most extraordinary reasons, i.e., as a regular habit among most nations, is such a horrid evil that the refusal of it automatically commands a certain amount of respect and sympathy.

We are not here concerned with the pacifism of some peculiar sect which in any case draws apart from the world to a certain extent, but with a pacifism of people in the world, who do not want to be withdrawn from it. For some of these, pacifism is prevented from being a merely theoretical attitude because they are liable to, and so are prepared to resist conscription; or are able directly to effect the attitude of some who are so liable.

A powerful ingredient in this pacifism is the prevailing image of Christianity. This image commands a sentimental respect among people who have no belief in Christianity, that is to say, in Christian dogmas; yet do have a certain belief in an ideal which they conceive to be part of "true Christianity." It is therefore important to understand this image of Christianity and to know how false it is. Such understanding is relevant, not merely to those who wish to believe Christianity, but to all who, without the least wish to believe, are yet profoundly influenced by this image of it.

According to this image, Christianity is an ideal and beautiful religion, impracticable except for a few rare characters. It preaches a God of love whom there is no reason to fear; it marks an escape from the conception presented in the Old Testament, of a vindictive and jealous God who will terribly punish his enemies. The "Christian" God is a *roi fainéant*, whose only triumph is in the Cross; his appeal is a goodness and unselfishness, and to follow him is to act according to the Sermon on the Mount—to turn the other cheek and to offer no resistance to evil. In this account some of the evangelical counsels are chosen as containing the whole of Christian ethics: that is, they are made into precepts. (Only some of them; it is not likely that someone who deduces the *duty* of pacifism from the Sermon on the Mount and the rebuke to Peter, will agree to take "Give to him that asks of you" equally as a universally binding precept.)

The turning of counsels into precepts results in high-sounding principles. Principles that are mistakenly high and strict are a trap; they may easily lead in the end directly or indirectly to the justification of monstrous things. Thus if the evangelical counsel about poverty were turned into a precept forbidding property owning, people would pay lip service to it as the ideal, while in practice they went in for swindling. "Absolute honesty!" it would be said: "I can respect that—but of course that means having no property; and while I respect those who follow that course, I have to compromise with the sordid world myself." If then one must "compromise with evil" by owning property and engaging in trade, then the amount of swindling one does will depend on convenience. This imaginary case is paralleled by what is so commonly said: absolute pacifism is an ideal; unable to follow that, and committed to "compromise with evil," one must go the whole hog and wage war *à outrance*.

The truth about Christianity is that it is a severe and practicable religion, not a beautifully ideal but impracticable one. Its moral precepts (except for the stricter laws about marriage that Christ enacted, abrogating some of the permissions of the Old Law) are those of the Old Testament; and its God is the God of Israel.

It is ignorance of the New Testament that hides this from people. It is characteristic of pacifism to denigrate the Old Testament and exalt the New: something quite contrary to the teaching of the New Testament itself, which always looks back to and leans upon the Old. How typical it is that the words of Christ "You have heard it said, an eye for an eye and a tooth for a tooth, but I say to you . . ." are taken as a repudiation of the ethic of the Old Testament! People seldom look up the occurrence of this phrase in the juridical code of the Old Testament, where it belongs, and is the admirable principle of law for the punishment of certain crimes, such as procuring the wrongful punishment of another by perjury. People often enough *now* cite the phrase to justify private revenge; no doubt this was as often "heard said" when Christ spoke of it. But no justification for this exists in the personal ethic taught by the Old Testament. On the contrary. What do we find? "Seek no revenge," (Leviticus xix, 18), and "If you find your enemy's ox or ass going astray, take it back to him; if you see the ass of someone who hates you lying under his burden, and would forbear to help him: you must help him" (Exodus xxiii, 4–5). And "If your enemy is hungry, give him food, if thirsty, give him drink" (Proverbs xxv, 21).

This is only one example; given space, it would be easy to shew how false is the conception of Christ's teaching as *correcting* the religion of the ancient Israelites, and substituting a higher and more "spiritual" religion for theirs. Now the false picture I have described plays an important part in the pacifist ethic and in the ethic of the many people who are not pacifists but are influenced by pacifism.

To extract a pacifist doctrine—i.e., a condemnation of the use of force by the ruling authorities, and of soldiering as a profession—from the evangelical counsels and the rebuke to Peter, is to disregard what else is in the New Testament. It is to forget St. John's direction to soldiers: "do not blackmail people; be content with your pay"; and Christ's commendation of the centurion, who compared his authority over his men to Christ's. On a pacifist view, this must be much as if a madam in a brothel had said: "I know what authority is, I tell this girl to do this, and she does it . . ." and Christ had commended her faith. A centurion was the first Gentile to be baptized; there is no suggestion in the New Testament that soldiering was regarded as incompatible with Christianity. The martyrology contains many names of soldiers whose occasion of martyrdom was not any objection to soldiering, but a refusal to perform idolatrous acts.

Now, it is one of the most vehement and repeated teachings of the Judaeo-Christian tradition that the shedding of innocent blood is forbidden by the divine law. No man may be punished except for his own crime, and those "whose feet are swift to shed innocent blood" are always represented as God's enemies.

For a long time the main outlines of this teaching have seemed to be merely obvious morality: hence, for example, I have read a passage by Ronald Knox complaining of the "endless moralizing," interspersed in records of meaness, cowardice, spite, cruelty, treachery and murder, which forms so much of the Old Testament. And indeed, that it is terrible to kill the innocent is very obvious; the morality that so stringently forbids it must make a great appeal to mankind, especially to the poor threatened victims. Why should it need the thunder of Sinai and the suffering and preaching of the prophets to promulgate such a law? But human pride and malice are everywhere so strong that now, with the fading of Christianity from the mind of the West, this morality once more stands out as a demand which strikes pride- and fear-ridden people as too intransigent. For Knox, it seemed so obvious as to be dull; and he failed to recognize the bloody and beastly records that it accompanies for the dry truthfulness about human beings that so characterizes the Old Testament.[3]

Now pacifism teaches people to make no distinction between the shedding of innocent blood and the shedding of any human blood. And in this way pacifism has corrupted enormous numbers of people who will not act according to its tenets. They become convinced that a number of things are wicked which are not; hence, seeing no way of avoiding "wickedness," they set no limits to it. How endlessly pacifists argue that all war must be *à outrance!* that those who wage war must go as far as technological advance permits in the destruction of the enemy's people. As if the Napoleonic wars were perforce fuller of massacres than the French war of Henry V of England. It is not true: the reverse took place. Nor is technological advance particularly relevant; it is mere squeamishness that deters people who would consent to area bombing from the enormous massacres *by hand* that used once to be committed.

The policy of obliterating cities was adopted by the Allies in the last war; they need not have taken that step, and it was taken largely out of a villainous hatred, and as corollary to the policy, now universally

[3] It is perhaps necessary to remark that I am not here adverting to the total extermination of certain named tribes of Canaan that is said by the Old Testament to have been commanded by God. That is something quite outside the provisions of the Mosaic Law for dealings in war.

denigrated, of seeking "unconditional surrender." (That policy itself was visibly wicked, and could be and was judged so at the time; it is not surprising that it led to disastrous consequences, even if no one was clever and detached enough to foresee this at the time.)

Pacifism and the respect for pacifism is not the only thing that has led to a universal forgetfulness of the law against killing the innocent; but it has had a great share in it.

4. The Principle of Double Effect

Catholics, however, can hardly avoid paying at least lip-service to that law. So we must ask: how is it that there has been so comparatively little conscience exercised on the subject among them? The answer is: double-think about double effect.

The distinction between the intended, and the merely foreseen, effects of a voluntary action is indeed absolutely essential to Christian ethics. For Christianity forbids a number of things as being bad in themselves. But if I am answerable for the foreseen consequences of an action or refusal, as much as for the action itself, then these prohibitions will break down. If someone innocent will die unless I do a wicked thing, then on this view I am his murderer in refusing: so all that is left to me is to weigh up evils. Here the theologian steps in with the principle of double effect and says: "No, you are no murderer, if the man's death was neither your aim nor your chosen means, and if you had to act in the way that led to it or else do something absolutely forbidden." Without understanding of this principle, anything can be—and is wont to be—justified, and the Christian teaching that in no circumstances may one commit murder, adultery, apostasy (to give a few examples) goes by the board. These absolute prohibitions of Christianity by no means exhaust its ethic; there is a large area where what is just is determined partly by a prudent weighing up of consequences. But the prohibitions are bedrock, and without them the Christian ethic goes to pieces. Hence the necessity of the notion of double effect.

At the same time, the principle has been repeatedly abused from the seventeenth century up till now. The causes lie in the history of philosophy. From the seventeenth century till now what may be called Cartesian psychology has dominated the thought of philosophers and theologians. According to this psychology, an intention was an interior act of the mind which could be produced at will. Now if intention is all important—as it is—in determining the goodness or badness of an action, then, on this theory of what intention is, a marvellous way offered itself of making any action lawful. You only had to "direct your intention" in a suitable way. In practice, this means making a little speech to yourself: "What I mean to be doing is. . . ."

This perverse doctrine has occasioned repeated condemnations by the Holy See from the seventeenth century to the present day. Some examples will suffice to shew how the thing goes. Typical doctrines from the seventeenth century were that it is all right for a servant to hold the ladder for his criminous master so long as he is merely avoiding the sack by doing so; or that a man might wish for and rejoice at his parent's death so long as what he had in mind was the gain to himself; or that it is not simony to offer money, not *as a price* for the spiritual benefit, but only *as an inducement* to give it. A condemned doctrine from the present day is that the practice of *coitus reservatus* is permissible; such a doctrine could only arise in connexion with that "direction of intention" which sets everything right no matter what one does. A man makes a practice of withdrawing, telling himself that he *intends* not to ejaculate; of course (if that is his practice) he usually does so, but then the event is "accidental" and *praeter intentionem*: it is, in short, a case of "double effect."

This same doctrine is used to prevent any doubts about the obliteration bombing of a city. The devout Catholic bomber secures by a "direction of intention" that any shedding of innocent blood that occurs is "accidental." I know a Catholic boy who was puzzled at being told by his school master that it was an accident that the people of Hiroshima and Nagasaki were there to be killed; in fact, however absurd it seems such thoughts are common among priests who know that they are forbidden by the divine law to justify the direct killing of the innocent.

It is nonsense to pretend that you do not intend to do what is the means you take to your chosen end. Otherwise there is absolutely no substance to the Pauline teaching that we may not do evil that good may come.

5. Some Commonly Heard Arguments

There are a number of sophistical arguments, often or sometimes used on these topics, which need answering.

Where do you draw the line? As Dr. Johnson said, the fact of twilight does not mean you cannot tell day from night. There are borderline cases, where it is difficult to distinguish, in what is done, between means and what is incidental to, yet in the circumstances inseparable from, those means. The obliteration bombing of a city is not a borderline case.

The old "conditions for a just war" are irrelevant to the conditions of modern warfare, so that must be condemned out of hand. People who say this always envisage only major wars between the Great Powers, which Powers are indeed now "in blood stepp'd in so far" that it is unimaginable for there to be a war between them which is not a set of enormous massacres of civil populations. But these are not the only wars. Why is Finland so far free? At least partly because of the "posture of military preparedness" which, considering the character of the country, would have made subjugating the Finns a difficult and unrewarding task. The offensive of the Israelis against the Egyptians in 1956 involved no plan of making civil populations the target of military attack.

In a modern war the distinction between combatants and noncombatants is meaningless, so an attack on anyone on the enemy side is justified. This is pure nonsense, even in war, a very large number of the enemy population are just engaged in maintaining the life of the country, or the sick, or aged, or children.

It must be legitimate to maintain an opinion—viz. that the destruction of cities by bombing is lawful—if this is argued by competent theologians and the Holy See has not pronounced. The argument from the silence of the Holy See has itself been condemned by the Holy See (Denzinger, 28th Edition, 1127). How could this be a sane doctrine in view of the endless twistiness of the human mind?

Whether a war is just or not is not for the private man to judge: he must obey his government. Sometimes, this may be, especially as far as concerns causes of war. But the individual who joins in destroying a city, like a Nazi massacring the inhabitants of a village, is too obviously marked out as an enemy of the human race, to shelter behind such a plea.

Finally, horrible as it is to have to notice this, we must notice that even the arguments about double effect—which at least show that a man is not willing openly to justify the killing of the innocent—are now beginning to look old-fashioned. Some Catholics are not scrupling to say that *anything* is justified in defence of the continued existence and liberty of the Church in the West. A terrible fear of communism drives people to say this sort of thing. "Our Lord told us to fear those who can destroy body and soul, not to fear the destruction of the body" was blasphemously said to a friend of mine; meaning: "so, we must fear Russian domination more than the destruction of people's bodies of obliteration bombing."

But whom did Our Lord tell us to fear, when he said: "I will tell you whom you shall fear" and "Fear not them that can destroy the body, but fear him who can destroy body and soul in hell"? He told us to fear God the Father, who can and will destroy the unrepentant disobedient, body and soul, in hell.

A Catholic who is tempted to think on the lines I have described should remember that the Church is the spiritual Israel: that is, that

Catholics are what the ancient Jews were, salt for the earth and the people of God—and that what was true of some devout Jews of ancient times can equally well be true of us now: "You compass land and sea to make a convert, and when you have done so, you make him twice as much a child of hell as yourselves." Do Catholics sometimes think that they are immune from such a possibility? That the Pharisees—who sat in the seat of Moses and who were so zealous for the true religion—were bad in ways in which we cannot be bad if we are zealous? I believe they do. But our faith teaches no such immunity, it teaches the opposite. "We are in danger all our lives long." So we have to fear God and keep his commandments, and calculate what is for the best only within the limits of that obedience, knowing that the future is in God's power and that no one can snatch away those whom the Father has given to Christ.

It is not a vague faith in the triumph of "the spirit" over force (there is little enough warrant for that), but a definite faith in the divine promises, that makes us believe that the Church cannot fail. Those, therefore, who think they must be prepared to wage war with Russia involving the deliberate massacre of cities, must be prepared to say to God: "We had to break your law, lest your church fail. We could not obey your commandments, for we did not believe your promises."

IV

Cases of Necessity

Alan Donagan

Common morality, as it is conceived in the Hebrew-Christian tradition, is almost certainly consistent as a system, although some received precepts may be inconsistent with one another, and need to be revised. Of course, consistency is no more than a necessary condition of truth. Besides the internal problem of consistency, common morality is confronted with the external problem of the hard cases to which it gives rise. Yet up to a point, hard cases confirm it. On any serious view, tragedy is part of human life; and morality goes hand in hand with tragedy.

Admittedly, a sense of proportion is necessary. Concerning the Torah of Moses, Maimonides wrote:

> Should an idolater arise and coerce an Israelite to violate any one of the commandments mentioned in the Torah under threat that otherwise he would put him to death, the Israelite is to commit the transgression rather than suffer death; for concerning the commandments it is said, "which, if a man do them, he shall live by them" (*Leviticus*, 18:5): "*Live* by them," and not die by them.[1]

However, this permission had two kinds of exception. First, it did not apply to the prohibitions of idolatry, inchastity, or murder. Second, the idolater's purpose must be personal advantage, and not to bring about a violation of the Law for its own sake. If his purpose is to abolish the Jewish religion or any of its precepts, "it is the Israelite's duty to suffer death and not violate any one," even of the lesser commandments.[2]

---

[1] Maimonides, *Mishneh Torah*, I, 1, 5, 1 (Hyamson, p. 40a).

[2] Ibid., I, 1, 5, 2–3 (Hyamson, p. 40a).

Similar exceptions are implicit in common morality. Respect for human beings as rational creatures does not require a man, under credible threat of being killed if he disobeys a command to take something that does not belong to him, to refuse to obey that command; but it does require him to refuse to rape, mutilate, or murder anybody. Indeed, in picking up and removing what does not belong to you, if you are under threat of death or serious injury, you do not steal; for you, as distinct from whoever coerces you, do not appropriate what is not yours. As a rough generalization, you may, under coercion, be an involuntary accomplice (in the colloquial sense of "involuntary") to a wrong, provided that your action does not irreparably violate what is due to some human being as such.

Even allowing for these implicit exceptions, two external objections to common morality are made. The first is that observing it would sometimes lead to irreparable disaster for the individual who observes it. In such "cases of necessity," it is argued, it is reasonable to break any moral precept whatever. The second is that public men, in gaining, keeping, and exercising public authority, must sometimes break the moral law in the common interest. Any member of a civil society may conceivably have a public responsibility thrust upon him; and if he refuses to dirty his hands in the common interest when he has such a responsibility, he falls short in doing his duty as a member of that society.

Should either of these objections be conceded to be valid, then it would follow that common morality, as conceived in the Hebrew-Christian tradition, is not what it claims to be; is not, that is, a law binding upon every human being as a rational creature. It may possibly be binding under certain conditions, but not unconditionally. And what, if any, the conditions are under which it is binding, and what is binding absolutely or unconditionally, may be discovered by investigating what is binding when it breaks down. Since, *ex hypothesi*, it will have broken down because of certain consequences which follow from observing its precepts, what will be binding absolutely will be determined by those consequences. This new absolute system will therefore be, in Anscombe's term, "consequentialist."[3] Unfortunately, consequentialist systems turn out to be, not one, but legion.

But does common morality break down when confronted with alleged cases of necessity, or with what has been called "the problem of dirty hands"?

A classic budget of cases of necessity, first investigated by the Stoics, is introduced by reflection on what it is permissible to do to a shipwrecked man, neither harming nor threatening to harm anybody, who is keeping himself afloat by clinging to a plank. Even if he has no

---

[3] Anscombe (1958), p. 12; cf. pp. 9–13.

hope of rescue, it would clearly be murder for somebody clinging to another plank to dislodge him. But would it be murder, would it even be culpable, for somebody without anything to support him to try to wrest away the plank? When ships are wrecked, the survivors often struggle over the possession of flotsam that may support one or two, but not more. Is it reasonable to denounce so wholly natural an action as murder?

The following variations on this theme, preserved by Cicero from a lost work by the Stoic Hecato of Rhodes, were to become familiar topics in Christian casuistry.

> "Suppose that a man who has clung to a plank from a wrecked ship is a fool, shall a sage wrest it away, if he can?" [Kirk glosses "a fool" as "to the Stoic, as to the Jewish moralist, . . . always a moral degenerate"; and "a sage" as "the man of real moral value to the community."]
>
> [Hecato] denies it, as being wrongful [*iniuriam*].
>
> "Well, shall the owner of the ship not repossess his own property?"
>
> "Not in the least, any more than he may decide, at sea, to throw a passenger overboard, on the ground that [the ship] is his. For until they have reached [the port] for which the ship was chartered, the passengers rather than the owner have the right to use it."
>
> "Well, if there is one plank, and two shipwrecked men, both sages, may each seize it for himself, or should each yield to the other?"
>
> "One should yield, but to the one whose life is more valuable, either in itself, or for the sake of the general good [*rei publicae*]."
>
> "But what if in those respects the value of each is equal?"
>
> "Then there will be no struggle, but one will yield to the other as though he had lost a draw or a tossup."[4]

In his opinion about how two sages ought to conduct themselves in such a situation—*Nullum erit certamen*—Hecato in part anticipated the Jewish and Christian view: everybody ought to do what he can to survive; but he ought also to be prepared to die if he must, and he ought not to buy his life at the price of another's.

Nevertheless, the implications of common morality for such questions are not exhausted by this first-order doctrine. Materially, it is wrong for a shipwrecked man to save his own life by dislodging somebody else from a plank and fending him off, so that he drowns. Formally, how culpable is such an action? Although the other's death is not intended, the agent did act voluntarily. Yet the blame falling to him on that account is generally allowed, in the Hebrew-Christian tradition, to be mitigated by the circumstance that he acted in fear of immediate death. Whewell explained why.

---

[4] Cicero, *De Officiis*, III, 23 (84–90). There is a valuable historical discussion in Kirk, *Conscience and Its Problems*, pp. 138–49, esp. pp. 146–47.

> [S]uch a fear, in most persons, [he wrote] produces a paroxysm and agony of terrour and trouble which subvert the usual balance of mind, and the usual course of thought and action. What is done under such circumstances, may be considered as an exception to the common condition of the man's being.[5]

Even though the fear of immediate death probably would not deprive a man of the power to act voluntarily, actions performed in a state of such fear are apt to be uncharacteristic and ill-considered, especially if the danger is sudden and unexpected, or the manner of the impending death horrible. Yet what has been said earlier about fear as diminishing the voluntariness of an action applies here. Although fear exculpates only if it deprives the agent of the power to act voluntarily, it always, according to its nature and degree, diminishes responsibility.

That the danger of imminent death, and the extreme fear arising from it, may mitigate blame but cannot exculpate, was forcibly explained by a Victorian chief justice, Lord Coleridge, in the celebrated case of *R. v. Dudley and Stephens*.[6] His judgment has some claim to be considered a classic expression of the position of common morality.

A jury had rendered a special verdict, finding the facts of the case to be substantially as follows, but referring them to the High Court for a ruling as to the law.

> The prisoners, able-bodied English seamen, and the deceased, an English boy between seventeen and eighteen years of age, the crew of an English yacht, were cast away in a storm on the high seas sixteen hundred miles from land, and were compelled to put into an open boat. The food they took with them was all consumed in twelve days, and having been for eight days without food, and for six days without water, the prisoners killed the boy. The boy when killed was lying at the bottom of the boat quite helpless and weak, and unable to make any resistance, and did not assent to his being killed. The prisoners and another man who was with them, fed upon the body and blood of the boy for four days, when they were picked up by a passing vessel. The verdict went on thus: 'That if the men had not fed upon the body of the boy, they probably would not have survived to be so picked up and rescued . . . ; that the boy, being in a much weaker condition, was likely to have died before them; . . . that, under the circumstances, there appeared to the prisoners every probability that unless they then fed, or very soon fed, upon the boy or one of themselves, they would die of starvation; that there was no appreciable chance of saving life except by killing someone for the others to eat; that, assuming any necessity to kill anybody, there was no greater necessity for killing the boy than any of the other three men.'[7]

---

[5] Whewell, *Elements of Morality*, § 314 (p. 173).

[6] *Reports of Cases in Criminal Law*, vol. 15, 1882–84 (London: Horace Cox, 1886), pp.624–38.

[7] Ibid., p. 624.

The submission of the defence was that various authorities, in their definitions of murder, imply that, in order to save your life, it is not unlawful to take the life of another, even though that other neither attacks nor threatens your life, nor is guilty of any other wrongful action.

This contention appeared to the court, "new and strange";[8] and, upon consideration, they utterly rejected it.

> [I]t is admitted [Lord Coleridge wrote] that the deliberate killing of this unoffending and unresisting boy was clearly murder, unless the killing can be justified by some well-recognised excuse admitted by the law. It is further admitted that there was in this case no such excuse, unless the killing was justified by what has been called necessity. But the temptation to the act which existed here was not what the law has ever called necessity. Nor is this to be regretted.[9]

In law, that is, in the English Common Law, the necessity that justifies killing is the exculpating necessity of defending oneself or others from physical violence. When it is necessary to do so in order to save one's own life, the temptation to kill another, who commits no offence, may be almost impossible to overcome; but, "if the temptation to murder in this case were to be held by law an absolute defence of it," there would be "an absolute divorce of law from morality," fatal in its consequences.[10]

Yet the court recognized that simply to have declared what the law is on the question would have been monstrous. After alluding to the Sovereign's prerogative of mercy, Lord Coleridge continued as follows.

> It must not be supposed that, in refusing to admit temptation to be an excuse for crime, it is to be forgotten how terrible the temptation was, how awful the suffering, how hard in such trials to keep the judgment straight and the conduct pure. We are often compelled to set up standards we cannot reach ourselves, and to lay down rules which we could not ourselves satisfy. But a man has no right to declare temptation to be an excuse, though he might himself have yielded to it, nor allow compassion for the criminal to change or weaken in any manner the legal definition of the crime.[11]

Murder had been done, but in such circumstances that the normal punishment for murder would have been altogether unjust and inappro-

---

[8] Ibid., p. 632.

[9] Ibid., p. 636.

[10] Ibid., p. 636.

[11] Ibid., p. 637.

priate. The final note in the report of the case reads, "The prisoners were afterwards respited and their sentence commuted to one of six months' imprisonment without hard labour."[12]

Alike in its definition of the material precept and in its appraisal of culpability, Lord Coleridge's judgement is a model of how cases of necessity are treated according to common morality. It is therefore of some interest that adversaries of common morality have for the most part preferred to argue from other cases, usually imaginary ones.

In recent discussions, variations upon the following imaginary case have won a good deal of attention.[13] A rockfall occurs, catching the first of a group of potholers who are making their way out of a cave, in which water is rising rapidly. The man caught in the rocks is not seriously injured and may expect to be rescued in a day or two by search parties. Those behind him, however, will be drowned in a few hours by the rising water unless they make a passage through the fallen rocks. They can do so, but only by blasting the rocks away with the explosives they have with them, which will cause the death of the man caught in the rocks.

Of this case, Kai Nielsen has written as follows.*

> If there really is no other way of unsticking our . . . man, and if plainly, without blasting him out, everyone in the cave will drown, then, innocent or not, he should be blasted out. This . . . does not reveal a callousness toward life, for the people involved are caught in a desperate situation in which, if such extreme action is not taken, many lives will be lost and far greater misery will obtain. . . . Surely we must choose between evils here, but is there anything more reasonable, more morally appropriate, than choosing the lesser evil when doing or allowing some evil cannot be avoided?[14]

Nielsen's argument is twofold: first, that since it is evident that in this case the stuck potholer ought to be blasted out, and since that is incompatible with the traditional moral doctrine that no (materially) innocent person may be killed under any circumstances, the traditional doctrine must be repudiated; and second, that the true moral doctrine is plain from the case, namely, that whenever a certain number of

---

[12] Ibid., p. 638, n. (b).

[13] Two versions of it are given in Foot (1967), p. 7, as "well-known to philosophers," although my own acquaintance with it began with this paper. Nielsen gives another version in Nielsen (1972), p. 228. Both Foot's and Nielsen's versions contain the comic irrelevancy of making the man fat, and the sole obstruction his body.

* [See p. 170 this volume.—Ed.]

[14] Nielsen (1972), pp. 228–29.

human lives can be saved, but only by taking a smaller number of such lives, the lesser evil is to be chosen and the smaller number taken.

The second part of this argument is unpersuasive, because the moral doctrine advanced is far stronger than the case requires. For example, it sanctions the murder of the ship's boy by Dudley and Stephens, although that would horrify many who would blast out the stuck potholer. And weaker doctrines are to hand that do not have such implications. For example, on Grisez's theory of the double effect, the crucial considerations would be that the blasting away of the obstructing rocks and the killing of the man caught in them is a unitary act, and that, since the sole intention of that act would be to save life, the unintended evil of killing somebody can be disregarded, as being a consequence outside the scope of the agents' intention, for which there is a proportionately serious reason. The action of Dudley and Stephens cannot be justified in this way; for killing the boy was a necessary part of what they intended, and not outside its scope.

However, Grisez's theory of the double effect [notwithstanding], the system of common morality we have developed cannot be reconciled by means of it to the blasting out of Nielsen's stuck potholer. Can it be reconciled to it by any means at all?

I think it can. Human beings are not morally forbidden to risk their lives on suitably serious enterprises, of which it is not unthinkable that potholing is one. And, although it is not beyond dispute, it does not appear to be impermissible for a group of human beings embarking on such an enterprise to agree that, if in the course of it, through nobody's fault, they should be confronted with a choice between either allowing certain of their number to be killed, or doing something that would, against everybody's will, cause the deaths of fewer of their number, the latter should be chosen. In so agreeing, each member of the group would act in his own probable interest. And so, if the situation contemplated came about, and the agreement were put into effect, it would not be a case of one subgroup, because it was larger, sacrificing the lives of another that was smaller. An agreement of the kind described would have force even if it was tacit: that is, even if, without saying so, all members of the group take it as accepted by all that they should conduct themselves in accordance with it. And perhaps it would have force even if it were virtual: that is, even if all members of the group, were they to think about it, would agree that everybody in the group would think that so to conduct themselves was the only rational course. If this is correct, then in any group of potholers in which such an agreement is in force, actually or virtually, it is permissible, in the circumstances of Nielsen's example, to blast out one of their number who is stuck. And with most such groups, such agreements will be in force.

Is the intuitive plausibility of Nielsen's verdict in cases like that of the potholers to be explained in this way? Evidence that it is may be found in the fact that, in relevantly similar cases in which the possibility is excluded of even a virtual agreement that the fewer are to die, verdicts like his are not plausible at all. Imagine the following situation. A sizable group of people are trapped in an excavation by the collapse of the one passage leading out of it. However, there is a shaft for a periscope, which they can ascend by ladder to within six feet of the earth's surface. At this point the periscope goes through to the surface in an airtight steel pipe. Water is rising in the excavation, and they will all be drowned before they are rescued, unless they can rapidly break through the six feet of earth between the top of the periscope shaft and the surface. They can do so only by blasting it with explosives left in the excavation. However, if they do, as they can see through the periscope, they will blow up a small party of picnickers, who are lunching by the periscope's "eye." Signals through the periscope are not understood, and its shaft is too strongly built to be dismantled in time for them to call through its pipe to give warning.

Whether, in this case, Nielsen would reaffirm his unrestricted principle that the lesser evil is to be chosen, because otherwise "many lives will be lost, and far greater misery will obtain."[15] I do not know. However, many who would sanction the blasting out of the stuck potholer would intuitively condemn the blowing up of the innocent picnickers as murder, however great the temptation to commit it. And if in both cases the many should choose to die, I suspect that the released potholer would, perhaps with irrational guilt, think himself the beneficiary of an act of supererogation, but that the spared picnickers would not.

Although moral intuition is an unreliable and corruptible guide, the doctrine of the legitimacy of consent to possible sacrifice in a common enterprise supplies a ground for the intuitive difference between the two cases—a ground consistent with common morality. By contrast, Nielsen's unrestricted principle of the least evil implies that there is no significant difference between them, or between both and the case of Dudley and Stephens. But that is not made explicit in his discussion.

Every moral system gives rise to hard cases, in which those who accept it must, contrary to their desire, cause harm or permit it. And to the best of my knowledge, no alleged case of necessity among small groups of individuals which has ever been shown to arise in common morality is more than a hard one: none of them compels us to abandon common morality for some alternative like Nielsen's, or to add to it "some form of 'disastrous consequences' clause, allowing prima facie obligations to be overridden when the consequences of keeping them are sufficiently bad."[16] Traditional moralists recognize that there are

---

[15] Ibid., p. 229.

[16] Brock (1973), p. 251 n. 13. By chance Brock's paper was to hand when I sought

cases in which the consequences of abiding by common morality will be terrible, and in which almost anybody would succumb to temptation. But they maintain that such consequences as that more die rather than fewer, although tragic, are morally acceptable. Lord Coleridge did not venture to say that, in the place of Dudley and Stephens, he would have acted better than they did; but he thought he had no choice but to say that there was a better way of acting.

The Problem of Dirty Hands

Cases in which the choice of evils is between the destruction of a whole community, or grave injury to it, and the death or grave injury of one of its members, are on a different footing from cases in which the choice is between the death or suffering of a larger or of a smaller number of individuals. The welfare of a genuine community is a good common to all its members, and most of them will acknowledge that they ought to be prepared, at need, to make sacrifices for it. Yet although there is a distinction between the two kinds of case, it must not be assumed that the sacrifice of an individual for the good of the community is justified; and that if common morality forbids it, then common morality must be superseded. Although the example may be suspect as Christian, one is given pause by the recollection that the high-minded and noble-sounding principle "It is expedient that one man should die for the people," was advanced by the high priest Caiaphas to justify the judicial murder of Jesus.[17]

We may begin by disposing of a class of cases with which a number of moral philosophers have recently occupied themselves, apparently in the hope of breaking down the deep and still prevalent conviction that there are some things a man absolutely must not do. All members of the class have a common form: a very powerful person or society (usually, a wicked dictator) threatens to bring a calamity upon a whole community (usually, its destruction by nuclear bombardment) unless it will do something abominable by the standards of common morality (say, to procure the judicial murder of an innocent man).

Such cases of threats to a whole community must be distinguished from imaginary cases in which the devilish tyrant threatens, say to torture all a man's children to death unless the man himself personally tortures one of them to death. These cease to be very persuasive when one perceives their underlying theme—that anybody sufficiently powerful "who wants us to do something we think wrong has only to

an example of the position criticized. Other examples of it are too many to count. Brock's proposed escape clause is further examined in 6.5 of *The Theory of Morality*.

[17] John, 18:4.

threaten that otherwise he will do something we think worse."[18] And besides, even from a consequentialist point of view, complying with such threats is not prudent. On the one hand, if you refuse, the tyrant may relent; on the other hand, you cannot rely on him to keep his word even if you comply with his threat—the inductive evidence of previous cases would not be a safe ground for prediction.

In cases of threats to a whole community, not only are the threats more terrible, they are also as a rule rational. In consequence, pertinent nonimaginary examples can be given. During and after the Roman persecutions which followed the Jewish revolts in A.D. 66–70 and 132–135, the Jewish rabbis were confronted with problems of demands made, both by an irresistible government and by hostile gangs of bandits, upon communities and groups of a people disarmed and helpless. It was accepted as Halachah, or binding rabbinic law, that when a company of Jews was threatened with death unless they surrendered one of their number, "though they all be killed, they shall not surrender a single soul from Israel."[19] The word "surrender" (*masar*) is here used in its usual pejorative sense, which implies treachery, by contrast with the neutral "give up" (*yehabh*) and "give" (*nathan*).[20] There are cases in which the giving up of a man by a community would not be "surrendering" him, and it fell to the rabbis to define the difference.

Just as there are Christians who do not discriminate between any voluntary homicide and murder, so there were rabbis who maintained that to give up anybody under any circumstance, was to "surrender" him; but the received opinion was that there are distinctions, and that they differ according as the demand is to hand over a man to be killed, or a woman for defilement.

In the former case, the accepted rule was as follows.

> If a company of Jews . . . is threatened by heathens who say, "Give us one of you that we may kill him, otherwise we shall kill you all," they must rather all be killed. However, if the demand is for a named individual, like Sheba son of Bichri, then, in order to avoid wholesale slaughter, he should be surrendered.[21]

The rationale of this ruling, as Daube explains it, was this. A demand for a named individual would normally be made in the name of some institution claiming civil authority, because the individual demanded was, rightly or wrongly, held to have transgressed its laws, or the commands of its officials, in some way deemed capital. In such cases the man would often be quite innocent by Jewish law. But, since

[18] Foot (1967), p. 10.

[19] Daube, *Collaboration with Tyranny in Rabbinic Law*, p. 19. My account of rabbinic teaching is derived from this work.

[20] Cf. ibid., pp. 7, 25–26.

[21] Ibid., pp. 18–19.

presumably his relations with the authority he offended were voluntary, he could not expect a whole company to die rather than give him up. Even in such a case, however, one rabbi, Resh Laquish, held that the company should not give anybody up unless it had satisfied itself that, from the point of view of the authority making it, the demand was justified.[22] And nobody denied that a demand for an unnamed man could only be made out of cruelty or hatred for Jews as such, and was never to be complied with.

The rule for treating a demand to hand over a woman for defilement was different. First, it is limited to companies consisting only of women, presumably for the reason Daube gives: "where men are present, Oriental men, there is no need to lay down that not one woman may be handed over."[23] And second, there is no exception for a named woman; for that a particular woman was wanted for purposes of defilement could not possibly imply any special responsibility on her part. However, two exceptions are allowed: a company of Jewish women, to whom such a demand is made, may hand over one "already unclean" or a slave, that is, a harlot or one already presumably used for concubinage.[24]

These rulings in rabbinic law, although they are disputable and were disputed, show far better than any moralist known to me has done how common morality would deal with the same questions. As Daube writes of one set of such rulings, and might have written of nearly all, the rabbi who made them (in this case Judah ben Ilai)

> implied no abdication of ethical standards. Fervently desirous of preventing the abolition of Palestinian Jewry, he did draw the line where reprieve would be bought at the price of moral cohesion and self-respect.[25]

This comment anticipates the reply that must be made, from the point of view of common morality, against the external objection that it is irrational to stick to common morality if it brings about the destruction of one's community.

Common morality is outraged by the consequentialist position that, as long as human beings can remain alive, the lesser of two evils is always to be chosen. Its defenders maintain, on the contrary, that there are minimum conditions for a life worthy of a human being, and that nobody may purchase anything—not even the lives of a whole community—by sacrificing those conditions. A community that surrenders its members at the whims of tyrants ceases to be anything

---

[22] Ibid., pp. 40–43.

[23] Ibid., p. 83.

[24] Ibid., pp. 76–79.

[25] Ibid., p. 39.

properly called by that name; and individuals willing to accept benefits at the price of crimes committed upon other individuals degrade their humanity. Common morality allows a certain room for compliance with tyrannical external force, when resistance has become impossible; but there is a line that must be drawn beyond which compliance is excluded, and the example of rabbinic teaching is a guide in drawing it.

Contemporary consequentialists have gone far beyond licensing such actions as betrayal and murder by communities desperate to preserve a remnant in face of irresistible external threats. Impressed by Machiavellian arguments that a state may flourish more under rulers who do not regard themselves as bound by common morality than under rulers who do, they have drawn the Machiavellian conclusion that it is a ruler's duty as a ruler to disregard morality when it collides with *raison d'Etat*. On this view, a good ruler is not a man of what Kant called *gute Wille* but one of what Machiavelli called *virtù*. That is, of "vitality, or energy and courage without regard for their objects, energy and courage both for good and for evil."[26] And every successful ruler whose success was not an accident will have the same confession to make as Hoerderer, the Communist leader in Sartre's *Les Mains sales*.

> I have dirty hands right up to the elbows. I've plunged them in filth and blood. Do you think you can govern innocently?[27]

If this is so, then common morality is not for humanity's true representatives, the leaders who, by holding themselves above the petty scruples of the led, make possible a better life for them.

The superiority of political leaders to ordinary moral scruples has been depicted romantically. Michael Walzer, for example, has recently revived Max Weber's portrait of the successful politician as a tragic hero, in whom the genius of politics lives in discord with the god of love; and who, when that discord breaks out in irreconcilable conflict, chooses to save the public rather than his own soul.[28] It is true that he wistfully adds that it would be a good idea if successful politicians were to be called upon to end their careers with a public penance, in the same way as Camus's anarchist assassins willingly submit to their executioners. But if Weber's portrait is a true one, to exact such a penance would be hypocritical. If citizens are unwilling to forgo what

---

[26] John Plamenatz, *Man and Society*, vol. 1, p. 29.

[27] Quoted in Walzer (1973), p. 161, from J.-P. Sartre, *Dirty Hands*, in "*No Exit*" *and Three Other Plays*, tr. Lionel Abel (New York, n.d.), p. 224.

[28] Walzer cites Max Weber, "Politics as a Vocation," in Hans Gerth and C. Wright Mills, eds., *From Max Weber: Essays in Sociology* (New York, 1946), pp. 77–128, esp. 125–26. (See Walzer [1973], pp. 163–64, 176–78.)

can only be obtained by actions they are unwilling to do themselves, they are not entitled to exact penance from anybody they appoint to do them on their behalf.

Hence R. B. Brandt and R. M. Hare have argued* irresistibly against Walzer that, if no consideration outweighs the ends of good government, and if the ends of good government can be accomplished only by sometimes traversing the precepts of common morality, then whatever validity common morality has, it has conditionally, within the scope of a more embracing consequentialist system.[29] If they are right, successful politicians are not tragic heroes, but simply good intelligent men making hard decisions, as good intelligent men sometimes must. The notion that they are sinning on our behalf must be rejected, as proceeding from an uncritical and primitive conception of morality.

Before succumbing to the arguments of Brandt and Hare, it is well to scrutinize the Machiavellian assumption on which they rest: that in politics nobody succeeds except by getting his hands dirty.

This is not the truism that politicians are men, not angels, which no moral theory has ever denied. It is rather the proposition that the political goods that matter, liberty, prosperity, and peace, can only be procured by courses of action which involve grave violations of common morality, if not in the use of power, then in its acquisition. Although this bit of cynicism sometimes passes as popular wisdom, it is not seriously defensible.

Certainly no such conclusion follows from Hegel's valid observation that the major progressive movements of history are seldom foreseen by progressives as they in fact come about, and that they are as often traceable to wicked or imprudent actions as to good or prudent ones, and to motives that are anything but progressive. It is a fallacy to infer, because a wicked action was necessary to a politically good result, that it could have been part of a rationally justifiable political program.

Hegel went on to maintain that not only are "the miseries that have overwhelmed the noblest of nations and polities, and the finest exemplars of private virtue, . . . a fatality which no intervention could alter," but also that "the vast congeries of volitions, interests, and activities" which bring those miseries about are "the instruments and means of the World-Spirit for attaining its object."[30] Both positions depend upon a vulgar illusion. Hegel's eyes, like those of most historians, were drawn to the events that have led up to the great periods in the culture of the past, and especially to the period he considered the greatest known to him—his own present. But since he simply dismissed the possibility that things could have happened otherwise, he gratui-

* [See pp. 237ff and 253ff this volume.—Ed.]

[29] Cf. Brandt (1972), and Hare (1972b).

[30] Hegel, *The Philosophy of History*, tr. Sibree, pp. 22, 25.

tously denied what common morality presupposes, that no great political and cultural goods yet brought into existence could not have been brought into existence in other ways. That good has come about through crime does not show that it could only have come about through crime. Furthermore, by approaching the crimes and follies of history through the goods to which they give rise, he averted his attention from the evils to which they also give rise. It need not be disputed that a number of political goods were conferred on Europe by Napoleon; but history is largely silent about the long-term miseries directly produced by his aggressive wars, and yet more silent about the connection between his career and the fatal forms taken by the militarization of Europe in the following century and a half. No philosophy of history has produced any evidence worth the name either that, in the long run, any great political good could only have come about through barbarous or oppressive means, or that the barbarous and oppressive actions without which some political goods would not have come about have not also brought about compensating evils.

To be fair, Walzer does not offer historical justifications of the great historical crimes: aggressive wars, religious persecution, slavery, despotism, economic oppression. His chosen examples are lesser, more personal misdeeds, of kinds which occur in ordinary "bourgeois-liberal" politics. He does not pretend that any great political good has ever been attained by the methods of Stalin, or Napoleon, or Robert Clive, but he cannot rid himself of the Machiavellian conviction that common morality incapacitates ordinary politicians in constitutional states for acting effectively when confronted with unscrupulousness or criminal violence.

The weakness of his case sufficiently appears from his two chief examples. The first is of a reforming politician, who would govern effectively and well if elected to office, but who cannot be elected "unless he makes a deal with a dishonest ward boss, involving the granting of contracts over the next four years."[31] Walzer agrees that effective reformers must sometimes make such deals, but maintains that they dirty their hands in doing so. Common morality, I think, is subtler.

A case of judicial bribery examined by Richard Baxter is a close parallel to Walzer's. In a state in which public officials regularly demand bribes, may a man bribe court officials to do him justice, or to keep them from doing him injustice?

> You may not in case your cause be bad, give any thing to procure injustice against another; no nor speak a word for it nor desire it: this I take as

[31] Walzer (1973), p. 165.

> presupposed. You may not give money to procure justice, when the law of the land forbiddeth it, and when it will do more hurt accidentally to others than good to you; when it will harden men in the sin of bribery, and cause them to expect the like from others. But except it be when some such accidental greater hurt doth make it evil, it is as lawful as to hire a thief not to kill me; when you cannot have your right by other means, you may part with a smaller matter for a greater.[32]

The principle underlying Baxter's ruling resembles that by which self-defence is allowed. Even in a society in which corruption is normal and lawful, it is wrong to initiate the corruption of others or to harden them in it; but it is not wrong to defend yourself by means of corruption against corruption already initiated by others.

There is much that a reforming politician in the situation Walzer describes may not do without dirtying his hands. He may not initiate the corruption of a previously honest ward boss. He may not promise to secure him a contract unless he can do so lawfully; and he may not make other wrong or unlawful promises, for example, to arrange to have work contracted for inadequately inspected. Moreover, the harm done in granting the contract—presumably that the public will pay more than it would with another contractor—must be outweighed by good gained by means of it. Yet Carl Sandburg has recorded that it was by "patronage gifts that would have raised a high and noisy scandal if known by the opposition" that Abraham Lincoln procured the passage through the House of Representatives of the constitutional amendment abolishing slavery.[33] And Sandburg, like Baxter, and like most ordinary decent men, would rightly have been taken aback at the suggestion that by doing so Lincoln violated common morality.

Walzer's second example is that of an honest politician who has seized power in an imperialist country during a disastrous colonial war, with a pledge to decolonize. In going to the colony to treat with the rebels, he finds that terrorists have hidden bombs in a number of apartment buildings in the capital, which are set to be detonated within a day. Shall he order the torture of a captured terrorist, to find where the bombs are, or shall he permit many people to be killed by their explosion?

Walzer appears to think it the politician's political duty to have the terrorist tortured, even though torture is always and in all circumstances abominable.[34] Yet as he has described the situation, it is far from evident that torture would even be expedient. Could not the buildings be evacuated and searched?

---

[32] Baxter, *Christian Directory*, IV, 19, dir. 9 (*P. W.*, pp. vi, 295).

[33] Carl Sandburg, *Abraham Lincoln* (abridged ed., New York: Dell, 1959), vol. 3, p. 739.

[34] Walzer (1973), pp. 167–68; cf. p. 174.

Let it be the case that they cannot. Let it also be the case that the information by which alone the explosions can be prevented is in fact locked in the bosom of a certain terrorist. Would it even then be expedient to torture him? The answer, I think, turns on whether he is known to possess the information—known, not suspected. I assume that Walzer would agree that, given civilized political aims, it is not expedient to sanction torture in order to extract information from those not known to possess it.

An additional circumstance should not be forgotten; namely, what the law of the land is. Although this study allows no scope for entering into political questions, I assume that no legal system can permit the use of torture for any purpose and also secure to those who live under it that immunity from arbitrary mistreatment that is necessary to civilized life. And if a law forbidding the use of torture is in force, it is doubtful whether any officer of state may expediently break it, even in a case such as that described. However, by stipulating that his politician has assumed power in a disastrous colonial war, and is acting in the colony, Walzer entitles us to presume that, in the case under consideration, laws safeguarding personal liberties have been suspended. Correspondingly, rebels and revolutionaries whose cause is just would not be bound by the laws of the society against which they were fighting.

Given that the political ends of the politician under consideration are civilized and that he keeps all of them in mind, even in situations of the kind described there can be few sets of circumstances in which he could reasonably conclude that to torture the captured terrorist would be politically expedient. Yet it cannot be denied that there are some such sets of circumstances. Suppose that such a set was to occur, is Walzer's assumption correct that to torture the prisoner would be morally impermissible?

Walzer's reason is curious: namely, that even those responsible for terrorist campaigns do not deserve to be tortured. In itself, his point is a good one. Torture is impermissible as punishment; for it degrades the person tortured, and to degrade a culprit violates the respect due to him as a rational creature. But, since the problem in our example is not one of punishment, the desert of the prisoner is irrelevant. The politician in question wants to know whether it violates the conditional immunity from violence owed to every rational creature, to wring by torture from a prisoner known to be withholding it, and from whom it can be obtained in no other way, information necessary for saving the lives and limbs of many innocent people. He is resolved to obey the precept. *Thou shalt not stand idly by the blood of thy neighbor*: and his question is whether, in the case before him, that precept sanctions the use of torture.

The answer must turn on whether or not the prisoner satisfies the conditions for immunity to violence. And unless positive law prohibits it (and in the case described it does not) it is hard to discern how the terrorist in question could be supposed to satisfy them. For one condition of immunity to violence is that one not be participating in an attempt on the lives or the bodily security of other innocent persons; and the terrorist *ex hypothesi* is so participating: he is, at the very least, deliberately allowing innocent persons to be killed and mutilated by withholding his knowledge; and if he had a hand in placing the bombs, he is allowing the consummation of murders and mutilations he himself has set in train. Until the nineteenth century, positive law and moral opinion joined in permitting torture in such a case. In the past century and a half, torture has come to be prohibited by law in all civilized countries; and rightly, because it has been found practically impossible, while allowing it at all, to confine its use to the very few cases in which it would be morally permissible. But we must not confound the moral prohibitions deriving from a good positive law with prohibitions of common morality per se.

And so the problem of dirty hands dissolves. It arises from a twofold sentimentalization: of politics, imagining it as an arena in which moral heroes take hard (that is, immoral) decisions for the good of us all; and of common morality, ignoring the conditions it places on the immunities it proclaims.

Consequentialist Theories

Even though unprejudiced investigation discloses that Hebrew-Christian common morality does not lack defensible ways of treating cases, not only of necessity but also of institutional corruption and of grave public danger, the tragic choices it sometimes calls for remain disquieting. Perhaps traditional morality is so constructed that observing it will not lead to disaster, but is it not rational to look for something better? Any acceptable moral system exalts benevolence. Of course, false conceptions must be corrected, in which benevolence is confounded with willingness to barter fundamental human goods for mere animal survival. But, those corrections made, is not the way open for a traditional morality of benevolence, the principle of which would be that human good—genuine and not merely apparent human good—is to be maximized?

In terms of the theory of action presupposed in our investigation of traditional morality,* a theory of morality founded on benevolence would distinguish a right action from a wrong one solely on the ground

* [Donagan, *A Theory of Morality*, pp. 37–52.—Ed.]

that its consequences, in the extended sense in which not all consequences are causal, are better than the consequences of any alternative action open to its agent. With respect to the properties directly mentioned in their minimal or basic descriptions, such goodness or badness as actions possess is insignificant. Virtually all the good or evil produced by human beings is to be found, not in their actions in themselves, but in the consequences of their actions. Hence a truly rational system of morality, so it may be argued, must begin with the principle that actions are right if and only if their consequences are better than those of any other actions that could be done instead.

I shall speak of all moral theories deriving from this principle as "consequentialist." The word was introduced into technical philosophical English by G. E. M. Anscombe, in a paper which for many of us remains a landmark.[35] There, she applied it to any theory according to which it is right to violate any rule or precept, as long as the foreseen consequences of abiding by it are sufficiently horrible.[36] But such a usage is arbitrarily restrictive. The theories that are "consequentialist" according to it constitute only one species of theories according to which actions are judged morally solely according to the nature of their consequences per se, and it seems preferable to use the word "consequentialist" for the genus rather than for the species. . . .

Utilitarianism

The strength or weakness of the structure of consequentialism may be tested most effectively by exploring its most persuasive and most thoroughly investigated variety: utilitarianism. Utilitarianism is that species of consequentialism in which better consequences are held to be consequences involving more happiness. Accordingly, the principle of utilitarianism is that actions are right if and only if their consequences involve greater happiness than those of any other actions that could be done instead. . . .

Critics of utilitarianism like Bernard Williams, and chastened utilitarians like R. M. Hare, even as they embrace moral systems very like the traditional one, tend to think of them as justified by their acceptance utility.[37] And they retain their distrust of any system of rules advanced as absolute.

Whenever a defender of traditional morality protests that there are moral rules which, whatever the consequences, must not be broken, such as the rule prohibiting murder—the killing of the materially

[35] Anscombe (1958).

[36] Ibid., p. 12; cf. pp. 10–13. Cf. Foot (1967), p. 10.

[37] Williams, *Critique*, pp. 134–35; Hare (1972a), p. 14.

innocent—a natural reaction is to confront him with imaginary horror upon imaginary horror, and to inquire whether it would not be permissible, nay right, to commit murder if these horrors would be the consequences of his not committing it. And so it has come to seem natural to accept as much of utilitarianism as this: that no moral system can be philosophically acceptable unless it is supplemented by an escape clause, to the effect that, in all cases of a choice of evils, if one of those evils is so great that incurring it rather than any of the others would be calamitous, and if it can only be avoided by taking a certain action, then that action is to be taken even if it is in breach of a precept of the system.[38]

Our investigation of the hard cases to which traditional common morality gives rise has shown why it rejects such an escape clause as crude and unnecessary. For, in laying down that its precepts are to be observed no matter what the consequences, traditional morality does not imply that they are to be observed, let us say, if the consequences should be the death of everybody on earth. It has been constructed at every point with careful attention to the nature both of human action and of the world in which it takes place. The worst efforts of "situation ethics" to invent situations in which the consequences of abiding by traditional morality would be some world calamity have resulted in nothing but absurd fantasies. In short, the nature of traditional morality is such that observing it cannot, except by unpredictable accidents, have calamitous consequences. However, since observing it can have tragic consequences—consequences that would tempt almost anybody to deviate from it—it commands that, after you have pondered what bad consequences may flow from abiding by it, and made what dispositions you can to avoid them, you are to disregard them. You are to obey, "whatever the consequences." This is sometimes expressed hyperbolically, as in the precept: *Fiat justitia, ruat caelum*. That precept was enunciated in a culture in which it was held to be impossible that the heavens should fall as a consequence of your doing what you ought. Its sufficiently plain sense is that you are to do what you ought, no matter what tragedy may befall. But such a precept can only be taken seriously if it is understood that nothing beyond tragedy will be a consequence of justice.

While it repudiates escape clauses by which its precepts may be violated if the consequences of observing them are "bad enough," traditional moral theory does not concede that the consequences of generally accepting such an escape clause would be better than those of rejecting it. Nor, in refusing this concession, does it rely on general considerations about the incalculability of acceptance utilities. For there are direct objections to the argument for such escape clauses.

[38] Cf. Hare (1972b), pp. 177–78; Brock (1973), p. 252; Williams, *Critique*, p. 90.

That argument reduces to this: the only difference between the consequences of the general acceptance of traditional morality, and the consequences of its general acceptance when supplemented by an escape clause, will be that, in cases in which observing it in its unsupplemented form would be a calamity, that calamity would be avoided, together with the good educational consequences of perceiving that fact. And the chief objection to it is that, since nearly everybody's judgement is disturbed by the anticipation of calamity, it is probable that much of what is done on the ground of such escape clauses will be mistaken.

The examples commonly offered in support of escape clauses conceal this fact by imputing to the agents a knowledge they cannot possess. Consider the following, from Bernard Williams's attack on utilitarianism.*

> Jim finds himself in the central square of a small South American town. Tied up against the wall are a row of twenty Indians, most terrified, a few defiant, in front of them several armed men in uniform. A heavy man in a sweat-stained khaki shirt turns out to be the captain in charge and, after a good deal of questioning of Jim which establishes that he got there by accident while on a botanical expedition, explains that the Indians are a random group of the inhabitants who, after recent acts of protest against the government, are just about to be killed to remind other possible protesters of the advantages of not protesting. However, since Jim is an honoured visitor from another land, the captain is happy to offer him a guest's privilege of killing one of the Indians himself. If he accepts, then as a special mark of the occasion, the other Indians will be let off. Of course, if Jim refuses, then there is no special occasion, and Pedro here will do what he was about to do when Jim arrived, and kill them all. . . . The men against the wall, and the other villagers, understand the situation, and are obviously begging him to accept. What should he do?[39]

What is objectionable about this is its implication that the situation described must be one in which the death of twenty Indians will be the consequence of Jim's refusal.

How might somebody in such a situation reasonably appraise it? I submit that he might well reason as follows. "In Latin countries, the office of executioner is not an honored one; so the offer of the 'privilege' of executing a prisoner is probably not in good faith. Moreover, officers in military regimes customarily pretend that anybody they execute is guilty of rebellion or some serious crime: that he is eager to exhibit what he proposes to do as something generally considered atrocious seems to imply that he doesn't expect me to

* [See p. 104 this volume.—Ed.]

[39] Williams, *Critique*, pp. 98–99.

report what happened. Yet what could stop me? Well, the whole thing may be a particularly nasty hoax—the gun he'll give me may be loaded with blanks. Or he may intend to murder me. Or he may think to make me an accomplice: if I should kill one prisoner, he could kill the others with impunity; for my testimony would incriminate myself as well." Were Jim to act upon these reasonable reflections, he would presumably intercede for all the prisoners, flattering the captain as patriotic but humane, while trying to present himself as somebody of credit and integrity; but he would on no account agree to kill anybody.

In a given case, the consequences of acting on this reasoning may be tragic: the heavy man in the sweat-stained shirt may turn out not to be bluffing, and may be deaf to persuasion. But would not general acceptance of the rule that one is to comply with such invitations to murderous complicity be more likely to have bad results than not? Fifty years ago, seeking a case in which a breach of the rule forbidding lying might be permissible (that there might be a permissible breach of the rule forbidding murder seems not to have occurred to him), Bishop Kirk turned up "the well-known instance of the British officer, himself an atheist, who refused to save his life from his Mohammedan captors by abjuring Christianity, lest it should bring the British name into discredit."[40] Juxtaposition of Williams's and Kirk's examples has left me suspecting, perhaps quite wrongly, that even in our time, the acceptance utility of simple Victorian rectitude would be high.

The duty of beneficence in the Hebrew-Christian tradition is not the indiscriminate and unlimited maximizing of good imposed by utilitarianism. It is the duty to do what good one reasonably can, without omitting any perfect duty. The religious ideal of charity goes far beyond it. But beneficence and charity alike have to do only with those consequences of actions that are within human foresight. Nor is that all. Some portion of the evil in the world is a consequence of human wrongdoing and culpable folly; of that portion, at least some does not fall upon the blameless but returns to plague its inventors. Utilitarianism pays little attention to this. The task it lays upon the benevolent is to maximize good; and it will not relieve them of that task even if it may happen largely to consist in rescuing the idle, the headstrong, and the wicked from the ill consequences of their own conduct. Williams has denounced utilitarianism as an attack on human integrity, because it reduces each individual to "a channel between the input of everyone's projects, including his own, and an output of optimific decision."[41] That is perhaps extreme. Nobody's integrity is attacked

---

[40] Kirk, *Conscience and Its Problems*, p. 340. In a note, Kirk acknowledged that the officer's assertion was not a lie, but added that a lie was "virtually . . . implied" by it. In my opinion, one cannot lie by virtual implication: cf. 3.4 *The Theory of Morality*.

[41] Williams, *Critique*, p. 116.

by requiring him to defer his own projects in order to shield some innocent from violence or fraud. But at bottom it is an unanswerable criticism of the utilitarian concept of benevolence. Genuine benevolence, or willing the well-being of others, is willing that they live a decent human life, and so being prepared to help them in their efforts to do so; it is not an interminable bondage to alleviating the woes brought upon themselves by those who make little or no effort to live well.

If its theory is sound, strict adherence to traditional common morality will never, except by unforeseeable accident, have calamitous consequences, although it may now and then have tragic ones. Yet it does not follow that the general acceptance of any other system in preference to it would have better consequences. It may or may not, depending on circumstances; but, either way, we cannot know. That is why attempting to choose a moral system by its consequences is not only a mistake in moral theory but also futile.[42]

[42] The argument of the concluding paragraphs of this chapter owes much to criticism by Gertrude Ezorsky, in conversation, of an unpublished paper of mine.

V

The Moral Law and the Law of God

Peter Geach

In modern ethical treatises we find hardly any mention of God; and the idea that if there really is a God, his commandments might be morally relevant is wont to be dismissed by a short and simple argument that is generally regarded as irrefutable. 'If what God commands *is not* right, then the fact of his commanding it is no moral reason for obedience, though it may in that case be dangerous to disobey. And if what God commands *is* right, even so it is not God's commanding it that makes it right; on the contrary, God as a moral being would command only what was right apart from his commanding it. So God has no essential place in the foundations of morals.'

The use of this argument is not confined to a recent or narrowly local school of philosophers; it was used by the British Idealists when they dominated British philosophy, and, as we shall see, it was used much earlier than that. Nor is its use confined to people who do not believe in God; on one occasion when I attacked the argument, my chief opponents were not atheists but professing Christians. This is not surprising; for the argument was used by Christians of an earlier generation, the Cambridge Platonists, as a stick to beat that dreadful man Hobbes with. (I shall have more to say about Hobbes later on.) And they in turn got the argument from Plato's *Euthyphro*.

Let me summarize that dialogue. Euthyphro and Socrates are discussing the trial in which Euthyphro is to appear as prosecutor of his own father. Euthyphro's father had tied up a peasant who killed another peasant in a drunken brawl, notified the authorities, thrown the prisoner into a ditch, and put the matter out of his mind; meanwhile the prisoner died of hunger and cold. Euthyphro (Mr. Right-mind, as Bunyan might have called him) feared lest the gods might punish him if he sat at meat with a man who had done such a deed, unless he set matters right by prosecuting the offender. He must have known that this would be an ineffectual gesture; the old-fashioned Homeric idea that Zeus will punish men for callous insolence to the poor was not going to impress the Athenian court.

Socrates (that is, I presume, Plato) finds it outrageous that a man prosecutes his own father over the death of a no-good peasant (he reiterates this term *'thēs'* to rub it in how little the man's death mattered) and he tries to dissuade Euthyphro by tricky arguments, in a style much admitted and imitated by modern moral philosophers. Euthyphro is easily tied in knots by asking him whether pious deeds are pious because they please the gods, or please the gods because they are pious deeds; whether men ever disagree except about moral matters, for which there is no decision procedure like arithmetical calculation or physical measurements; and so on. But Mr. Right-mind is not convinced; again and again he cuts himself loose from these dialectical knots with the assertion that it doesn't matter who was the murderer and what relation he was to the prosecutor and whether the victim was a peasant, but only whether a man was foully done to death in a way that all the gods must hate. The dialogue ends with Euthyphro telling Socrates he has no more time for discussion and going off on his legal business.

Was this, as the received view represents, a victory for Socrates? Or was it a victory for simple piety over sophistical tricks? Euthyphro admittedly had one weak point: he believed in many gods who were sometimes at variance with one another and so might command different things. But this is irrelevant for our purposes; for Euthyphro's unswerving fidelity to the divine law would be no less objectionable to modern moral philosophers if he had believed in one God. The main issue is whether a man's moral code ought to be influenced in this way by beliefs about Divine commands.

In the first place, I want to reject a view—which some Christians have at least approached—that all our appraisals of good and bad logically depend on knowledge of God. To get a clear and indisputable example I shall take a bad sort of act. For there is a logical asymmetry between good and bad acts: an act is good only if everything about it is good, but may be bad if *anything* about it is bad; so it might be risky to say we knew an act to be good *sans phrase*, rather than to have some good features. But there is no such risk in saying that we know certain kinds of act to be bad. Lying, for example, is bad, and we all know this; giving a man the lie is a deadly insult the world over.

If a philosopher says he doubts whether there is anything objectionable in the practice of lying, he is not to be heard. Perhaps he is not sincere in what he says; perhaps his understanding is debauched by wickedness; perhaps, as often happens to philosophers, he has been deluded by a fallacious argument into denying what he really knows to be the case. Anyhow, it does not lie in his mouth to say that here I am abandoning argument for abuse; there is something logically incongruous, to use Newman's phrase, if we take the word of a Professor of Lying that he does not lie. Let me emphasize that I am not saying a sane and honest man must think one should *never* lie; but I say that, even if he thinks lying is sometimes a necessary evil, a sane and honest man must think it an evil.

Now it is logically impossible that our knowledge that lying is bad should depend on revelation. For obviously a revelation from a deity whose 'goodness' did not include any objection to lying would be worthless; and indeed, so far from getting our knowledge that lying is bad from revelation, we may use this knowledge to test alleged revelations. Xenophanes rejected traditional Greek religious beliefs because the gods were represented as liars and cheats; and (if Browning could be trusted) it would be a fatal objection to the claims of the Druses' Messiah Hakim that he commanded his followers to lie about their religion under persecution. It is not that it would be too dreadful to believe in mendacious deities; a revelation destroys its own credibility if it is admitted to come from deities or from a prophet who may lie. We know lying to be bad before needing to examine any alleged revelation. Sir Arnold Lunn has jeered at unbelievers for esteeming truthfulness apart from any supernatural hopes or fears, and has quoted with approval a remark of Belloc that one can't be loyal to an abstraction like truth; a pagan Greek would have retorted that Lunn and Belloc were *akolastoi*, incorrigibly wicked, if they could not see directly the badness of lying.

The knowledge of God is thus *not* prerequisite to our having *any* moral knowledge. I shall argue however that we do need it in order to see that we must not do evil that good may come, and that this principle actually follows from a certain conception of God. If I can make this out, the sophistry from which I started will have been completely refuted; for accepting or rejecting this principle makes an enormous difference to one's moral code.

I must first clear up an ambiguity in the phrase 'doing evil that good may come'. We cannot ask whether e.g. Caesar's death was a good or bad *thing to happen*; there are *various* titles under which it may be called good or bad. One might very well say e.g. that a violent death was a bad *thing to happen to a living organism* but a good *thing to happen to a man who claimed divine worship*, and this would again leave it open whether doing Caesar to death was a good or bad *thing to do* for Brutus and the rest. Now when I speak of 'not doing evil that good may come', what I mean is that certain sorts of act are such *bad things to do* that they must never be done to secure any good or avoid any evil. For A to kill a man or cut off his arm is not necessarily a *bad thing to do*, though it is necessarily bad that such a thing should happen to a living organism. Only by a fallacy of equivocation can people argue that if you accept the principle of not doing evil that good may come, then you must be against capital punishment and surgical operations.

Suppose that A and B are agreed that adultery is a bad sort of behaviour, but that A accepts the principle of not doing evil that good may come, whereas B rejects it. Then in A's moral deliberations adultery is simply out: as Aristotle said, there can be no deliberating when and how and with whom to commit it (EN 1107a16). For B, on the other hand, the *prima facie* objection to adultery is defeasible, and in some circumstances he may decide: Here and now adultery is the best thing. Similarly, Sir David Ross holds that the objection to punishing the innocent, viz. that then we are not 'respecting the rights of those who have respected the rights of others', is only a *prima facie* objection; in the general interest it may have to be overruled, 'that the whole nation perish not'—a Scripture quotation that we may hope Sir David made without remembering who was speciously justifying whose judicial murder.

It is psychologically possible to hold the principle of not doing evil that good may come independently of any belief in Divine commandments: I have already cited the example of Aristotle on adultery. We have to see whether this is also logically consistent.

We must first settle what sort of answer is relevant if a man asks 'Why shouldn't I commit adultery?'; only then can we see what reason against, if any, is decisive. One obviously relevant sort of reply to a question 'Why shouldn't I?' is an appeal to something the questioner wants, and cannot get if he does so-and-so. I maintain that only such a reply is relevant and rational. In post-Kantian moral theory another sort of reply has been offered as relevant—an appeal not to an agent's Inclinations but to his Sense of Duty. Now indeed you can so train a man that 'You *must* not', said in a peculiar manner, strikes him as a sufficient answer to 'Why shouldn't I?'; he may feel a peculiar awe at hearing this from others, or even on saying it himself; it may even be part of the training to make him think he *must* not ask why he *must* not. (Cf. Lewis Carroll's juvenile poem 'My Fairy'.) The result of such training is what people like Sir David Ross call "apprehending obligation'. When I speak of the Sense of Duty (in capitals) I shall always be referring to this notion.

Now, as we know, a totalitarian regime can make a man 'apprehend' all sorts of things as his 'obligations', if Providence does not specially protect him. But on the Sense of Duty theory a man so trained is admirable if he does what he thinks he *must* do, regardless of the nature and quality of his acts; for is he not acting from the highest of motives, the Sense of Duty? If a young Nazi machine-guns a column of refugees till he bleeds to death, instead of retiring for medical treatment, is not his Sense of Duty something to fill us with awe?

To myself, it seems clear that although *'You mustn't'* said in this peculiar way may psychologically work as a final answer to 'Why shouldn't I?', it is no rational answer at all. This Sense of Duty, as Bradley said (*Appearance and Reality*, c. 25) 'is empty self-will and self-assurance, which swollen with private sentiment or chance desire, wears the mask of goodness. And hence that which professes itself moral would be the same as mere badness, if it did not differ, even for the worse, by the addition of hypocrisy. We may note here that our country, the chosen home of Moral Philosophy, has the reputation abroad of being the chief home of hypocrisy and cant.'

Let us forget about the Sense of Duty, for I think it can be shown that an action's being a good or bad thing for a human being to do is of itself a fact calculated to touch an agent's inclinations. I shall here appropriate the powerful arguments, in the spirit of Aristotle, recently developed by Mrs. Philippa Foot. Moral virtues, she argues, are habits of action and avoidance; and they are such as a man cannot rationally choose to go without, any more than he can rationally choose to be blind, paralytic, or stupid; to choose to lack a virtue would be to choose a maimed life, ill-adapted to this difficult and dangerous world. But if you opt for virtue you opt for being the sort of man who *needs* to act virtuously (just as if you choose to take up smoking you opt to be the kind of man who *needs* to smoke); moreover, you cannot decide at the outset to act virtuously only when it is not too awkward or dangerous or unpleasant—that is deciding not to have the habit of virtue at all. If, for example, you opt for courage, you may perish through facing danger a coward would have shirked; but our world is such that it is not even safe not to be brave—as Horace said, death pursues after cowards too. And if you opt for chastity, then you opt to become the sort of person who *needs* to be chaste; and then for you, as Aristotle said, there can be no deliberating when and with whom to commit adultery; adultery is out.

But somebody might very well admit that not only is there something bad about certain acts, but also it is desirable to become the sort of person who needs to act in the contrary way; and yet *not* admit that such acts are to be avoided in all circumstances and at any price. To be sure, a virtuous person cannot be ready in advance to do such acts; and if he does do them they will damage his virtuous habits and perhaps irreparably wreck his hard-won integrity of soul. But at this point someone may protest 'Are you the only person to be considered? Suppose the price of your precious integrity is a most fearful disaster! Haven't you got a hand to burn for your country (or mankind) and your friends?'. This sort of appeal has not, I think, been adequately answered on Aristotelian lines, either by Aristotle or by Mrs. Foot.

It is just at this point, I think, that the law of God becomes relevant. I shall not argue as to the truth of the theological propositions I shall use in the following discussion; my aim in this essay is to show that *if* a man accepts them he may rationally have quite a different code from someone who does not. And the propositions I shall use all belong to natural theology; in Hobbes's language, I am considering only 'the Kingdom of God by Nature'.

If God and man are voluntary agents, it is reasonable to believe that God will not only direct men to his own ends willy-nilly like the irrational creatures, but will govern them by command and counsel. The question is then whether God has given laws to man which forbid whole classes of actions, as human laws do. There appear strong reasons for doubting whether God's commands could be like this.

> Laws have to be framed in broad general terms because the foresight of legislation is limited, and because the laws would be unmanageably complicated if the legislators even tried to bring in all the contingencies they could themselves foresee; nor can there be somebody always at every man's elbow to give him commands suiting the particular contingency. But God is subject to none of these human limitations; so is it not a grossly anthropomorphic view of God to imagine him legislating in general terms because hard cases make bad law?

It is not a question, I reply, of God's knowledge and power, but of man's. Man's reason can readily discern that certain practices, like lying, infanticide, and adultery, are generally undesirable, even to the point that it is generally desirable that men should not *think* of resorting to them. But what man is competent judge in his own cause, to make exception in a particular case? Even apart from bias, our knowledge of the present relevant circumstances is grossly fallible; still more, our foresight of the future. Some men, like Dr. Buchman's disciples, have claimed to have Divine guidance in all conjunctures of life; but such claims are open to doubt, and certainly most men are not thus favoured. So unless the rational knowledge that these practices are *generally undesirable* is itself a promulgation of the Divine law *absolutely forbidding* such practices, God has left most men without any promulgation of commands to them on these matters at all: which, on the theological premises I am assuming, is absurd.

The rational recognition that a practice is generally undesirable and that it is best for people on the whole not even to think of resorting to it is thus *in fact* a promulgation to a man of the Divine law forbidding the practice, even if he does not realise that this is a promulgation of the Divine law, even if he does not believe there is a God.

This is not a paradox. You have had a city's parking regulation promulgated to you by a No Parking notice, even if you are under the illusion that you may ignore the notice and think it has been put up by a neighbour who dislikes cars. And similarly anyone who can see the general objectionableness of lying and adultery has had God's law against such actions promulgated to him, even if he does not recognize it as God's law.

This means that the Divine law is in some instances promulgated to all men of sound understanding. No man can sincerely plead ignorance that lying, for example, is generally objectionable. I am *not* saying that a sane and honest man must see that lying is *absolutely excluded*; but he must have some knowledge of the *general objectionableness* of lying, and this is in fact a promulgation to him of the Divine law against lying. And he can advance from this knowledge to recognition of the Divine law as such, by a purely rational process.

To make this point clearer, let us consider a modern ethical philosopher who says 'I do on the whole object to lying, but this is just a practical attitude I take up—it is quite wrong to call it "knowledge" '. I do *not* say of him what I should of a man who professed to have no special objection to lying: that he is just a vicious fellow, or a fool talking at random, who deserves no answer. What I do say is that his very protest shows that he does possess that sort of knowledge which is in fact God's promulgation of a law to him. His erroneous philosophy will not allow him to call it knowledge; but that does not prevent it from *being* knowledge—philosophers in fact know many things that their own theories would preclude them from knowing. And since he has this knowledge, he has had God's law against lying promulgated to him, even if he does not believe in God.

Thus, whatever a man may think, his rational knowledge that it is a bad way of life for a man to be a liar or an adulterer is in fact a promulgation to him of the Divine law; and he is able to infer that it is such a promulgation if he rightly considers the matter. As Hobbes said:

> These dictates of reason men use to call by the name of laws, but improperly: for they are but conclusions or theorems concerning what conduceth to the conservation and defence of themselves: whereas law, properly, is the word of him that by right hath command over others. But yet if we consider the same theorems as delivered in the word of God that by right commandeth over all things, then are they properly called laws.

There is a current malicious interpretation of Hobbes on which 'the word of God' would mean whatever the sovereign chooses to decree to be canonical Scripture. High-minded people are prepared to talk about Hobbes with reckless disregard of the truth: the late Lord Lindsay, in his Preface to the Everyman *Leviathan*, perpetrated a horrid mangling of Hobbes' text, giving the false text an air of authenticity by the use of antique spelling.[1] But what Hobbes himself says

[1] p. xvi of Everyman edition. Lindsay's version confounds Law and Right of

elsewhere is: 'God declareth his laws by the dictates of natural reason.' As an historical footnote I add that a very similar line of reasoning is to be found in Berkeley's youthful sermon on Passive Obedience. The debt Berkeley owes to Hobbes is quite obvious: but no doubt a clergyman could hardly cite such an authority explicitly without destroying the edifying effect of his discourse.

But what if somebody asks 'Why should I obey God's Law?' This is really an insane question. For Prometheus to defy Zeus made sense because Zeus had not made Prometheus and had only limited power over him. A defiance of an Almighty God is insane: it is like trying to cheat a man to whom your whole business is mortgaged and who you know is well aware of your attempts to cheat him, or again, as the prophet said, it is as if a stick tried to beat, or an axe to cut, the very hand that was wielding it. Nebuchadnezzar had it forced on his attention that only by God's favour did his wits hold together from one end of a blasphemous sentence to another—and so he saw that there was nothing for him but to bless and glorify the King of Heaven, who is able to abase those who walk in pride. To quote Hobbes again 'God is King, though the nations be angry: and he that sitteth upon the cherubim, though the earth be moved. Whether men will or no they must be subject always to the Divine power. By denying the existence or Providence of God, men may shake off their ease, but not their yoke.'

This reasoning will not convince everybody; people may still *say* that it makes sense, given that there is a God, to defy him; but this is so only because, as Prichard said, you can no more make a man think than you can make a horse drink. A moral philosopher once said to me: 'I don't think I am morally obliged to obey God unless God is good: and surely it is a synthetic proposition that God is good.' I naturally asked him how he understood the proposition that God is good; he replied 'Well, I have no considered view how it should be analysed; but provisionally I'd say it meant something like this: God is the sort of God whom I'd choose to be God if it were up to me to make the choice.' I fear he has never understood why I found the answer funny.

I shall be told by such philosophers that since I am saying not: It is your supreme moral duty to obey God, but simply: It is insane to set about defying an Almighty God, my attitude is plain power-worship. So it is: but it is worship of the Supreme power, and as such is wholly different from, and does not carry with it, a cringing attitude towards earthly powers. An earthly potentate does not compete with God, even unsuccessfully: he may threaten all manner of afflictions, but only

---

Nature; which Hobbes emphatically distinguishes in the very passage (c. 14 *ad init.*) that Lindsay claims to be quoting!

from God's hands can any affliction actually come upon us. If we fully realize this, we shall have such fear of God as destroys all earthly fear: 'I will show you whom you shall fear', said Jesus Christ to his disciples.

'But now you are letting your view of the facts distort your values.' I am not sure whether this piece of claptrap is meant as moral reprobation or as a logical objection; either way, there is nothing in it. Civilized men know that sexual intercourse is liable to result in child-bearing; they naturally have quite different sexual morals, one way or another, from savages who do not know this. And they are logically justified in evaluating sexual intercourse differently; for they have a different view of what sort of act it is. Now for those who believe in Almighty God, a man's every act is an act either of obeying or of ignoring or of defying that God; so naturally and logically they have quite different standards from unbelievers—they take a different view as to what people are in fact doing.

'But suppose circumstances are such that observance of one Divine law, say the law against lying, involves breach of some other absolute Divine prohibition?'—If God is rational, he does not command the impossible; if God governs all events by his Providence, he can see to it that circumstances in which a man is inculpably faced by a choice between forbidden acts do not occur. Of course such circumstances (with the clause 'and there is no way out' written into their description) are consistently describable; but God's Providence could ensure that they do not in fact arise. Contrary to what unbelievers often say, belief in the existence of God does make a difference to what one expects to happen.

Let us then return to our friend Euthyphro. Euthyphro regarded his father's act of leaving a poor man to die forgotten in a ditch as not just *prima facie* objectionable, but as something *forbidden* by the gods who live for ever; and he was horribly afraid for himself if he went on living with the offender as if nothing had happened. He did well to be afraid, the fear of God is the beginning of wisdom. To be sure, it is not all of wisdom.

The fear of God of which I have spoken is such fear as restrains even the wish to disobey him; not merely servile fear, which restrains the outward act, but leaves behind the wish 'If only I could do it and get away with it!' And, as is proper in a paper of this kind, I have confined myself to what Hobbes called the Kingdom of God by Nature. It is no part of our merely natural knowledge of God that we can boldly call God our Father and serve him in filial love: we are his children, if we are, purely by his free gift of the Spirit of adoption, and not by birthright: and the fear of God for his power irresistible is at least the *beginning* of wisdom—without it there is only pitiable folly. I agree, indeed, with Hobbes that gratitude for God's benefits would not be a sufficient ground for *unreserved* obedience if it were severed from fear of God's irresistible power.

That fear is an ultimate suasion. We cannot balance against our obedience to God some good to be gained, or evil to be avoided, by disobedience. For such good or evil could in fact come to us only in the order of God's Providence; we cannot secure good or avoid evil, either for ourselves or for others, in God's despite and by disobedience. And neither reason nor revelation warrants the idea that God is at all likely to be lenient with those who presumptuously disobey his law because of the way they have worked out the respective consequence of obedience and disobedience. Eleazer the scribe (2 Maccabees 6), with only Sheol to look forward to when he died, chose rather to go there by martyrdom—*praemitti se velle in infernum*—than to break God's law. 'Yet should I not escape the hand of the Almighty, neither alive nor dead.'

The wicked can for the moment use God's creation in defiance of God's commandments. But this is a sort of miracle or mystery; as St. Paul said, God has made the creature subject to vanity against its will. It is reasonable to expect, if the world's whole *raison d'être* is to effect God's good pleasure, that the very natural agents and operations of the world should be such as to frustrate and enrage and torment those who set their wills against God's. If things are not at present like this, that is only a gratuitous mercy, on whose continuance the sinner has no reason to count. 'The world shall fight with him against the unwise. . . . Yea, a mighty wind shall stand up against them, and like a storm shall blow them away.'

VI

Right and Wrong as Absolute

Charles Fried

Ordinary moral understanding, as well as many major traditions of Western moral theory, recognize that there are some things which a moral man will not do, no matter what. The harming of innocent people, lying, enslavement, and degradation—these are all things decent people shrink from, though great good might seem to come in particular cases from resorting to them. Consequentialists acknowledge this deep thrust, and the arguments they offer to account for it come down to this: The category of the good is the single overriding moral category, identifying those states of affairs which we should wish to obtain. All other moral concepts are secondary and derivative. Right and wrong are the derivative categories directing choice, but they do so under the sovereign mandate of the category of the good. Thus, if there is any apparent divergence between the right and the good, this is only because sometimes the greatest good is attained if individuals do not pursue it directly. An example is the economic theory of Adam Smith, which holds that it is right for individuals to pursue their own advantage because by doing so they are more likely to contribute to the greatest good of the greatest number, more likely than if they were enjoined to pursue the greatest good directly. So also consequentialism may promulgate the view that certain traditional wrongs—for instance, lying, killing innocent people—are "absolutely" wrong, not because they are indeed always wrong or because their avoidance is to be elevated above the pursuit of the greatest good, but because if the prohibition is given in this forceful way, imperfect human agents are on the whole more likely to avoid doing unjustified harm.

On what basis, the consequentialist asks, can one admit the independence of moral categories competing with the category of the good? It is states of the world, including states of mind, which we care about, choose, and therefore value. And so it is states of the world which must determine utterly the contents of morality. Surely we must be able to say whether one state of the world is better than another and which one is best of all. Whatever the conception of that end state, the consequentialist asserts that it cannot be rational to be concerned with how the end state comes about, except as that concern bears upon the very production of that end state. In short, it is ends not means which determine morality. Moreover, consequentialism is driven to hold that there is some one single end state, or type of end state, or characteristic of end states which is morally significant, for then this characteristic provides a criterion for choosing between end states, a criterion which is itself consequentialist.

The opposing conception of right and wrong, the conception that there are some things we must not do no matter what good we hope to accomplish, has always stood as a provocation and a scandal to consequentialism. If a state of the world is the best possible state and we bring it about at the least possible cost, what else can matter? Yet the opposing conception (the deontological) holds that how one achieves one's goals has a moral significance which is not subsumed in the importance and magnitude of the goals. Whether we get to the desired end state by deliberately hurting innocent people, by violating their rights, by lies and violence, is intensely important. And yet the deontologist does not deny that states of the world are sources of value and even agrees that the good inherent in states of the world (including our own states of mind) is the only *good*. If a happy state of the world existed that had been brought about through wrong and violation of right, and if those wrongs could no longer be righted, there is nothing that says that this happiness would not count as real happiness and should not be enjoyed; still, if this happiness had been ours to choose only by wrongful means, we would have had to wave it away. We would have to wave it away because right and wrong are the foundations of our moral personality. We choose our goods, but if what we choose is to have value as a good, then the entity doing the choosing must have value, and the process of choice must be such that what comes out of it has value. In the view I shall elaborate, right and wrong have an independent and overriding status because they establish our basic position as freely choosing entities. That is why nothing we choose can be more important than the ground—right and wrong—for our choosing. Right and wrong are the expressions of respect for persons—respect for others and self-respect.

For both views, then, right and wrong are directive concepts, addressed in the second person, as it were, to an agent choosing a course of action. Good and bad, on the other hand, evaluate states of the world in general, however produced, whether as a product of choice or not. The difference between the views is that consequentialism subordinates the right to the good, while for deontology the two realms, while related, are distinct. The goodness of the ultimate consequences does not guarantee the rightness of the actions which produced them. The two realms are not only distinct for the deontologist, but the right is prior to the good. How this priority works out, and particularly how it works out in light of the obvious fact that action is, after all, directed at producing results, are questions which will be considered. . . .*

Right and Wrong as Absolute

It is part of the idea that lying or murder are wrong, not just bad, that these are things you must not do—no matter what. They are not mere negatives that enter into a calculus to be outweighed by the good you might do or the greater harm you might avoid. Thus the norms which express deontological judgments—for example, Do not commit murder—may be said to be absolute. They do not say: "Avoid lying, other things being equal" but "Do not lie, period." This absoluteness is an expression of how deontological norms or judgments differ from those of consequentialism. But absoluteness is only a suggestive first approximation of a much more complex characteristic. This characteristic can only be fully appreciated as a number of such norms are considered in detail and contrasted with their consequentialist versions. In every case the norm as boundaries and what lies outside those boundaries is not forbidden at all. Thus lying is wrong, while withholding a truth which another needs may be perfectly permissible—but that is because withholding truth is not lying. Murder is wrong but killing in self-defense is not. The absoluteness of the norm is preserved in these cases, but only by virtue of a process which defines its boundaries. That process is different from the process by which good and bad are weighed in consequentialism, and so the distinctiveness of judgments of right and wrong is preserved.†

* My attention will be directed particularly to wrongs, those things which we must not do. The concept of right is more general. In its general significance it is used in philosophical terminology to refer to the whole domain of the obligatory, the domain of duty, the domain of deontology as opposed to the domain of the good. But it can mean a variety of other things as well. Often it is used in the negative as an equivalent of wrong: "Lying is not right." When something is said to be right, this does not mean invariably that it must be done, but perhaps only that it may be done, that is, that it is not wrong. Finally, one may speak of *a right*, as in the right to vote. This last use, the sense in which one speaks of *rights*, is theoretically related to the first, but grammatically distinct. In this work [*Right and Wrong*] I shall consider the right in general and rights, but not the concept of right contained in usages such as "the right thing to do."

† Consider this case: Is it wrong to take another's property? Well, what of

Even within such boundaries we can imagine extreme cases where killing an innocent person may save a whole nation. In such cases it seems fanatical to maintain the absoluteness of the judgment, to do right even if the heavens will in fact fall. And so the catastrophic may cause the absoluteness of right and wrong to yield, but even then it would be a non sequitur to argue (as consequentialists are fond of doing) that this proves that judgments of right and wrong are always a matter of degree, depending on the relative goods to be attained and harms to be avoided. I believe, on the contrary, that the concept of the catastrophic is a distinct concept just because it identifies the extreme situations in which the usual categories of judgment (including the category of right and wrong) no longer apply. At the other end of the spectrum, there is the concept of the trivial, the *de minimis* where the absolute categories do not yet apply. And the trivial also does not prove that right and wrong are really only a matter of degree. It is because of these complexities and because the term absolute is really only suggestive of a more complex structure, that I also refer to the norms of right and wrong not as absolute but as categorical.*

When we say that one must not grievously harm an innocent person, that one must not lie, these are categorical prohibitions in the sense that (within limits) no amount of good can justify them. But they are not absolute in the sense that we may never be justified in doing acts which have these very results—the death of an innocent person, the propagation of false beliefs—as a consequence. They are absolute in the sense that they point out certain *acts* we must not perform. They are not absolute in the consequentialist's sense; they do not state that a certain state of the world is of such supreme importance that the

---

emergencies, as when I need your car to get to the hospital and you won't consent? Perhaps what is wrong in that case is not taking the car but taking it without compensating you for its use. What if I do not have the moeny? Perhaps what is wrong is not compensating you when I can. Though qualified in various ways, the judgment still seems to be absolute.

* It is ironic that it is the dominant form of consequentialism—hedonistic utilitarianism—which is really absolutist. Hedonistic utilitarianism offers a single criterion, the sovereign standard of pleasure and pain, in terms of which all choice is absolutely determined. Consequences and only consequences count because pleasure and pain are themselves consequences, and the consequences of consequences. Utilitarianism is supremely pragmatic about the worth of all the particular things people do, seek, and avoid—beauty, knowledge, food, friendship, mutual aid, truth-telling and lying, revenge, punishment, death—for all these things are good and bad only and insofar as they do or do not conduce to the one sovereign good. And other forms of consequentialism—for instance religious ethics, which substitute beatitude for Bentham's pleasure, or ethics that view survival of the species as the sovereign good—display exactly the same logical structure. It is this logical structure that makes consequentialism peculiarly susceptible to mathematicization. Moral choice can be modeled as a mathematical exercise, the point of which is to find the maximum of a function, given the initial conditions of choice.

value of everything else must be judged by its tendency to produce that state. So here we see a complex relation between deontological judgments on what we *do* and evaluative (axiological) judgments on states of the world—with which we are also concerned. We must indeed be concerned with producing good in the world, but without violating the absolute norms of right and wrong.

It is a crucial thesis . . . , then, that there are categorical norms, and that judgments of right and wrong take the form of categorical norms. Given the centrality of this concept, I offer this specification. First, a *norm* is a judgment addressed to an agent, directing choice. Thus a norm differs from value judgments in general in that value judgments do not necessarily direct choice, although choices may be made by reference to them. If I say that the August moon is particularly beautiful or that Hadrian was a wise emperor, consistency requires that I take the opportunity to gaze upon the moon in August when nothing stands in the way or emulate Hadrian should I find myself in his situation, but it is obviously not the point of these judgments to prescribe such conduct. To say, however, that lying is wrong is just to direct all potential auditors to avoid lies. Second, a norm is *categorical* when its application is not contingent upon the agent's adopting some other independent end, which the norm will lead him to attain; it is not like the norm "If you wish to live to be ninety, don't smoke." This is Kant's distinction between categorical and hypothetical imperatives. But third, my conception contains a further element, which is captured (though with more rigor than I ultimately intend) by the term absoluteness. A categorical norm does more than direct that a particular value be given weight in making choices. It is not like the directive that the suffering of animals be taken into account in one's choices, and that if the cost is not too great that their suffering be minimized. Rather, a categorical norm displaces other judgments in its domain, so that other values and ends may not be urged as reasons for violating the norm. It is preemptive. This latter characteristic of categorical norms is the most distinctive and the most troublesome. In fact, I have already indicated that in a sense it is an approximation of a more complex notion. A categorical norm may be overwhelmed by extreme circumstances. So also it may be underwhelmed, as it were, by the triviality of the instance of its application. But so long as the consequences fall within a very broad range, the categorical norm holds, no matter what those consequences. To propound a categorical norm, to argue that an action is wrong, is to invite inquiry into the kinds of action intended to be covered, but not an inquiry into the costs of compliance.

Finally, there is the question whether all deontological norms are absolute or categorical. These are judgments of right and wrong which in their very statement invite the weighing of consequences and of competing considerations. Individuals have a right to a fair share of scarce resources and a duty to contribute to a regime of fair shares, but what share is fair will vary with the circumstances and is in part a matter of the consequences of what each person does. Similarly, it is wrong to expose the person or property of another to undue risk of harm, but what risk is undue is a function of the good to be attained and the likelihood and magnitude of the harm. Yet these judgments too are categorical, though in a complex way which I will elaborate only after I have developed the analysis of intentional harms. Briefly the idea is that, even where the specification of the wrong (taking more than one's fair share, subjecting others to undue risk) includes a weighing of consequences, once the weighing has been done then it is also absolutely wrong to go against the conclusion of that process. Where, as in the case of fairness, consequences are weighed in a special way (for example, in order to equalize rather than maximize net benefits) then the absoluteness of the obligation is one that forbids sacrificing equality for any amount of greater net benefits. Finally, there are many cases where the only right thing to do is to maximize net good consequences—usually subject to certain constraints. And in those cases it is wrong to do anything else.

The Complexity of Deontological Systems

Although the inexorable nature of the norms of right and wrong makes the moral system based on them seem harsh and rigid, the opposite is in fact the case. Deontologic systems are typically complex, consisting of a number of specific norms. Though there are connections between these norms and they are all generated by a common general conception of moral personality, still they reduce neither to each other nor to some single overriding moral precept. The domain of right can no more be exhausted by some one all-inclusive norm than the concept of human happiness can be boiled down to some particular enjoyment. Moreover, even as a system, categorical norms do not take up the totality of moral space. One cannot live one's life by the demands of the domain of right. After having avoided wrong and done one's duty, an infinity of choices is left to be made. Indeed, it is consequentialist systems like utilitarianism which are oppressive in the totality of the claim they make on moral agents. For utiliarians there is always only one right thing to do, and that is to promote in all possible ways at every moment the greatest happiness of the greatest number.* To stop

* Utility theory, a modern version of utilitarianism, seems to escape this criticism by standing ready to recognize any number of distinct values related in whatever complex ways one wishes. The mediating, homogenizing entity of utility is posited as a theoretical entity only. In utility theory no one aims at utility as such or even cares about it. Utility is postulated as the mathematical expression of the relative

even for a moment or to rest content with a second best is a failure of duty. And if we seek to excuse ourselves by saying that everyone needs a rest from time to time, or as Bernard Williams put it, everyone needs to knock off doing good works occasionally, the utilitarian will allow that too, *if* this is how we best maintain our efficiency in the pursuit of overall utility. In contrast to this oppressive, obsessive regime the limited absolutism of deontology is a positive relief.

That the system of right and wrong is both limited and multifarious is a large part of what makes it appealing and true to the complex facts of our moral life. Now, the term absolute certainly has a nasty, pervasive ring to it, and it is important to see exactly how it is that right and wrong, absolute though they are, keep from spreading out and taking over the whole of our moral lives. They do not, but in speculating how they might and why they do not, we shall come to a better understanding of the domain of right and wrong in general. We shall see how the very *form* of categorical norms (norms of right and wrong) expresses the same conception of human personality as do the *contents* of the norms. Consider the norms "Do not lie" or "Kill no innocent person." It is intuitively obvious that these are distinct norms which do not boil down to versions of each other or of some third norm—this is the multiplicity of categorical norms. Also, it is obvious that in most situations there is a great deal of choice left over, even after we have complied in scrupulous detail with these norms—this is the limited nature of the norms. But it might be otherwise. If, for instance, we looked at the norm about killing as a consequentialist might, we would see it as describing a bad state of affairs: the death of an innocent person. How would the consequentialist go on to give it absolute or categorical force? He might say that the death was bad in itself, which means that its badness is not just a function of some further states (fear, grief, lost opportunities) to which it tended to conduce, but that standing alone it was bad. This, however, would hardly capture the force of the judgment that the killing was categorically wrong. For to say that the death of an innocent person is bad in

---

strengths of the material ends people do pursue. So long as the relation between material ends can take any logical form at all, including the logical forms of deontology, there is no harm in this view, and very little bite. It does no more than report the structure of ends that a person may or does have. It may be, however, that this presentation of the system of ends as formally equivalent to the maximization of some very complexly related set of preferences is much less illuminating than a presentation in terms of right and wrong, good and bad. It may miss, for instance, the reason *why* the ends are related as they are. Also, there is the danger that certain complex relations of ends, such as obtain in a deontological system, will be distorted in the name of a more convenient mathematical presentation, which will then be asserted to be more rational. Or perhaps the reader or theorist will forget that utility is no more than an ex post, explanatory, theoretical entity, which is no part of anyone's actual system of ends.

itself commits you to no more than concluding that, other things equal, it should be avoided, that as a moral negative it must be outweighed to be permissible. But this says nothing at all about how easily it may be outweighed, what good can justify this bad. It may be, for instance, that almost any good at all might justify killing an innocent person, and still we can say the death is bad in itself. Nor is anything much changed if we say that what is bad in itself is not the death but the actual act of killing—for we must know what negative weight the killing has and not just that it has a negative weight. Can this killing be justified, for instance, as a way of preventing two killings by someone else?

Would the consequentialist express this absoluteness of the norm by saying that the result of the killing, the death, is not only bad in itself but somehow absolutely bad, where this must mean that it is so bad a consequence that nothing can outweigh it? That would certainly be very categorical, but it obviously goes too far. For if the death of an innocent person really were that bad, then the norm would be no longer a limited, but a pervasive one. What, for instance, if some action of mine carried a very slight risk of causing the death of an innocent person? If the absoluteness of the norm is to be interpreted as making the fact of death so overwhelmingly bad, it seems clear that I must not take even the slightest risk of killing an innocent person. But really everything I do carries some risk that it will contribute to the death of an innocent person. Indeed, we cannot even save the situation by limiting our calculations to foreseeable consequences, for the limits of the foreseeable are set by what we are obliged to look out for. If the consequence is as bad as all that, then we must also hunt about to see if there is any conceivable way that we might inadvertently be facilitating it. Of course there will always be some conceivable way, and that will be enough to stop us.

This line of analysis is enough to show that some quite plausible interpretations of absolute norms lead to impossibly stringent conclusions, lead in fact to total paralysis. But the case is in fact even worse. For if the absoluteness of the norm is interpreted to mean that the consequence—such as the death of an innocent person—is overwhelmingly bad, then not only are we forbidden to do anything, for anything carries with it a risk of death, we are indeed required to do nothing but seek out ways to minimize the deaths of innocent persons. For if such a death is so bad that no good can outweigh it, we are surely not justified in pursuing some good, even if that good does not present this risk, when we might instead be *preventing* this most undesirable of all consequences. So this interpretation is not actually a prescription for paralysis, it is more like an obsession. The norm, by virtue of this view of its absoluteness, takes over the whole of our moral life. Finally, since every action will endanger the life of some innocent, even an action intended to rescue some *other* innocent, we cannot escape the further corollary of this interpretation that we must choose that course and only that course of action expected to produce the greatest net saving of life—including, if need be, the deliberate, cold-blooded killing of an innocent person.

The situation is worse still, for this interpretation is not only obsessive, it also opens the possibility of insoluble contradictions within any system containing more than one absolute norm. The judgment that it is categorically wrong to lie would be interpreted in an analogous way to mean that a false belief is absolutely bad—that is, so bad that nothing can justify producing or even not eradicating it. But obviously, telling the truth will very often increase to some small extent the chances that an innocent person will die, and in any event the time spent in eradicating false belief will *not* be spent in warding off the danger of death from innocent persons.

Now, deontological systems avoid the paralysis, obsession, and contradiction of this interpretation. They are at once less and more stringent. They would not allow killing an innocent even to save several innocents from death; but the consequentialist interpretation would require the killing. Obviously, the interpretation of categorical norms in terms of consequences is profoundly inappropriate (it is a consequentialist interpretation of absolute norms), but how are the norms of right and wrong to be interpreted so as to avoid these results? How are they to be contained and specified? These questions bring us back to the notion of personal and limited responsibility with which this work began. They bring us back to the vision of the proper domain of human choice, which generates both the form and contents of the system of right and wrong.

A first approximation of the domain of categorical norms is the domain of actions. It is a good start to see that what is condemned as wrong is not some consequence, some state of affairs (a man dead, a false belief—these things are bad, not wrong) but the *action* which produces these states of affairs. Now, this is all right for any action which includes all its morally relevant features within the description of the action itself. Thus, for example, a norm condemning a certain sexual practice as wrong could be taken to condemn only the proscribed action without reference to any of its possible consequences. And of course such a categorical norm easily escapes the problems of paralysis, obsession, and contradiction. There are many things one can do other than engage in the forbidden action. If lying is defined as the act of asserting as true what is believed to be false, this provides another example. There is no problem in principle about forbidding that act absolutely. Since it is not consequences or states of the world as such that are proscribed, it is irrelevant that we might be causing, risking causing, or failing to avoid the same consequences (such as false beliefs) as tend to be caused by the forbidden action. Since we are not enjoined to minimize false beliefs at all costs but only not to lie at all costs, we can honor the prohibition and still have ample room left over for other things.

Thus there is no problem about prohibitions of actions which are defined by a close description of the gestures involved in accomplishing them, but most significant actions in our lives are defined in terms of their consequences. As to these, categorical prohibitions threaten to land us once more in obsession, paralysis, and contradiction. Killing an innocent person, for instance, or violating another's rights is a perfectly general description of any action at all that produces that particular result. We do not say that it is wrong to stab, strangle, club, or shoot an innocent person, but just to kill. So also consider humiliating another. There are no narrowly specified ways of doing this; yet it is wrong. And in general, right and wrong are concerned with the most important aspects of our lives, not just with a few ritual observances, and the consequences we produce or suffer are intensely important. Accordingly, most important norms, whether categorical or not, are concerned with the production of particular consequences and not with the gestures that bring them about. They have the form "Do not do *that*" where "that" is not a gesture, like picking your nose, but the production of a result. The trouble is that once judgments of right and wrong take this form, how are we to maintain their categorical force without falling into the traps and absurdities I have sketched?

Causation and Negative Duties

It has recently been proposed that we avoid these difficulties and focus our moral vision by considering not the undefined, unlimited range of all possible consequences of our actions but rather just those harmful consequences of which we are the *cause*.* But the concept of cause is at once too wide and too narrow a focusing criterion of what it is wrong to do. It is too wide, since when we are still considering what to do, the causal criterion scarcely narrows the range of our concerns at all. If, for instance, it is wrong to *cause* the death of an

* Particularly, it is claimed that this causal criterion would exclude responsibility in three classes of situations: (1) where we might have prevented the bad state of affairs from happening but did not ourselves set in motion the train of events which led to the unfortunate outcome; (2) where some act of ours did set the fatal train in motion, but the course of events by which it arrived at that destination was so unpredictable and bizarre that the result could not reasonably be laid at our doorstep; and (3) where the result came about through the deliberate choice of another responsible agent, for whom our action at most provided the occasion or opportunity to accomplish his own purposes. See, generally, H.L.A. Hart and A. M. Honoré, *Causation in the Law* (Oxford: Oxford University Press, 1959).

innocent person, then we are still faced with the fact that any act might be the cause of death, and if all such acts are absolutely wrong, no act is permitted.* And the causal criterion is too narrow if it excludes every case where a forbidden result occurs by way of the deliberate act of another—for instance, if we bribe or persuade another to act as our agent. Finally, the concept of cause is itself highly controversial and problematic. Why exactly is it that when I fail to perform some act, knowing that I could have prevented a bad result, I am not said—in the absence of some preexisting duty—to have caused that result? And if I did act, but the result would have happened irrespective of my act, can I be said to have caused it? In any event, the causal criterion turns out to be proposed primarily to limit the range of consequences for which a person may be held responsible *after* he has acted, and particularly the range of harmful consequences for which an agent should be made to pay compensation. Now, this is not necessarily the same question as what it is right and wrong to do. For instance, a person may have acted quite properly in engaging in some useful but hazardous activity, but still he should be responsible to the innocent victims of the accidental harm he causes. Norms of right and wrong, however, are addressed first of all to choice, to an agent before he acts.

Another suggestion to account for the stringency of what I call the

---

* Consider this variant of the causal thesis: An act is absolutely wrong only if the actor believes that the act is substantially certain to cause a forbidden result.

Does this not allow the causal criterion to specify an absolute norm without what I call the danger of obsession? Perhaps, but there are grave difficulties encountered in following this route. How "substantial" must the certainty be? If the answer is that substantiality is a matter of moral judgment, then it is clear that the norm is not absolute after all, since how certain the result must be will be a function of *normative* issues such as the magnitude of the harm, its probability, and the importance of the other ends being pursued. But that is precisely the judgment which the consequentialist demands every time. If substantiality is a non-normative approximation, such as 99 per cent, this objection is avoided, but at a great price in plausibility. For now what is to be a difference in moral kinds—between absolute and consequentialist types of norms—will depend on a highly arbitrary non-moral difference of degree. We shall have to say that acting where the result is believed to be 99 per cent certain is absolutely forbidden, but where the result is believed to be only 98 per cent certain, the consequentialist balancing is in order. The intentionality test I shall propose avoids this anomaly: between an intended and a foreseen consequence is a difference in kind which mirrors the difference in kind between categorical and consequentialist judgments. Finally, the causal criterion will have to reimport intention after all. For it would be absurd to say that one who intends the forbidden result but knows his chances of success are slim does not violate an absolute prohibition while one who does not intend that result but knows his chances are great acts absolutely wrongly. To avoid this anomaly, the causal criterion would have to be amended by adding the clause "or intends to cause that result," but then, of course, whatever difficulties about intention were sought to have been avoided reappear and one might just as well speak of intention straightaway.

norms of right and wrong is the distinction offered by Philippa Foot between positive and negative duties.* The proposal is that positive duties—duties to confer benefits or to prevent harm from occurring—are more easily outweighed (for instance by our wish to pursue our own interests) than are negative duties. Negative duties, duties *not* to harm others, Foot asserts, are far more insistent. This distinction would explain why it may be forbidden to ward off evil from one person by inflicting even a lesser evil on another. This distinction between positive and negative duties is obviously related to the distinction, familiar in both legal and moral contexts, between acts and omissions. It is generally true that a person is neither civilly nor criminally liable for harm unless the harm came about through his action. The mere fact that he failed to prevent the harm will not generally ground liability unless there was some special duty—a duty which the mere opportunity to be of service does not of itself create. Indeed the positive/negative duty distinction might be seen as the forward-looking, directive version of the act/omission distinction.

Both Foot's distinction and the distinction between acts and omissions suffer from the same defects as the more general causal criterion. Indeed, they depend on the concept of cause. Foot's negative duties, after all, must include negative duties not to cause certain results. That alone is not disastrous: in moral philosophy we may often be forced to swallow some quite unchewed metaphysical morsels, and we should be prepared to do so, provided only that the morsels appear to have a strong intuitive grounding. But we have the further problem that as soon as the negative duty is specified in terms of results (for example, the duty not to cause the death of an innocent person) it is obviously far too demanding—considered beforehand, anything at all might cause that result. So without some further attenuation, the danger of paralysis, obsession, or contradiction looms once again. Foot is able to avoid these difficulties only because for her, even negative duties are not absolute or categorical; they are simply more stringent than, they tend to override, positive duties. But for my argument, if the force of categorical norms is to be maintained and yet absurdity avoided, some other or further way must be found to limit the range of consequences to which the norms apply.

Intention: The Person as Agent and Object

Intention. Categorical norms are morally possible because they are concerned with what we do, rather than with what we allow to happen. To be sure, morality is concerned in some way or another with all the

* [See p. 154 this volume.—Ed.]

consequences to which we might contribute or which we might avoid. The categorical norms, however, designate what it would be wrong to *do* (in this way the concept resembles that of negative duties), but their absolute force attaches only to what we intend, and not to the whole range of things which come about as a result of what we do intentionally. This link of intentionality between a moral agent and what he accomplishes, a link which is crucial in the application of these norms, is simply another aspect, the procedural aspect, of the substantive contents of the norms. Both aspects express an underlying moral conception of the person. It is respect for persons as the ultimate moral particulars which is expressed by the contents of categorical norms. The mode of application, the procedural aspect, expresses this same centrality of the individual's personal efficacy as a moral agent.

This procedural aspect of categorical norms, by distinguishing what we do from what we merely allow to happen, allows the norms to retain their categorical force while avoiding the hazards of paralysis, obsession, and contradiction. This procedural aspect allows us to move beyond descriptions of acts as gestures to bring consequences within the ambit of absolute norms, without, however, forcing us to an obsessive or paralyzing concern with those effects. For so long as the bad effect just happens, then we have not violated an absolute norm by allowing that effect to happen, even if we could have prevented it, even if it came about as a side effect of something we were doing. But, of course, the notion of doing as opposed to allowing to happen, suggestive though it may be, is vague and requires further specification. This specification is provided by the concept of intention.

The norms of right and wrong proscribe *intentionally* bringing about the forbidden result. If that result occurs inadvertently or as a more concomitant of one's conduct or because one failed to seize an opportunity to prevent that result, then whatever else may be said of the conduct—it may be careless or callous, and may be condemned for that reason—it does not violate the categorical prohibition. This distinction between intended and unintended but possibly foreseen consequences necessarily occurs whenever bringing about a particular result is condemned as categorically wrong. Thus, for instance, David Daube writes of the Talmudic injunction against handing over a hostage to be killed or a woman to be molested, noting that the injunction holds even if the refusal results in a similar fate for a greater number of equally innocent persons. The handing over is an intentional act of betrayal, for the consequences of which the betrayer is responsible, while the still more dire consequences of not betraying are not his responsibility. Similarly, some legal doctrines condemn, or judge more severely, or permit a more limited range of excuses for intentionally bringing about certain harmful results. The international law of war condemns intentional infliction of civilian casualties, while permitting the causing of such casualties as a side effect, even a certain one, of military action against military targets. Finally, this distinction is formalized in the so-called law of double effect, by which certain bad results—for example, the death of an innocent person, the sinful act of another—may not be "directly" willed, that is, chosen either as one's ultimate goal or as the means to one goal, though they may be tolerated in appropriate circumstances as the foreseen concomitants of one's chosen means or ends.

This emphasis on intention has the virtues both of the causal proposal and of the distinctions between act and omission, between positive and negative duties. It has their virtues, but without their defects.* Now, one intends a result if that result is chosen either as one's ultimate end or as one's means to that end. One intends a result just in case one can say that one acted (or failed to act) in order to produce that result, just in case one would have to include that result in answer to the question "Why did you do that?" or "Why did you fail to do that?" Moreover, there are consequences of one's acting which, though foreseen with ever so much likelihood, are not intended at all. These results are mere side effects and one does not violate a categorical norm just by causing mere side effects to occur. The concept of intention comes into every categorical norm which is couched in terms of results. "Do not do *X*" (where *X* is an effect of one's actions) becomes "Do not intend *X*" or "Do not choose *X* either as your end or as the means to your end." Of course, there are categorical norms which speak in terms of actions *tout court*. For instance, the norm forbidding lying or perhaps some explicitly described sexual practice does not speak in terms of results at all, and so the need to confine an absolute norm of this kind to intended results does not arise. But even in such cases the act itself is in its very

* Thus the intention criterion would absolve the legislator who passes a beneficial law, knowing it will provide occasions for corruption, though we would condemn a legislator who corrupted voters or officials for the purpose of obtaining this legislation. This is because the incidental corruption is not part of his intention. The causal criterion would reach the same conclusion—that the legislator is not responsible for the corruption—because he did not cause it; that is, because it was a result of the choice of responsible agents. But, as we have seen, this is not quite sound—if the legislator had persuaded his cronies to use bribery and corruption, we would want to condemn him in that case too, and we could do so on the intention criterion although the bribery ran through the choices of independent moral agents. Similarly, if we fail to do something with the intention, for the purpose, of harming an innocent person, the intention criterion condemns us as severely as if we wielded the instrument of harm in our hands, but the act/omission or positive/negative duty distinction may not. Finally, intention provides a needed limitation of any supposed negative duty not to harm others—with that limitation the duty can sensibly be claimed to be categorical.

conception intentional: One who says something false believing it to be true does not lie.

Problems about Intention. There are serious difficulties in any systematic use of the concept of intention, and the literature is replete with criticisms and refutations. The two major forms of criticism relate (1) to the coherence of the distinction between what we intend and what we merely allow to happen—the extent to which we can state the principle of distinction so as to determine in all cases whether a particular result is intended as the agent's end or means to his end or whether it is a mere concomitant of his plans—and (2) to its moral relevance—even if we could discover a principle of application or if we had sufficient confidence in our intuitive ability to distinguish what is intended from mere concomitants of what is intended, the question would still remain why we should make such a distinction, what morally relevant feature such a distinction picks out.

The principal objection to the coherence of the intention concept acknowledges the importance of *ultimate ends* but denies the possibility of distinguishing *means* from side effects, where neither are desired for their own sake. Here are two cases which have been adduced to point out this difficulty:

> I. A, seeking to free his friend from prison, explodes a charge under the wall, knowing that a guard stationed on top of the wall will be killed in the explosion, though this death is immaterial to his plan. May we say that he did not intend the death of the guard, but that if he had shot the guard to obtain his keys he did so intend? Putting aside the point of making such a distinction, on what criterion is the distinction made?
>
> II. A party of explorers is trapped in a cave, in whose narrow opening a rather fat member of the party is lodged, and the waters are rising. If a member of the party explodes a charge next to the fat man, should we say that he intended the fat man's death as a means or that it is a mere side effect of (a) freeing the party, (b) removing the fat man's body from the opening, or most implausibly, (c) blowing him to atoms? How can we tell; why should we care?

There is a traditional criterion for distinguishing an intended means from an unintended but foreseen concomitant, the counterfactual test: if the morally relevant result at issue (in Case I, the death of the guard) could somehow miraculously be prevented and events thereafter allowed to take their natural course, would the actor still have chosen to act as he did? The gruesome case of the fat man in the cave is supposed to show that this means of discrimination can prove anything and everything. Since it is not by virtue of the fat man's *death* that the plan fails but only by virtue of the continued presence of his body in the mouth of the cave, then if the fat man did not die, the blaster would still have lit the fuse on the dynamite. Unfortunately, one may always be able to designate some aspect of the result as the chosen means and another aspect as an undesired side-effect. And the gambit can be blocked only if we find some way of saying that certain consequences come in such tightly bound units that they may not be disaggregated—blowing the fat man to atoms cannot be severed in analysis from killing him.

I do not have a foolproof criterion for identifying the results we intend and distinguishing them from those we merely allow to happen, for distinguishing—in Thomas Nagel's phrase—between "what one does to people and what merely happens to them as a result of what one does." The counterfactual test, for instance, is not incorrect but is defective in that in the hardest cases it appears to depend on the very concepts—intention, purpose—it is meant to explicate. Crucial as intention is, I must be content to leave it unanalyzed, a primitive term. This is a less unsatisfactory state in which to leave the argument than might first appear. The argument I shall be developing will explicate this formally unanalyzed concept of intention to a considerable extent. And after all, I am not interested in the concept of intention in the abstract, but as it serves to specify the absolute norms of right and wrong. There may very well not be a satisfactory analysis of intention for every domain of human activity—from literary criticism to the behavior of large groups—or at any rate not one single analysis. Indeed, I suggest that the concept of intended as opposed to foreseen consequences has its clearest application just in respect to actions and results which invoke the stringent norms of right and wrong.

Intention as Efficacious Desire. There is a connection between intention and the contents of categorical norms. The two illuminate each other. The central concept in each case is that of respect for persons. It is wrong to do those things which violate the integrity of other persons, but whether we have indeed done wrong will depend on whether as agents we have engaged our persons in causing harm to another. It is striking that the state of the world ends up being the same whether that state was produced as a means or as a mere concomitant. (The guard is just as dead in either version of case I.) Since the resulting states of the world themselves offer no clue as to why the production of one as a means and the other as a side effect should invoke different moral judgments, can we find the difference in the heart of the agent? But what do we look for there? Not his intention, surely: that would make the circle of argument so close as to be ludicrous. Is it his desire, then? Is it what he appears to value or take pleasure in? But this also will not do. We have no more reason in the case of a means than in the case of a side effect to believe that the agent desired the result for its own sake, while we can be sure in both cases that the agent at least was willing that the relevant result occur as a price of achieving his ultimate goal.*

The concept of intention closes this gap between states of the world and the agent's state of mind. Right and wrong are clearly not determined solely by states of the world. The badness of bad states of the world does not account for the whole force of categorical norms. If we add the agent's state of heart to our state descriptions, we still have a gap to close. And even if we relate the two states, so that we speak of the special superstate which consists of an evil state of mind followed by the bad state of affairs, we still have not closed the gap. The gap is closed only if we realize (1) that judgments of right and wrong are judgments speaking to individuals and guiding their actions—they do not evaluate states (or even superstates) of the world and (2) that in guiding actions these judgments speak neither just about the outcomes of actions nor just about states of mind regarding those outcomes, but about a unity of mind and efficacy which is represented by the concept of intention. Absolute norms relate to the efficacious *choice* of good and evil. The absolute norms are not even primarily concerned with desires. To desire evil may be morally bad, but it is not murder, theft, rape. It is the special union of results and desire in intentional action which calls forth the types of moral rules I have called absolute.

Now, here is an apparent paradox: the result is not wrong, and the desire for the result is not wrong, and even being the causal agency of the result is not *necessarily* wrong (as in the case of unintended side effects); yet bringing the result about intentionally is wrong. How can this be? Is not intention the compound of causal efficacy and desire? And if so, why is the whole here more (evil) than the sum of its parts? The answer is that the "whole" is not simply a compound of those two parts—causal efficacy plus desire; at any rate, the moral quality of the whole is not simply the sum of the moral qualities of the two parts. Intentional action is the primary unit, and notions like desire and wish are incomplete notions when abstracted from this unit. They are like aiming without the target; they need action to complete them.†

---

* An argument has been offered to explain why the law may distinguish intended from merely foreseen results. An agent who chooses an evil as his means has shown himself disposed to persist in seeking to produce the harmful result if he fails at first, while in the case of a mere concomitant it is at least conceivable for the agent to be relieved if the harm does not eventuate. This argument has no application to the case where the unintended but foreseen result was sure to happen. And at any rate it is inapposite to moral norms designed to tell agents what they may or may not do.

† Gilbert Harman has recently sketched an account of practical reasoning and intention which seems to me to complement the conception of intention and its relation to ethics I offer here. ("Practical Reasoning," *Review of Metaphysics* 29 [1976]: 431). Harman distinguishes, as I do, between intended consequences and

Intentional action is the primitive concept of human efficacy. Desire and consequences are different aspects (at opposite ends, as it were) of that concept. Counterfactual and dispositional tests tease out, clarify these aspects—"Would you have acted anyway, even if . . ." But these tests too are not the *meaning* of intention. We view our own agency differently from the agency of natural objects in the world. We have purposes and we know these purposes. We know these purposes in a special way, as we know ourselves. We do not need to observe or infer them. It is part of our faith in ourselves that our purposes do issue in changes in the world, but it is not as if we wielded our bodies as tools when we acted. Our bodies, actions, motions are not themselves the result of our actions, they are our actions. There is no more basic action which sits behind these.

Morality is about the good and the right way of our being in the world *as human beings*. We relate to the world as human beings as we pursue our purposes in the world, as we act intentionally. Thus, just as it is a mistake to separate more than provisionally desire from action, so it is a mistake to separate more than provisionally moral judgment on our desires from moral judgment on the results we produce in the world. The paradigmatic moral judgment is on intentional action as such. That is why the most stringent, the absolute,

---

foreseen but unintended consequences. His example is that of a sniper who in firing his gun knowingly heats the barrel and alerts the enemy, neither of which he intends to do. Harman adds the following refinement: One who attempts something which is not reasonably in his power to bring about—such as hitting a target at a great distance—also does not intend that result, even if he succeeds. (Harman does say that in both instances—the foreseen but unintended result and the attempted but unlikely result—the actor acts intentionally, though he does not intend the result.) Now, the argument Harman offers for this set of distinctions seems very close to mine: "Intentions are primitive in the sense that they are not to be analyzed away in terms of reasons, beliefs, desires, and behavior" (p. 436). Intending or forming an intention is a way of bringing about the intended result, thus distinguishing intentions from predictions, desires, or hopes. This special efficacy of intentions also explains why an actor has not done what she intended if the desired result comes about in some unexpected way. "Mabel intends to drive to Ted's house, to find him, and to kill him. By chance, Ted happens to walk by as Mabel backs out of her driveway and she runs him down without seeing him . . . She does not kill him intentionally . . . Her intention is not simply 'to kill Ted' . . . It also includes a plan specifying how that intention will lead her to do what she intends" (p. 444).

Finally, it is this special efficacy of intention which explains the means/side-effect distinction, on which I insist as well. "An intention is a conclusion of practical reasoning that says that the very conclusion guarantees [the result]" (p. 483). This distinguishes intention from belief or prediction, which is the conclusion of theoretical reasoning. The sniper intends to kill his victim and his intention brings about that result. That his shot will alert the enemy and heat the barrel of his gun are, by contrast, at most predictions, conclusions of theoretical reasoning. Further, we can see why, in this view of intention as plan, means as well as ultimate goals are contrasted to mere concomitants.

judgments are on acts which are defined by a unity of intentionality and result. This primacy of intention explains why in law and morals a sharp line is drawn between the results (intended either for their own sake or as means) and the concomitants (even foreseen and certain concomitants) of our action. We see a paradox in this distinction only if we assume that because the consequences in the world are the same in the two cases, the judgment of them must be the same. Intention gives prominence to the central conception of human efficacy, which is efficacy according to purpose; at the same time, intention contrasts to that kind of efficacy the causality of which merely runs through my person or my movements but is not invested with the personal involvement of purpose.*

This argument does not prove too much. It does not lead to the conclusion that there may never be grounds for condemning an agent who knowingly causes harm he does not intend. Indeed, as I have suggested already, to expose others to undue risks of harm is wrong, as it may be wrong on occasion to stand by indifferently while another person suffers a preventable injury. Nevertheless, in such cases, where one does not do injury but the injury comes about as a result of what one does (or does not do), the condemnation depends on a different and more complex argument. In such cases we must inquire not only into the degree of the risk but also into the agent's reason for creating that risk. And the conclusion of that inquiry will depend not just on the relative discounted magnitudes of the good pursued weighed against the concomitant risks. It will be a question, too, of whether the agent had a right to be pursuing a particular end and whether the potential victim had some particular claim to the special care or benevolence of the agent. A crude utilitarian balancing of benefits and burdens is no more appropriate in the domain of unintentional than intentional harm. But the determination of the structures of judgment depends on our having in hand a theory of rights and particularly positive rights, the positive claims we may have to each other's care or effort. Such a theory of rights must use as one of its points of departure

* There is a sentimental correlate of consequentialism which holds that just as we really should be accountable equally for all the consequences of our actions, still if we should enter into questions of the heart then it should be only by our ultimate ends—and not also by our chosen means—that we are to be judged. This notion of ultimate ends, however, is not really clear—it is said to refer to those things which we pursue for their own sake and for no other reason. But what is it that is pursued for its own sake, really? It turns out that ultimate ends have a way of receding into some unifying abstraction like pleasure, utility, or the good. The view I propose, on the other hand, makes not ultimate ends—whatever they may be—central, but rather the more concrete, particular conception of a plan, project, or purpose. So where a man acts, intending a result though only as a means, it is as important that he intended that result as that he intended it while intending something beyond it.

the notion that there are some things we may not do to each other, no matter what, some things that are categorically wrong. Once that conception is in hand we may proceed to consider more complex and balanced wrongs—from unduly risky conduct to failing to make a sufficient effort to cure the defects of an unjust form of government.

Respect for Persons

Just as the concepts of right and wrong imply a special conception of efficacy which is personal efficacy, so also the substantive contents of the norms of right and wrong express the value of persons, of respect for personality. What we may not do to each other, the things which are wrong, are precisely those forms of personal interaction which deny to our victim the status of a freely choosing, rationally valuing, specially efficacious person, the special status of moral personality. To lie or to do intentional, grievous harm to the body of another represents a denial of the personal status of that other, a denial not necessarily implicit in allowing that harm to come about as a mere concomitant of our actions. If we use harming another as the means to our end, then we assert that another person may indeed be our means, while if we merely accept the risk that others will be harmed as we pursue our ends, and do not make that harm a part of our projects, then it is still possible to assert that those others are not reduced to the status of means in our system. . . . When we accomplish our purposes through lies, it is not so much that among the consequences of our action must be counted the fact that another person entertains a false belief—after all, that may be trivial enough—but rather that we have asserted that the mind, the rationality of another, is available to us as the track on which the train of our purposes may run.

Thus, what constitutes doing wrong to another may also be regarded as a denial of the respect owed another's moral personality. And it is a principal hypothesis of mine that the absolute quality of categorical norms (what one might call their logic), the concepts of action and intention necessary to the application of those norms (the psychology of the system), and the substantive moral basis of the norms, the respect for persons, all fit together in a system. Though I have identified respect for persons as a value, the connection between that respect and the concept of right and wrong shows that this value is wholly different from all other values. All other values gather their moral force as they determine choice. By contrast, the value of personhood, far from being chosen, is the presupposition and substrate of the very concept of choice. And that is why the norms surrounding respect for person may not be compromised, why these norms are absolute in respect to the various ends we choose to pursue.

VII

A Critique of Consequentialism

Bernard Williams

No one can hold that everything, of whatever category, that has value, has it in virtue of its consequences. If that were so, one would just go on for ever, and there would be an obviously hopeless regress. That regress would be hopeless even if one takes the view, which is not an absurd view, that although men set themselves ends and work towards them, it is very often not really the supposed end, but the effort towards it on which they set value—that they travel, not really in order to arrive (for as soon as they have arrived they set out for somewhere else), but rather they choose somewhere to arrive, in order to travel. Even on that view, not everything would have consequential value; what would have non-consequential value would in fact be travelling, even though people had to think of travelling as having the consequential value, and something else—the destination—the non-consequential value.

If not everything that has value has it in virtue of consequences, then presumably there are some types of thing which have non-consequential value, and also some particular things that have such value because they are instances of those types. Let us say, using a traditional term, that anything that has that sort of value, has *intrinsic* value.[1] I take it to be the central idea of consequentialism that the only kind of thing that has intrinsic value is states of affairs, and that anything else that has value has it because it conduces to some intrinsically valuable state of affairs.

How much, however, does this say? Does it succeed in distinguishing

[1] The terminology of things 'being valuable', 'having intrinsic value', etc., is not meant to beg any questions in general value-theory. Non-cognitive theories, such as Smart's, should be able to recognize the distinctions made here.

consequentialism from anything else? The trouble is that the term 'state of affairs' seems altogether too permissive to exclude anything: may not the obtaining of absolutely anything be represented formally as a state of affairs? A Kantian view of morality, for instance, is usually thought to be opposed to consequentialism, if any is; at the very least, if someone were going to show that Kantianism collapsed into consequentialism, it should be the product of a long and unobvious argument, and not just happen at the drop of a definition. But on the present account it looks as though Kantianism can be made instantly into a kind of consequentialism—a kind which identifies the states of affairs that have intrinsic value (or at least intrinsic moral value) as those that consist of actions being performed for duty's sake.[2] We need something more to our specification if it is to be the specification of anything distinctly consequentialist.

The point of saying that consequentialism ascribes intrinsic value to states of affairs is rather to *contrast* states of affairs with other candidates for having such value: in particular, perhaps, actions. A distinctive mark of consequentialism might rather be this, that it regards the value of actions as always consequential (or, as we may more generally say, derivative), and not intrinsic. The value of actions would then lie in their causal properties, of producing valuable states of affairs; or if they did not derive their value in this simple way, they would derive it in some more roundabout way, as for instance by being expressive of some motive, or in accordance with some rule, whose operation in society conduced to desirable states of affairs. . . .

To insist that what has intrinsic value are states of affairs and not actions seems to come near an important feature of consequentialism. Yet it may be that we have still not hit exactly what we want, and that the restriction is now too severe. Surely *some* actions, compatibly with consequentialism, might have intrinsic value? This is a question which has a special interest for utilitarianism, that is to say, the form of consequentialism concerned particularly with happiness. Traditionally utilitarians have tended to regard happiness or, again, pleasure, as experiences or sensations which were related to actions and activity as effect to cause; and, granted that view, utilitarianism will indeed see the value of all action as derivative, intrinsic value being reserved for the experiences of happiness. But that view of the relations between action and either pleasure or happiness is widely recognized to be inadequate. To say that a man finds certain actions or activity pleasant, or that they make him happy, or that he finds his happiness in them, is certainly not always to say that they induce certain sensations in him,

[2] A point noted by J. J. C. Smart, "A Critique of Utilitarianism," in *Utilitarianism: For and Against,* J. J. C. Smart and Bernard Williams (Cambridge: Cambridge University Press, 1977), p. 13.

and in the case of happiness, it is doubtful whether that is ever what is meant. Rather it means such things (among others) as that he enjoys doing these things for their own sake. It would trivialize the discussion of utilitarianism to tie it by definition to inadequate conceptions of happiness or pleasure, and we must be able to recognize as versions of utilitarianism those which, as most modern versions do, take as central some notion such as *satisfaction*, and connect that criterially with such matters as the activities which a man will freely choose to engage in. But the activities which a man engages in for their own sake are activities in which he finds intrinsic value. So any specification of consequentialism which logically debars action or activity from having intrinsic value will be too restrictive even to admit the central case, utilitarianism, so soon as that takes on a more sophisticated and adequate conception of its basic value of happiness.

So far then, we seem to have one specification of consequentialism which is too generous to exclude anything, and another one which is too restrictive to admit even the central case. These difficulties arise from either admitting without question actions among desirable states of affairs, or blankly excluding all actions from the state of affairs category. This suggests that we shall do better by looking at the interrelations between states of affairs and actions.

It will be helpful, in doing this, to introduce the notion of the *right* action for an agent in given circumstances. I take it that in any form of direct consequentialism, and certainly in act-utilitarianism, the notion of the right action in given circumstances is a maximizing notion:[3] the right action is that which out of the actions available to the agent brings about or represents the highest degree of whatever it is the system in question regards as intrinsically valuable—in the central case, utilitarianism, this is of course happiness. In this argument, I shall confine myself to direct consequentialism, for which 'right action' is unqualifiedly a maximizing notion.

The notion of the right action as that which, of the possible alternatives, maximizes the good (where this embraces, in unfavourable circumstances, minimizing the bad), is an objective notion in this sense, that it is perfectly possible for an agent to be ignorant or mistaken, and non-culpably ignorant or mistaken, about what is the right action in the circumstances. Thus the assessment by others of whether the agent did, in this sense, do the right thing, is not bounded by the agent's state of knowledge at the time, and the claim that he did the wrong thing is compatible with recognizing that he did as well as anyone in his state of knowledge could have done.[4] It might be suggested that, contrary to this, we have already imported the subjec-

[3] Cf. Smart's definition, loc. cit., p. 45.

[4] In Smart's terminology, loc. cit., the 'rational thing': pp. 46–7.

tive conditions of action in speaking of the best of the actions *available to him*: if he is ignorant or misinformed, then the actions which might seem to us available to him were not in any real sense available. But this would be an exaggeration; the notion of availability imports some, but not all, kinds of subjective condition. Over and above the question of actions which, granted his situation and powers, were physically not available to him, we might perhaps add that a course of action was not really available to an agent if his historical, cultural or psychological situation was such that it could not possibly occur to him. But it is scarcely reasonable to extend the notion of unavailability to actions which merely did not occur to him; and surely absurd to extend it to actions which did occur to him, but where he was misinformed about their consequences.

If then an agent does the right thing, he does the best of the alternatives available to him (where that, again, embraces the least bad: we shall omit this rider from now on). Standardly, the action will be right in virtue of its causal properties, of maximally conducing to good states of affairs. Sometimes, however, the relation of the action to the good state of affairs may not be that of cause to effect—the good state of affairs may be constituted, or partly constituted, by the agent's doing that act (as when under utilitarianism he just enjoys doing it, and there is no project available to him more productive of happiness for him or anyone else).

Although this may be so under consequentialism, there seems to be an important difference between this situation and a situation of an action's being right for some non-consequentialist reason, as for instance under a Kantian morality. This difference might be brought out intuitively by saying that for the consequentialist, even a situation of this kind in which the action itself possesses intrinsic value is one in which the rightness of the act is derived from the goodness of a certain state of affairs—the act is right *because* the state of affairs which consists in its being done is better than any other state of affairs accessible to the agent; whereas for the non-consequentialist it is sometimes, at least, the other way round, and a state of affairs which is better than the alternatives is so because it consists of the right act being done. This intuitive description of the difference has something in it, but it needs to be made more precise.

We can take a step towards making it more precise, perhaps, in the following way. Suppose *S* is some particular concrete situation. Consider the statement, made about some particular agent

(1) In *S*, he did the right thing in doing *A*. For consequentialists, (1) implies a statement of the form

(2) The state of affairs *P* is better than any other state of affairs accessible to him;

where a state of affairs being 'accessible' to an agent means that it is a state of affairs which is the consequence of, or is constituted by, his doing an act available to him (for that, see above); and *P* is a state of affairs accessible to him only in virtue of his doing *A*.[5]

Now in the exceptional case where it is just his doing *A* which carries the intrinsic value, we get for (2).

(3) The state of affairs which consists in his doing *A* is better than any other state of affairs accessible to him.

It was just the possibility of this sort of case which raised the difficulty of not being able to distinguish between a sophisticated consequentialism and non-consequentialism. The question thus is: if (3) is what we get for consequentialism in this sort of case, is it what a non-consequentialist would regard as implied by (1)? If so, we still cannot tell the difference between them. But the answer in fact seems to be 'no'.

There are two reasons for this. One reason is that a nonconsequentialist, though he must inevitably be able to attach a sense to (1), does not have to be able to attach a sense to (3) at all, while the consequentialist, of course, attaches a sense to (1) only because he attaches a sense to (3). Although the non-consequentialist is concerned with right actions—such as the carrying out of promises—he may have no general way of comparing states of affairs from a moral point of view at all. Indeed, the emphasis on the necessary comparability of situations is a peculiar feature of consequentialism in general, and of utilitarianism in particular.

A different kind of reason emerges if we suppose that the non-consequentialist does admit, in general, comparison between states of affairs. Thus, we might suppose that some non-consequentialist would consider it a better state of things in which more, rather than fewer, people kept their promises, and kept them for non-consequentialist reasons. Yet consistently with that he could accept, in a particular case, all of the following: that *X* would do the right thing only if he kept his promise; that keeping his promise would involve (or consist in) doing *A*; that several other people would, as a matter of fact, keep their promises (and for the right reasons) if and only if *X* did not do *A*. There are all sorts of situations in which this sort of thing would be true: thus it might be the case that an effect of *X*'s doing *A* would be to provide some inducement to these others which would lead them to break promises which otherwise they would have kept. Thus a non-

[5] 'Only' here may seem a bit strong: but I take it that it is not an unreasonable demand on an account of his doing *the* right thing in *S* that his action is uniquely singled out from the alternatives. A further detail: one should strictly say, not that (1) implies a statement of the form (2), but that (1) implies *that there is* a true statement of that form.

consequentialist can hold both that it is a better state of affairs in which more people keep their promises, and that the right thing for *X* to do is something which brings it about that fewer promises are kept. Moreover, it is very obvious what view of things goes with holding that. It is one in which, even though from some abstract point of view one state of affairs is better than another, it does not follow that a given agent should regard it as his business to bring it about, even though it is open to him to do so. More than that, it might be that he could not properly regard it as his business. If the goodness of the world were to consist in people's fulfilling their obligations, it would by no means follow that one of my obligations was to bring it about that other people kept their obligations.

Of course, no sane person could really believe that the goodness of the world just consisted in people keeping their obligations. But that is just an example, to illustrate the point that under non-consequentialism (3) does not, as one might expect, follow from (1). Thus even allowing some actions to have intrinsic value, we can still distinguish consequentialism. A consequentialist view, then, is one in which a statement of the form (2) follows from a statement of the form (1). A non-consequentialist view is one in which this is not so—not even when the (2)-statement takes the special form of (3).

This is not at all to say that the alternative to consequentialism is that one has to accept that there are some actions which one should always do, or again some which one should never do, *whatever the consequences*: this is a much stronger position than any involved, as I have defined the issues, in the denial of consequentialism. All that is involved, on the present account, in the denial of consequentialism, is that with respect to some type of action, there are some situations in which that would be the right thing to do, even though the state of affairs produced by one's doing that would be worse than some other state of affairs accessible to one. The claim that there is a type of action which is right *whatever the consequences* can be put by saying that with respect to some type of action, assumed as being adequately specified, then *whatever* the situation may (otherwise) be, that will be the right thing to do, *whatever* other state of affairs might be accessible to one, however much better it might be than the state of affairs produced by one's doing this action.

If that somewhat Moorean formulation has not hopelessly concealed the point, it will be seen that this second position—the *whatever the consequences* position—is very much stronger than the first, the mere rejection of consequentialism. It is perfectly consistent, and it might be thought a mark of sense, to believe, while not being a consequentialist, that there was no type of action which satisfied this second condition: that if an adequate (and non-question-begging) specification of a type of action has been given in advance, it is always possible to think of some situation in which the consequences of doing the action so specified would be so awful that it would be right to do something else.

Of course, one might think that there just *were* some types of action which satisfied this condition; though it seems to me obscure how one could have much faith in a list of such actions unless one supposed that it had supernatural warrant. Alternatively, one might think that while logically there was a difference between the two positions, in social and psychological fact they came to much the same thing, since so soon (it might be claimed) as people give up thinking in terms of certain things being right and wrong whatever the consequences, they turn to thinking in purely consequential terms. This might be offered as a very general proposition about human thought, or (more plausibly) as a sociological proposition about certain situations of social change, in which utilitarianism (in particular) looks the only coherent alternative to a dilapidated set of values. At the level of language, it is worth noting that the use of the word *'absolute'* mirrors, and perhaps also assists, this association: the claim that no type of action is 'absolutely right'—leaving aside the sense in which it means that the rightness of anything depends on the value-system of a society (the confused doctrine of relativism)—can mean either that no type of action is right—whatever-its-consequences, or, alternatively, that 'it all depends on the consequences', that is, in each case the decision whether an action is right is determined by its consequences.

A particular sort of psychological connexion—or in an old-fashioned use of the term, a 'moral' connexion—between the two positions might be found in this. If people do not regard certain things as 'absolutely out', then they are prepared to start thinking about extreme situations in which what would otherwise be out might, exceptionally, be justified. They will, if they are to get clear about what they believe, be prepared to compare different extreme situations and ask what action would be justified in them. But once they have got used to that, their inhibitions about thinking of everything in consequential terms disappear: the difference between the extreme situations and the less extreme, presents itself no longer as a difference between the exceptional and the usual, but between the greater and the less—and the consequential thoughts one was prepared to deploy in the greater it may seem quite irrational not to deploy in the less. *A fortiori*, someone might say: but he would have already had to complete this process to see it as a case of *a fortiori*.

One could regard this process of adaptation to consequentialism, moreover, not merely as a blank piece of psychological association, but as concealing a more elaborate structure of thought. One might have the idea that the *unthinkable* was itself a moral category; and in more than one way. It could be a feature of a man's moral outlook that he regarded certain courses of action as unthinkable, in the sense that he would not entertain the idea of doing them: and the witness to that might, in many cases, be that they simply would not come into his head. Entertaining certain alternatives, regarding them indeed as *alternatives*, is itself something that he regards as dishonourable or morally absurd. But, further, he might equally find it unacceptable to consider what to do in certain conceivable situations. Logically, or indeed empirically conceivable they may be, but they are not to him morally conceivable, meaning by that their occurrence as situations presenting him with a choice would represent not a special problem in his moral world, but something that lay beyond its limits. For him, there are certain situations so monstrous that the idea that the processes of moral rationality could yield an answer in them is insane: they are situations which so transcend in enormity the human business of moral deliberation that from a moral point of view it cannot matter any more what happens. Equally, for him, to spend time thinking what one would decide if one were in such a situation is also insane, if not merely frivolous.

For such a man, and indeed for anyone who is prepared to take him seriously, the demand, in Herman Kahn's words, to *think the unthinkable* is not an unquestionable demand of rationality, set against a cowardly or inert refusal to follow out one's moral thoughts. Rationality he sees as a demand not merely on him, but on the situations in, and about, which he has to think; unless the environment reveals minimum sanity, it is insanity to carry the decorum of sanity into it. Consequentialist rationality, however, and in particular utilitarian rationality, has no such limitations: making the best of a bad job is one of its maxims, and it will have something to say even on the difference between massacring seven million, and massacring seven million and one.

There are other important questions about the idea of the morally unthinkable, which we cannot pursue here. Here we have been concerned with the role it might play in someone's connecting, by more than a mistake, the idea that there was nothing which was right whatever the consequences, and the different idea that everything depends on consequences. While someone might, in this way or another, move from one of those ideas to the other, it is very important that the two ideas are different: especially important in a world where we have lost traditional reasons for resisting the first idea, but have more than enough reasons for fearing the second.

Negative Responsibility: And Two Examples

Although I have defined a state of affairs being *accessible* to an agent in terms of the actions which are *available* to him, nevertheless it is the former notion which is really more important for consequentialism. Consequentialism is basically indifferent to whether a state of affairs consists in what I do, or is produced by what I do, where that notion is itself wide enough to include, for instance, situations in which other people do things which I have made them do, or allowed them to do, or encouraged them to do, or given them a chance to do. All that consequentialism is interested in is the idea of these doings being *consequences* of what I do, and that is a relation broad enough to include the relations just mentioned, and many others.

Just what the relation is, is a different question, and at least as obscure as the nature of its relative, cause and effect. It is not a question I shall try to pursue; I will rely on cases where I suppose that any consequentialist would be bound to regard the situations in question as consequences of what the agent does. There are cases where the supposed consequences stand in a rather remote relation to the action, which are sometimes difficult to assess from a practical point of view, but which raise no very interesting question for the present enquiry. The more interesting points about consequentialism lie rather elsewhere. There are certain situations in which the causation of the situation, the relation it has to what I do, is in no way remote or problematic in itself, and entirely justifies the claim that the situation is a consequence of what I do: for instance, it is quite clear, or reasonably clear, that if I do a certain thing, this situation will come about, and if I do not, it will not. So from a consequentialist point of view it goes into the calculation of consequences along with any other state of affairs accessible to me. Yet from some, at least, non-consequentialist points of view, there is a vital difference between some such situations and others: namely, that in some a vital link in the production of the eventual outcome is provided by *someone else's* doing something. But for consequentialism, all causal connexions are on the same level, and it makes no difference, so far as that goes, whether the causation of a given state of affairs lies through another agent, or not.

Correspondingly, there is no relevant difference which consists *just* in one state of affairs being brought about by me, without intervention of other agents, and another being brought about through the intervention of other agents; although some genuinely causal differences involving a difference of value may correspond to that (as when, for instance, the other agents derive pleasure or pain from the transaction), that kind of difference will already be included in the specification of the state of affairs to be produced. Granted that the states of affairs have been adequately described in causally and evaluatively relevant terms, it makes no further comprehensible difference who produces them. It is because consequentialism attaches value ultimately to states of affairs, and its concern is with what states of affairs the world contains, that it essentially involves the notion of *negative responsibility*: that if I am ever responsible for anything, then I must be just as much responsible for things that I allow or fail to prevent, as I am for things that I myself, in the more everyday restricted sense, bring about.[6] Those things also must enter my deliberations, as a responsible moral agent, on the same footing. What matters is what states of affairs the world contains, and so what matters with respect to a given action is what comes about if it is done, and what comes about if it is not done, and those are questions not intrinsically affected by the nature of the causal linkage, in particular by whether the outcome is partly produced by other agents.

The strong doctrine of negative responsibility flows directly from consequentialism's assignment of ultimate value to states of affairs. Looked at from another point of view, it can be seen also as a special application of something that is favoured in many moral outlooks not themselves consequentialist—something which, indeed, some thinkers have been disposed to regard as the essence of morality itself: a principle of impartiality. Such a principle will claim that there can be no relevant difference from a moral point of view which consists just in the fact, not further explicable in general terms, that benefits or harms accrue to one person rather than to another—'it's me' can never in itself be a morally comprehensible reason.[7] This principle, familiar with regard to the reception of harms and benefits, we can see consequentialism as extending to their production: from the moral point of view, there is no comprehensible difference which consists just in my bringing about a certain outcome rather than someone else's producing it. That the doctrine of negative responsibility represents in this way the extreme of impartiality, and abstracts from the identity of the agent, leaving just a locus of causal intervention in the world—that fact is not merely a surface paradox. It helps to explain why consequentialism can seem to some to express a more serious attitude than non-consequentialist views, why part of its appeal is to a certain kind of high-mindedness. Indeed, that is part of what is wrong with it.

For a lot of the time so far we have been operating at an exceedingly abstract level. This has been necessary in order to get clearer in general terms about the differences between consequentialist and other outlooks, an aim which is important if we want to know what features

---

[6] This is a fairly modest sense of 'responsibility', introduced merely by one's ability to reflect on, and decide, what one ought to do. This presumably escapes Smart's ban (p. 54 loc. cit.) on the notion of 'the responsibility' as 'a piece of metaphysical nonsense'—his remarks seem to be concerned solely with situations of inter-personal blame.

[7] There is a tendency in some writers to suggest that it is not a comprehensible reason at all. But this, I suspect, is due to the overwhelming importance those writers ascribe to the moral point of view.

of them lead to what results for our thought. Now, however, let us look more concretely at two examples, to see what utilitarianism might say about them, what we might say about utilitarianism and, most importantly of all, what would be implied by certain ways of thinking about the situations. The examples are inevitably schematized, and they are open to the objection that they beg as many questions as they illuminate. There are two ways in particular in which examples in moral philosophy tend to beg important questions. One is that, as presented, they arbitrarily cut off and restrict the range of alternative courses of action—this objection might particularly be made against the first of my two examples. The second is that they inevitably present one with the situation as a going concern, and cut off questions about how the agent got into it, and correspondingly about moral considerations which might flow from that: this objection might perhaps specially arise with regard to the second of my two situations. These difficulties, however, just have to be accepted, and if anyone finds these examples cripplingly defective in this sort of respect, then he must in his own thought rework them in richer and less question-begging form. If he feels that no presentation of any imagined situation can ever be other than misleading in morality, and that there can never be any substitute for the concrete experienced complexity of actual moral situations, then this discussion, with him, must certainly grind to a halt: but then one may legitimately wonder whether every discussion with him about conduct will not grind to a halt, including any discussion about the actual situations, since discussion about how one would think and feel about situations somewhat different from the actual (that is to say, situations to that extent imaginary) plays an important role in discussion of the actual.

(1) George, who has just taken his Ph.D. in chemistry, finds it extremely difficult to get a job. He is not very robust in health, which cuts down the number of jobs he might be able to do satisfactorily. His wife has to go out to work to keep them, which itself causes a great deal of strain, since they have small children and there are severe problems about looking after them. The results of all this, especially on the children, are damaging. An older chemist, who knows about this situation, says that he can get George a decently paid job in a certain laboratory, which pursues research into chemical and biological warfare. George says that he cannot accept this, since he is opposed to chemical and biological warfare. The older man replies that he is not too keen on it himself, come to that, but after all George's refusal is not going to make the job or the laboratory go away; what is more, he happens to know that if George refuses the job, it will certainly go to a contemporary of George's who is not inhibited by any such scruples and is likely if appointed to push along the research with greater zeal than George would. Indeed, it is not merely concern for

George and his family, but (to speak frankly and in confidence) some alarm about this other man's excess of zeal, which has led the older man to offer to use his influence to get George the job . . . George's wife, to whom he is deeply attached, has views (the details of which need not concern us) from which it follows that at least there is nothing particularly wrong with research into CBW. What should he do?

(2) Jim finds himself in the central square of a small South American town. Tied up against the wall are a row of twenty Indians, most terrified, a few defiant, in front of them several armed men in uniform. A heavy man in a sweat-stained khaki shirt turns out to be the captain in charge and, after a good deal of questioning of Jim which establishes that he got there by accident while on a botanical expedition, explains that the Indians are a random group of the inhabitants who, after recent acts of protest against the government, are just about to be killed to remind other possible protestors of the advantages of not protesting. However, since Jim is an honoured visitor from another land, the captain is happy to offer him a guest's privilege of killing one of the Indians himself. If Jim accepts, then as a special mark of the occasion, the other Indians will be let off. Of course, if Jim refuses, then there is no special occasion, and Pedro here will do what he was about to do when Jim arrived, and kill them all. Jim, with some desperate recollection of schoolboy fiction, wonders whether if he got hold of a gun, he could hold the captain, Pedro and the rest of the soldiers to threat, but it is quite clear from the set-up that nothing of that kind is going to work: any attempt at that sort of thing will mean that all the Indians will be killed, and himself. The men against the wall, and the other villagers, understand the situation, and are obviously begging him to accept. What should he do?

To these dilemmas, it seems to me that utilitarianism replies, in the first case, that George should accept the job, and in the second, that Jim should kill the Indian. Not only does utilitarianism give these answers but, if the situations are essentially as described and there are no further special factors, it regards them, it seems to me, as *obviously* the right answers. But many of us would certainly wonder whether, in (1), that could possibly be the right answer at all; and in the case of (2), even one who came to think that perhaps that was the answer, might well wonder whether it was obviously the answer. Nor is it just a question of the rightness or obviousness of these answers. It is also a question of what sort of considerations come into finding the answer. A feature of utilitarianism is that it cuts out a kind of consideration which for some others makes a difference to what they feel about such cases: a consideration involving the idea, as we might first and very simply put it, that each of us is specially responsible for what *he* does, rather than for what other people do. This is an idea closely connected with the value of integrity. It is often suspected that utilitarianism, at least in its direct forms, makes integrity as a value more or less unintelligible. I shall try to show that this suspicion is correct. Of course, even if that is correct, it would not necessarily follow that we should reject utilitarianism; perhaps, as utilitarians sometimes suggest, we should just forget about integrity, in favour of such things as a concern for the general good. However, if I am right, we cannot merely do that, since the reason why utilitarianism cannot understand integrity is that it cannot coherently describe the relations between a man's projects and his actions.

Two Kinds of Remoter Effect

A lot of what we have to say about this question will be about the relations between my projects and other people's projects. But before we get on to that, we should first ask whether we are assuming too hastily what the utilitarian answers to the dilemmas will be. In terms of more direct effects of the possible decisions, there does not indeed seem much doubt about the answer in either case; but it might be said that in terms of more remote or less evident effects counterweights might be found to enter the utilitarian scales. Thus the effect on George of a decision to take the job might be invoked, or its effect on others who might know of his decision. The possibility of there being more beneficent labours in the future from which he might be barred or disqualified, might be mentioned; and so forth. Such effects—in particular, possible effects on the agent's character, and effects on the public at large—are often invoked by utilitarian writers dealing with problems about lying or promise-breaking, and some similar considerations might be invoked here.

There is one very general remark that is worth making about arguments of this sort. The certainty that attaches to these hypotheses about possible effects is usually pretty low; in some cases, indeed, the hypothesis invoked is so implausible that it would scarcely pass if it were not being used to deliver the respectable moral answer, as in the standard fantasy that one of the effects of one's telling a particular lie is to weaken the disposition of the world at large to tell the truth. The demands on the certainty or probability of these beliefs as beliefs about particular actions are much milder than they would be on beliefs favouring the unconventional course. It may be said that this is as it should be, since the presumption must be in favour of the conventional course: but that scarcely seems a *utilitarian* answer, unless utilitarianism has already taken off in the direction of not applying the consequences to the particular act at all.

Leaving aside that very general point, I want to consider now two types of effect that are often invoked by utilitarians, and which might be invoked in connexion with these imaginary cases. The attitude or tone involved in invoking these effects may sometimes seem peculiar; but that sort of peculiarity soon becomes familiar in utilitarian discussions, and indeed it can be something of an achievement to retain a sense of it.

First, there is the psychological effect on the agent. Our descriptions of these situations have not so far taken account of how George or Jim will be after they have taken the one course or the other; and it might be said that if they take the course which seemed at first the utilitarian one, the effects on them will be in fact bad enough and extensive enough to cancel out the initial utilitarian advantages of that course. Now there is one version of this effect in which, for a utilitarian, some confusion must be involved, namely that in which the agent feels bad, his subsequent conduct and relations are crippled and so on, *because he thinks that he has done the wrong thing*—for if the balance of outcomes was as it appeared to be *before* invoking this effect, then he has not (from the utilitarian point of view) done the wrong thing. So that version of the effect, for a rational and utilitarian agent, could not possibly make any difference to the assessment of right and wrong. However, perhaps he is not a thoroughly rational agent, and is disposed to have bad feelings, whichever he decided to do. Now such feelings, which are from a strictly utilitarian point of view irrational—nothing, a utilitarian can point out, is advanced by having them—cannot, consistently, have any great weight in a utilitarian calculation. I shall consider in a moment an argument to suggest that they should have no weight at all in it. But short of that, the utilitarian could reasonably say that such feelings should not be encouraged, even if we accept their existence, and that to give them a lot of weight is to encourage them. Or, at the very best, even if they are straightforwardly and without any discount to be put into the calculation, their weight must be small: they are after all (and at best) one man's feelings.

That consideration might seem to have particular force in Jim's case. In George's case, his feelings represent a larger proportion of what is to be weighed, and are more commensurate in character with other items in the calculation. In Jim's case, however, his feelings might seem to be of very little weight compared with other things that are at stake. There is a powerful and recognizable appeal that can be made on this point: as that a refusal by Jim to do what he has been invited to do would be a kind of self-indulgent squeamishness. That is an appeal which can be made by other than utilitarians—indeed, there are some uses of it which cannot be consistently made by utilitarians, as when it essentially involves the idea that there is something dishonourable about such self-indulgence. But in some versions it is a familiar, and it must be said a powerful, weapon of utilitarianism. One must be clear, though, about what it can and cannot accomplish. The most it can do, so far as I can see, is to invite one to consider how seriously, and for what reasons, one feels that what one is invited to do is (in these circumstances) wrong, and in particular, to consider that question from the utilitarian point of view. When the agent is not seeing the situation from a utilitarian point of view, the appeal cannot force him to do so; and if he does come round to seeing it from a utilitarian point of view, there is virtually nothing left for the appeal to do. If he does not see it from a utilitarian point of view, he will not see his resistance to the invitation, and the unpleasant feelings he associates with accepting it, *just* as disagreeable experiences of his; they figure rather as emotional expressions of a thought that to accept would be wrong. He may be asked, as by the appeal, to consider whether he is right, and indeed whether he is fully serious, in thinking that. But the assertion of the appeal, that he is being self-indulgently squeamish, will not itself answer that question, or even help to answer it, since it essentially tells him to regard his feelings just as unpleasant experiences of his, and he cannot, by doing that, answer the question they pose when they are precisely not so regarded, but are regarded as indications[8] of what he thinks is right and wrong. If he does come round fully to the utilitarian point of view then of course he will regard these feelings just as unpleasant experiences of his. And once Jim—at least—has come to see them in that light, there is nothing left for the appeal to do, since *of course* his feelings, so regarded, are of virtually no weight at all in relation to the other things at stake. The 'squeamishness' appeal is not an argument which adds in a hitherto neglected consideration. Rather, it is an invitation to consider the situation, and one's own feelings, from a utilitarian point of view.

The reason why the squeamishness appeal can be very unsettling, and one can be unnerved by the suggestion of self-indulgence in going against utilitarian considerations, is not that we are utilitarians who are uncertain what utilitarian value to attach to our moral feelings, but that we are partially at least not utilitarians, and cannot regard our moral feelings merely as objects of utilitarian value. Because our moral relation to the world is partly given by such feelings, and by a sense of what we can or cannot 'live with', to come to regard those feelings from a purely utilitarian point of view, that is to say, as happenings outside one's moral self, is to lose a sense of one's moral identity; to lose, in the most literal way, one's integrity. . . .

[8] On the non-cognitivist meta-ethic in terms of which Smart presents his utilitarianism, the term 'indications' here would represent an understatement.

VIII

What a Good Man Can Bring Himself to Do[1]

R. G. Frey

Are there some acts it would always be wrong to perform, no matter what the consequences? A positive answer to this question is usually taken to define a kind of moral absolutism, one that is formulated around the absolute prohibition of certain kinds of acts, e.g., the judicial execution of the innocent. Miss Anscombe defended an absolutism of this type in her well-known paper "Modern Moral Philosophy,"[2] and more recent absolutisms, such as those espoused by Stuart Hampshire in his Leslie Stephen lecture *Morality and Pessimism*[3] and by Thomas Nagel in his paper "War and Massacre,"[4] have likewise been variations on the prohibition theme. Indeed, it would not be far short of the truth to say that, so far as moral absolutisms have engaged the attention of contemporary moral philosophers at all, they have been of this prohibition type. This applies to critics as well as adherents: for example, Jonathan Bennett,[5] Kai Nielsen,[6] Richard Hare,[7]

---

[1] An earlier version of this paper was read to the Eastern Division of the American Philosophical Association in New York in December 1975. The same version was also read to a discussion group in Oxford, from which I received valuable assistance. I am grateful as well to R. H. Hare for his comments on this earlier paper.

[2] G. E. M. Anscombe, "Modern Moral Philosophy," *Philosophy*, vol. 43, 1958, pp. 1–19.

[3] S. Hampshire, *Morality and Pessimism* (Cambridge University Press, 1972). [See p. 119ff. this volume.—Ed.]

[4] T. Nagle, "War and Massacre," *Philosophy and Public Affairs*, vol. 1, 1972, pp. 123–144. [See p. 217ff. this volume.—Ed.]

[5] J. Bennett, "Whatever The Consequences," *Analysis*, vol. 26, 1966, pp. 83–102. [See p. 175ff. this volume.—Ed.]

[6] K. Nielsen, "The Search for Absolutes," in *Ethics Without God* (London, Pemberton Books, 1973), pp. 65–103.

[7] R. M. Hare, "Rules of War and Moral Reasoning," *Philosophy and Public*

and Richard Brandt[8] have all attacked moral absolutisms, in each case of the prohibition type.

Now what this exclusive attention to absolute prohibitions has masked is that another form of moral absolutism is possible, according to which there are some kinds of acts that a good man simply could not bring himself to perform. Such acts would be physically within his power, but fellow feeling would prevent him from performing them; so to speak, such acts would be physically possible but morally impossible. The result is a kind of moral absolutism, but one which is not formulated around the absolute prohibition of certain kinds of acts and so which is perhaps immune to many (if not all) of the sorts of criticisms brought against absolutisms of the prohibition type by Bennett and the others. This different type of absolutism can be found in Jonathan Edwards's *Freedom of the Will*;[9] but arguments in support of it there all become entwined with theological premises, which are difficult to untangle and evaluate, controversial in themselves, and apt, therefore, to divert attention away from the absolutism itself. Much more interesting, just because it is free of theological controversy, is an argument to be extracted from James Cargile's paper "On Consequentialism."[10] In what follows, I want to analyze this argument and to show why, though valid, it is nevertheless defective. My aim is not to make trouble for Cargile but to air some of the sorts of difficulties this interestingly different type of absolutism faces.

Argument

Cargile's argument is briefly put. The good man is motivated by fellow feeling, i.e., by feelings of sympathy with and concern for the happiness of others; but some acts (or kinds of acts) are so vicious, so completely cruel in their infliction of terrible suffering on others that they cannot be motivated by fellow feeling; therefore, anyone who performs one of these acts cannot be a good man. Given that "the good man" means "the man of good character," as it does for Cargile,[11] the argument may be recast more plainly as follows: if a man is of good character, he is motivated by fellow feeling; if anyone

---

Affairs, vol. 1, 1972, pp. 166–181; "Principles," *Proceedings of the Aristotelian Society*, vol. 72, 1972–73, pp. 1–18. [See pp. 253ff. this volume.—Ed.]

[8] R. B. Brandt, "Utilitarianism and the Rules of War," *Philosophy and Public Affairs*, vol. 1, 1972, pp. 145–165. [See pp. 237ff. this volume.—Ed.]

[9] J. Edwards, *Freedom of the Will* (Indianapolis, Bobbs-Merrill Co., 1969), parts III and IV.

[10] J. Cargile, "On Consequentialism," *Analysis*, vol. 29, 1969, pp. 78–88.

[11] *Ibid.*, p. 85.

performs an act of type V (vicious), he cannot be motivated by fellow feeling; therefore, anyone who performs an act of type V is not a man of good character. This argument is valid, but the truth of both of the premisses is doubtful.

Disclaimer

My doubts in this regard *have nothing to do* either with any disagreement over who is the good man or with my own, very strong inclination towards act-utilitarianism. Cargile takes the good man to be one who is disposed to act in ways conducive to human pleasure,[12] a characterization I accept; his crucial point is that there are restrictions on these ways, such that even if human pleasure were to be obviously maximized by performing an act of type V, a good man nevertheless could not bring himself to perform such an act. Restrictions of this sort are hardly likely to recommend themselves to act-utilitarians, though they accept that the good man is one disposed to act in ways conducive to human pleasure; but nothing in what follows turns upon the rejection of such restrictions by act-utilitarians. In order to doubt the truth of Cargile's premises, then, one is not forced to embrace act-utilitarianism.

Major Premise

"If a man is of good character, he is motivated by fellow feeling."

What if only once in my life, and that in very extreme circumstances, I inflict terrible suffering on another person in order to produce an immense number of good consequences? And that the rest of the time I behave as Cargile would have me? Cargile's estimate of me will be taken not from the run of cases but from the single case, in which the good man could not bring himself to do what I did; and my character will be tainted forever, on the strength of this case, since I have in fact done something that a good man could not have brought himself to do. In its more popular form, this is the view that the single, very serious case is the acid test of a man's character, that a person's "true character" emerges, so to speak, when "his back is to the wall." Now either this view is held in conjunction with a dispositional analysis of character or it is not. For Cargile, it is: he speaks, for example, of "actions which someone possessing the dispositions characteristic of a good man could not possibly perform in any circumstances."[13] But if

[12] *Ibid.*, p. 83.

[13] *Ibid.*, p. 87.

only once in my life, in very serious circumstances, I inflict terrible suffering in order to produce an immense number of good consequences, it cannot be said that I lack the dispositions characteristic of a good man; for a single case could not show whether I lacked (or, for that matter, possessed) disposition Ø. A range of cases in which I have opportunity to Ø and in which a good man would not Ø and in which I do Ø are required to establish this; but in the vast bulk of cases I do not Ø; in fact, there is only one case in which I do. So a single case is not going to show that I lack this disposition. Put differently, human personality traits, or dispositions need not manifest themselves at all moments: in saying that a man is of a sunny and cheerful disposition, we are not saying that in every waking moment of his life he exhibits these characteristics, that he never exhibits gloom and despair. Rather, we are saying that, more often than not, or in the vast run of cases, he is sunny and cheerful. Likewise, in saying that a man of good character is disposed to behave in a certain way or to be motivated by fellow feeling, we are not saying that this disposition manifests itself each and every time he has occasion to act, only that it manifests itself in the vast bulk of cases. If this is so, then it will not follow from the fact that I once inflict terrible suffering in order to produce an immense number of good consequences that I lack the dispositions characteristic of a good man, any more than it will follow, if I do *not* inflict terrible suffering in such a very serious case, that I possess the dispositions characteristic of a good man.

It may be claimed, of course, that if I can bring myself to inflict terrible suffering on another person once, I can bring myself to do so again. But the burden of proof here is not upon me; for this claim ignores the situation or circumstances in which I was able to bring myself to perform this terrible act. To be sure, if such very extreme circumstances arise again, then maybe I *will be able* to bring myself once more to inflict terrible suffering on another person; but this supposition about extreme circumstances does not license any additional supposition about what I will do when I am once again in *normal* circumstances. Given that I have to date, in normal circumstances, behaved as Cargile would have me, and that it is only in this one case of extreme circumstances, that I have been able to bring myself to inflict terrible suffering on another person, and then only because I knew an immense number of good consequences could be set against that suffering, one is not entitled simply to conclude that, in subsequent cases of *normal circumstances*, I am now likely or more likely than I would have been to break my established good habits. Argument, indeed, empirical evidence, is needed to reach this conclusion.

Nor is the case I am considering objectionable because it is simply *laid down* that an immense number of good consequences can be set against the harmful consequences of inflicting terrible suffering. The question is whether a good man could *ever* bring himself, *e.g.*, to torture; and the answer to this question must be framed not only on the basis of those cases where the good man knows or thinks the alternative to torture has obviously *better* consequences but also on the basis of those cases where he knows or thinks the alternative to torture has preponderantly or obviously *worse* consequences.

If the view that the single, very serious case is the acid test of a man's character is held, not in conjunction with a dispositional analysis of character, but rather on its own, then it is plain that it can yield what many of us will regard as an unacceptable result. What if, then, in a case of very serious, extreme circumstances, because of fellow feeling, I cannot bring myself to inflict terrible suffering on another person in order to produce an immense number of good consequences, yet in all the other, everyday affairs of life I behave abominably, *e.g.*, by repeatedly lying, stealing, *etc.*? To use the single case as the touchstone of character makes me out to be a good man, even though the vast run of cases indicates perfectly clearly that I lack those habits, practices, principles or whatever characteristic of a good man. It seems a distinctly objectionable treatment of character which gives the result that, provided I behave well in the acid test case, I can behave any way I please in other cases and remain a good man.

Minor Premise

"If anyone performs an act of type V (vicious), he cannot be motivated by fellow feeling."

There are obvious difficulties with this premise in respect of identifying acts of type V, that is, the acts or kinds of acts a good man could not bring himself to perform. For example, Cargile confines himself to a discussion of acts which involve the infliction of terrible suffering, and it is unclear whether he regards inflicting terrible suffering on others as a defining characteristic of the sorts of acts a good man could not bring himself to perform or merely as an example of such acts. If an example, then the range or extent of acts of type V remains to be delimited, and it becomes an open and important question, for any particular act other than one involving inflicting terrible suffering (euthanasia, performing an abortion), whether it is one a good man could bring himself to perform. On the other hand, if inflicting terrible suffering is a defining characteristic of the sorts of acts the good man will balk at, then presumably he will not balk at painless murder. This does *not* mean that he will perform such an act, only that it is not the sort of act he could not bring himself to perform, and so not the sort of act that is incompatible with being motivated by fellow feeling. But if painless murder is compatible with fellow feeling, then a host of other, equally painless yet equally pernicious acts will also be; and it begins to appear that, so long as terrible suffering can be prevented, the performance of any act will be compatible with fellow feeling. And this yields the result that there are *no* acts of type V, *no* acts which a good man, because of fellow feeling, could not bring himself to perform, provided in some way or other terrible suffering could be avoided.

Again, although Cargile's general solution to the problem of identifying those acts which we as good men could not bring ourselves to perform is that we consult our feelings of sympathy with and concern for the happiness of others, the truth is that we have scarcely any idea of how to conduct this consultation. Is an act a good man could not bring himself to perform one that is distasteful to him? Or must it engender a feeling of repugnance? Or perhaps an intense feeling of repugnance? Must this feeling of repugnance persist over a certain duration? Or does even a fleeting trace of repugnance suffice to prevent the good man from performing the act? And what are we to do if we first feel repugnance at performing a particular act but then cease to feel repugnance, *e.g.,* as the time for action approaches? What do we do if, as is often the case, our feelings are mixed, with some pulling in a different direction from others? The point is that, unless we know *how* to go about consulting our fellow feeling, we will not know how to *use* fellow feeling as the arbiter of what a good man can bring himself to do.

Counterexample

Now it is worth pointing out, in respect of this minor premise, that a man paying heed to his fellow feeling can very easily fail to perform that act that all except Cargilean good men would wish to see performed. In other words, the agent will fail to perform an act of type V when that is what we should wish him to perform.

Suppose, then, I find myself in a situation in which, unless my friend's leg is removed at once, gangrene poisoning will kill him. There is no medical or other person around except myself; there is no instrument available to do the job except a hack saw; and there are no drugs or whisky available to render my friend unconscious, nor dare I strike him a blow on the head, since he has been injured there also. What do I do? If I consider the consequences of not sawing off the leg, then I am likely to decide to saw it off. But what am I likely to decide if I pay heed to my fellow feeling? (The answer to this question must not be influenced by considerations of squeamishness; the fact that the act of sawing off the leg completely sickens me, with the blood and pus running and the bone perhaps splintering, has nothing to do with what fellow feeling tells me to do in this case; hence, there must be no imputation that the Cargilean good man is a squeamish man.) In fact, the intense suffering my friend will undergo produces in me an intense feeling of repugnance at performing the act. Every bit of fellow feeling in me wells up at the prospect of *this* degree of suffering, no matter how good the consequences that may result from sawing the leg off: I simply cannot bring myself to perform the act. Now if this is my decision, then my friend is going to die. Yet, no one can complain either that I failed to consult my deep feelings for humanity, since I did consult them, or that I failed to consult these feelings properly or in the required manner, since, in the absence of some account of how we are to go about consulting our feelings, there is no standard or paradigm that defines "proper" or "the required manner" in this context. So my decision not to saw off the leg is perfectly compatible with being motivated by fellow feeling, indeed, it is the decision fellow feeling leads me to make. But if I act upon this decision, will I not be failing to perform that act which all but Cargilean good men would wish to see performed? What I *should* do is overcome my intense feeling of repugnance at performing the act, overcome whatever qualms I may have about inflicting terrible suffering upon a fellow being, keep the good consequences of my act firmly in mind, and saw my friend's leg off. And my motive in behaving this way is a good one: it is to save my friend's life.

The two most prominent objections to this example fail completely. First, it may be contended that, if the suffering my friend will undergo through my sawing off his leg is estimated by me to be roughly commensurate (assuming such an estimate to be possible) with the suffering he will undergo through dying in the immediate future of gangrene poisoning, then I may as well decide, even as a result of consulting my fellow feeling, to saw off his leg. For a Cargilean good man, however, even if true, this consideration is not germane, since what he recoils from is not people *undergoing* terrible suffering but *his inflicting* terrible suffering on people. (In this connection, Cargile observes that "it is an essential feature of humanity that we recoil more strongly from directly inflicting pain than we do from merely knowing an equal amount of pain is inflicted."[14]) Thus, in my example, the important point for the Cargilean good man will not be that I know my friend is going to suffer a terrible death through gangrene poisoning but that I am not going to inflict a roughly commensurate amount of suffering upon him; it is simply not to the point, therefore, that the two amounts of suffering are estimated by me to be roughly equal. Second, it may be contended that my example is impaired because it involves my inflicting terrible suffering on another person from a good and not

[14] *Ibid.*, p. 88.

a bad motive, and that, therefore, my act is not a vicious one or an act of type V. This line of argument, however, is confused. Acts of type V are vicious acts, but it is important to bear in mind that "vicious" here refers to the quality of the act, as one involving the infliction of terrible suffering on another person, and not to the motive with which the act is performed, which may be, and, in my example, is a good one. To take a fantastic case, suppose I am told that unless I torture a small baby, twenty innocent people will be killed: Cargile's point is that, in this logically possible situation, a good man, even though he realized an immense number of good consequences would flow from torturing the baby, still could not bring himself so to act. Importantly, however, the good man's motives in this situation are, I think, clearcut: if he *does not torture* the baby, his motive is a good one, *viz.*, to forego the infliction of terrible suffering upon another human being; but if he *does torture* the baby, though he thereby inflicts terrible suffering, his motive is equally a good one, *viz.*, to save twenty lives. In other words, he will perform an act of type V, from a morally good motive, and his act will be "vicious" though he will not.

A Basic Defect

What divides most of us from the Cargilean good man in what we would do in the gangrene poisoning case points to what seems to be a basic defect in this different type of absolutism. Most of us want the good man to be a feeling man, certainly; but we also want him to be a man capable of considering carefully and thinking through the various contingencies of a situation and thinking out what he should do. This is not to suggest that he look to his head *rather than* his heart, only that a Cargilean good man who looks *only* to his heart gives a truncated picture of the good man. It will be said, of course, that the Cargilean good man looks to his heart only in those very few cases which involve inflicting terrible suffering; in all other cases, as in all his affairs of everyday life, he can be as much a thinking man, indeed, as much a calculator of consequences as anyone else. This is tantamount to saying, however, that it is only in the really difficult cases, *e.g.*, where concerns of life and death and terrible suffering are involved, that the good man is to give up trying to think out what he ought to do and to trust instead to his feelings. But *why* in these cases—and this is the really crucial point—do his feelings warrant the more trust? For even assuming his feelings are unmixed, and he can consult them in the required manner, with or without some calculus by which to determine intensity, duration, *etc.*, he is giving up the thinking out of cases in just those situations which, *because* of their difficulty and complexity, one would have considered the presence of close thought of paramount importance. Cargile provides no reason for our believing that our feelings are either more morally reliable or more likely to be morally reliable than our thinking out of cases; but, in the absence of such a reason, when I think through the consequences of the alternatives, and thus decide to saw off my friend's leg in order to save his life, there will be no reason for me to think or even to suspect that my decision, based on a consideration of consequences and not on paying heed to my feelings, will *in virtue of that fact* be less likely to be morally reliable.

Moreover, even the good man himself will require a case to be made for why his feelings warrant the degree of trust this different type of absolutism places in them, if he, as a good man, is *with confidence* really going to allow his feelings in difficult cases to dictate his behaviour. This will be especially true in the most difficult cases of all, namely, cases of conflict, in which, for example, there are only two alternatives open to the agent, both of which involve inflicting terrible suffering, involve, that is, the performance of acts of type V. In these cases, the Cargilean good man will be unable to bring himself to perform either alternative; he will simply collapse or break down. And surely even the good man himself is going to have to be convinced that breaking down in such a case is the appropriate thing for him to do. For I think a very great many of us would argue that the good man is precisely the individual who should not break down in difficult situations but who should be equipped to think out moral problems like this one; the last thing we want, it seems to me, is that he should collapse in the most trying cases of all.

IX

Absolutism and the Good Life

Stuart Hampshire

Each moral philosophy singles out some ultimate ground or grounds for unconditional praise of persons, and prescribes the ultimate grounds for preferring one way of life to another. This is no less true of a utilitarian ethics than of any other; the effectively beneficent and happy man is accounted by a utilitarian more praiseworthy and admirable than any other type of man, and his useful life is thought the best kind of life that anyone could have, merely in virtue of its usefulness, and apart from any other characteristics it may have. The utilitarian philosophy picks out its own essential virtues, very clearly, and the duties of a utiliarian are not hard to discern, even though they may on occasion involve difficult computations.

But there is one feature of familiar moralities which utiliarian ethics famously repudiates, or at least makes little of. There are a number of different moral prohibitions, apparent barriers to action, which a man acknowledges and which he thinks of as more or less insurmountable, except in abnormal, painful and improbable circumstances. One expects to meet these prohibitions, barriers to action, in certain quite distinct and clearly marked areas of action; these are the taking of human life, sexual relations, family duties and obligations, and the administration of justice according to the laws and customs of a given society. There are other areas in which strong barriers are to be expected; but these are, I think, the central and obvious ones. A morality is, at the very least, the regulation of the taking of life and the regulation of sexual relations, and it also includes rules of distributive and corrective justice: family duties: almost always duties of friendship: also rights and duties in respect of money and property. When specific prohibitions in these areas are probed and challenged by reflection, and the rational grounds for them looked for, the questioner will think that he is questioning a particular morality specified by particular prohibitions. But if he were to question the validity of any prohibitions in these areas, he would think of himself as challenging the claims of morality itself; for the notion of morality requires that there be some strong barriers against the taking of life, against some varieties of sexual and family relations, against some forms of trial and punishment, some taking of property, and against some distributions of rewards and benefits.

Moral theories of the philosophical kind are differentiated in part by the different accounts that they give of these prohibitions: whether the prohibitions are to be thought of as systematically connected or not: whether they are absolute prohibitions or to be thought of as conditional. Utilitarians always had, and still have, very definite answers: first, they *are* systematically connected, and, secondly, they are to be thought of as not absolute, but conditional, being dependent for their validity as prohibitions upon the beneficial consequences of observing them. Plainly there is no possibility of proof here, since this is a question in ethics, and not in logic or in the experimental sciences. But various reasons for rejecting the utilitarian position can be given.

All of us sometimes speak of things that cannot be done, or that must not be done, and that are ruled out as impossible by the nature of the case: also there are things that one must do, that one cannot not do, because of the nature of the case. The signs of necessity in such contexts mark the unqualified, unweakened, barrier to action, while the word 'ought', too much discussed in philosophical writing, conveys a weakened prohibition or instruction. The same contrast appears in the context of empirical statements, as in the judgments 'The inflation ought to stop soon' and 'The inflation must stop soon'. The modal words 'must' and 'ought' preserve a constant relation in a number of different types of discourse, of which moral discourse is only one, not particularly conspicuous, example: he who in a shop says to the salesman 'The coat must cover my knees', alternatively, 'The coat ought to cover my knees', speaks of a need or requirement and of something less: he who, looking at the mathematical puzzle, says 'This must be the way to solve it', alternatively 'This ought to be the way to solve it', speaks of a kind of rational necessity, and of something less: examples of 'ought' as the weaker variant of 'must' could be indefinitely prolonged into other types of contexts. So 'He must help him' is the basic, unmodified judgment in the context of moral discussion or reflection, and 'He ought to help him' is its weakened variant, as it is in all other contexts. To learn what a man's moral beliefs are entails learning what he thinks that he must not do, at any cost or at almost any cost.

The range of the utterly forbidden types of conduct amongst Stephen's friends would differ significantly, but not greatly, from the range of the forbidden and the impossible that would be acknowledged in this room. Social anthropologists may record fairly wide variations in the range of the morally impossible, and also, I believe, some barriers that are very general, though not quite universal; and historians similarly. For example, in addition to certain fairly specific types of killing, certain fairly specific types of sexual promiscuity, certain takings of property, there are also types of disloyalty and of cowardice, particularly disloyalty to friends, which are very generally, almost universally, forbidden and forbidden absolutely: they are forbidden as being intrinsically disgraceful and unworthy, and as being, just for these reasons, ruled out: ruled out because they would be disgusting, or disgraceful, or shameful, or brutal, or inhuman, or base, or an outrage.

In arguing against utilitarians I must dwell a little on these epithets usually associated with morally impossible action, on a sense of disgrace, of outrage, of horror, of baseness, of brutality, and, most important, a sense that a barrier, assumed to be firm and almost insurmountable, has been knocked over, and a feeling that, if this horrible, or outrageous, or squalid, or brutal, action is possible, then anything is possible and nothing is forbidden, and all restraints are threatened. Evidently these ideas have often been associated with impiety, and with a belief that God, or the Gods, have been defied, and with a fear of divine anger. But they need not have these associations with the supernatural, and they may have, and often have had, a secular setting. In the face of the doing of something that must not be done, and that is categorically excluded and forbidden morally, the fear that one may feel is fear of human nature. A relapse into a state of nature seems a real possibility: or perhaps seems actually to have occurred, unless an alternative morality with new restraints is clearly implied when the old barrier is crossed. This fear of human nature, and sense of outrage, when a barrier is broken down, is an aspect of respect for morality itself rather than for any particular morality, and for any particular set of prohibitions.

The notion of the morally impossible—'I cannot leave him now: it would be quite impossible.' 'Surely you understand that I *must* help him'—is distinct. A course of conduct is ruled out ('You cannot do that'), because it would be inexcusably unjust, or dishonest, or humiliating, or treacherous, or cruel, or ungenerous, or harsh. These epithets, specifying why the conduct is impossible, mark the vices characteristically recognised in a particular morality. In other societies, at other places and times, other specific epithets might be more usually associated with outrage and morally impossible conduct; but the outrage or shock, and the recognition of impossibility, will be the same in cases where the type of conduct rejected, and the reasons for the rejection, are rather different.

The utilitarian will not deny these facts, but he will interpret them differently. Shock, he will say, is the primitive, pre-rational reaction; after rational reflection the strength of feeling associated with a prohibition can be, and ought to be, proportional to the estimated harm of the immediate and remote consequences; and he will find no more in the signs of necessity and impossibility than an emphasis on the moral rules which have proved to be necessary protections against evil effects. The signs of necessity are signs that there is a rule. But the rational justification of there being a rule is to be found in the full consequences of its observance, and not in non-rational reactions of horror, disgust, shame, and other emotional repugnances.

But I believe that critical reflection may leave the notion of absolutely forbidden, because absolutely repugnant, conduct untouched. There may in many cases be good reflective reasons why doing such things, assuming such a character, may be abhorrent, and excluded from the range of possible conduct; there may be reflective reasons, in the sense that one is able to say why the conduct is impossible as destroying the ideal of a way of life that one aspires to and respects, as being, for example, utterly unjust or cruel or treacherous or corruptly dishonest. To show that these vices are vices, and unconditionally to be avoided, would take one back to the criteria for the assessment of persons as persons, and therefore to the whole way of life that one aspires to as the best way of life. A reflective, critical scrutiny of moral claims is compatible, both logically and psychologically, with an overriding concern for a record of unmonstrous and respectworthy conduct, and of action that has never been mean or inhuman; and it may follow an assessment of the worth of persons which is not to be identified only with a computation of consequences and effects.

There is a model of rational reflection which depends upon a contrast between the primitive moral response of an uneducated man, and of an uneducated society, and the comparatively detached arguments of the sophisticated moralist, who discounts his intuitive responses as being prejudices inherited from an uncritical past. Conspicuous in the philosophical radicals, in John Stuart Mill, and in the Victorian free-thinkers generally, this model in turn depended upon the idea that primitive, pre-scientific men are usually governed by strict moral taboos, and that in future intellectually evolved, and scientifically trained, men will be emancipated from these bonds, and will start again with clear reasoning about consequences. The word 'taboo', so often used in these contexts, shows the assumption of moral progress from primitive beginnings, and suggests a rather naive contrast between older moralities and the open morality of the future; empirical calculation succeeds a priori prejudice, and the calculation of consequences is reason.

But reflection may discover a plurality of clear and definite moral injunctions; injunctions about the taking of life, about sexual relations, about the conduct of parents towards children and of children towards parents, about one's duties in times of war, about the conditions under which truth must be told and under which it may be concealed, about rights to property, about duties of friendship, and so on over the various aspects and phases of a normal span of life. Such injunctions need not be inferrable from a few basic principles, corresponding to the axioms of a theory. The pattern that they form can have a different type of unity. Taken together, a full set of such injunctions, prohibiting types of conduct in types of circumstance, describes in rough and indeterminate outline, an attainable and recognisable way of life, aspired to, respected and admired: or at least the minimum general features of a respectworthy way of life. And a way of life is not identified and characterised by one distinct purpose, such as the increase of general happiness, or even by a set of such distinct purposes. The connection between the injunctions, the connection upon which a reasonable man reflects, is to be found in the coherence of a single way of life, distinguished by the characteristic virtues and vices recognised within it.

A way of life is a complicated thing, marked out by many details of style and manner, and also by particular activities and interests, which a group of people of similar dispositions in a similar social situation may share; so that the group may become an imitable human type who transmit many of their habits and ideals to their descendants, provided that social change is not too rapid.

In rational reflection one may justify an intuitively accepted and unconditional prohibition, as a common, expected feature of a recognisable way of life which on other grounds one values and finds admirable: or as a necessary preliminary condition of this way of life. There are rather precise grounds in experience and in history for the reasonable man to expect that certain virtues, which he admires and values, can only be attained at the cost of certain others, and that the virtues typical of several different ways of life cannot be freely combined, as he might wish. Therefore a reasonable and reflective person will review the separate moral injunctions, which intuitively present themselves as having force and authority, as making a skeleton of an attainable, respectworthy and preferred way of life. He will reject those that seem likely in practice to conflict with others that seem more closely part of, or conditions of, the way of life that he values and admires, or that seem irrelevant to this way of life.

One must not exaggerate the degree of connectedness that can be claimed for the set of injunctions that constitute the skeleton of a man's morality. For example, it is a loose, empirical connection that reasonably associates certain sexual customs with the observation of certain family duties, and certain loyalties to the state or country with the recognition of certain duties in respect of property, and in time of war. The phrase 'way of life' is vague and is chosen for its vagueness. The unity of a single way of life, and the compatibility in practice of different habits and dispositions, are learnt from observation, direct experience and from psychology and history: we know that human nature naturally varies, and is deliberately variable, only within limits: and that not all theoretically compatible achievements and enjoyments are compatible in normal circumstances. A reasonable man may envisage a way of life, which excludes various kinds of conduct as impossible, without excluding a great variety of morally tolerable ways of life within this minimum framework. The moral prohibitions constitute a kind of grammar of conduct, showing the elements out of which any fully respectworthy conduct, as one conceives it, must be built.

The plurality of absolute prohibitions, and the looseness of their association with any one way of life, which stresses a certain set of virtues, is to be contrasted with the unity and simplicity of utilitarian ethics. One might interpret the contrast in this way: to the utilitarian it is certain that all reasonable purposes are parts of a single purpose in a creature known to be governed by the pleasure principle or by a variant of it. The anti-utilitarian replies: nothing is certain in the *theory* of morality: but, at a pretheoretical level, some human virtues fit together as virtues to form a way of life aspired to, and some monstrous and brutal acts are certainly vicious in the sense that they undermine and corrupt this way of life; and we can explain why they are, and what makes them so, provided that we do not insist upon either precision or certainty or simplicity in the explanation.

The absolute moral prohibitions, which I am defending, are not to be identified with Kant's categorical moral injunctions; for they are not to be picked out by the logical feature of being universal in form. Nor are they prescriptions that must be affirmed, and that cannot be questioned or denied, just because they are principles of rationality, and because any contrary principles would involve a form of contradiction. They are indeed judgments of unconditional necessity, in the sense that they imply that what must be done is not necessary because it is a means to some independently valued end, but because the action is a necessary part of a way of life and ideal of conduct. The necessity resides in the nature of the action itself, as specified in the fully explicit moral judgment. The principal and proximate grounds for claiming that the action must, or must not, be performed are to be found in the characterisation of the action offered within the prescription; and if the argument is pressed further, first a virtue or vice, and then a whole way of life will have to be described.

But still a number of distinctions are needed to avoid misunderstandings. First, he who says, for example, 'You must not give a judgment about this until you have heard the evidence', or 'I must stand by my friend in this crisis', claiming an absolute, and unconditional, necessity to act just so on this occasion, is not claiming an overriding necessity so to act in all circumstances and situations. He has so far not generalised at all, as he would have generalised if he were to add 'always' or 'in all circumstances'. The immediate grounds for the necessity of the action or abstention are indicated in the judgment itself. These particular actions, which are cases of the general type 'respecting evidence' and 'standing by friends', are said to be necessary on this occasion in virtue of having just this character, and in virtue of their being this type of action. In other painful circumstances, and on other occasions, other unconditional necessities, with other grounds, might be judged to have overriding claims.

In a situation of conflict, the necessities may be felt to be stringent, and even generally inescapable, and the agent's further reflection may confirm his first feeling of their stringency. Yet in the circumstances of conflict he has to make a choice, and to bring himself to do one of the normally forbidden things, in order to avoid doing the other. He may finally recognise one overriding necessity, even though he would not be ready to generalise it to other circumstances. The necessity that is associated with types of action—e.g. not to betray one's friends—is absolute and unconditional, in the sense that it is not relative to, or conditional upon, some desirable external end: but it is liable occasionally to conflict with other necessities.

A second distinction must be drawn: from the fact that a man thinks that there is nothing other than X which he can do in a particular situation it does not follow that it is intuitively obvious to him that he must do X. Certainly he may have reached the conclusion immediately and without reflection; but he might also have reached the very same conclusion after weighing a number of arguments for and against. A person's belief that so-and-so must be done, and that he must not act in any other way, may be the outcome of the calculation of the consequences of not doing the necessary thing: always provided that he sees the avoidance of bringing about these consequences as something that is imposed on him as a necessity in virtue of the character of the action. The reason for the necessity of the action sometimes is to be found in its later consequences, rather than in the nature and quality of the action evident at the time of action. In every case there will be a description of the action that shows the immediate ground for the necessity, usually by indicating the virtue or vice involved.

Different men, and different social groups, recognise rather different moral necessities in the same essential areas of moral concern. This is no more surprising, or philosophically disquieting, than the fact that different men, and different social groups, will order the primary virtues of men, and the features of an admirable way of life, differently. That the poverty stricken and the destitute must be helped, just because they suffer, and that a great wrong does not demand a great punishment as retribution, are typical modern opinions about what must be done. Reasoning is associated with these opinions, as it is also with the different orderings of essential virtues; there are no conclusive proofs, or infallible intuitions, which put a stop to the adducing of new considerations. One does not expect that everyone should recognise the same moral necessities; but rather that everyone should recognise some moral necessities, and similar and overlapping ones, in the same, or almost the same areas, of moral concern.

A man's morality, and the morality of a social group, can properly be seen as falling into two parts, first, a picture of the activities necessary to an ideal way of life which is aspired to, and, second, the unavoidable duties and necessities without which even the elements of human worth, and of a respectworthy way of life, are lacking. The two parts are not rationally unconnected. To take the obvious classical examples: a betrayal of friends in a moment of danger, and for the sake of one's own safety, is excluded from the calculation of possibilities; one may lose perhaps everything else, but this cannot be done; the stain would be too great. And one may take public examples: an outrage of cruelty perpetrated upon undefended civilians in war would constitute a stain that would not be erased and would not be balanced against political success.

How would a sceptical, utilitarian friend of Stephen's, a philosophical friend of the utilitarians, respond to these suggestions? Among other objections he would certainly say that I was turning the clock back, suggesting a return to the moral philosophies of the past: absolute prohibitions, elementary decencies, the recognition of a plurality of prohibitions which do not all serve a single purpose: and with nothing more definite behind them than a form of life aspired to; this is the outline of an Aristotelian ethics: ancient doctrine. Modern utilitarians thought that men have the possibility of indefinite improvement in their moral thinking, and that they were confined and confused by their innate endowments of moral repugnances and emotional admirations. There was a sense of the open future in all their writing. But hope of continuing improvement, if it survives at all now, is now largely without evidence. Lowering the barriers of prohibition, and making rational calculation of consequences the sole foundation of public policies, have so far favoured, and are still favouring, a new callousness in policy, a dullness of sensibility, and sometimes moral despair, at least in respect of public affairs. When the generally respected barriers of impermissible conduct are once crossed, and when no different unconditional barriers, within the same areas of conduct, are put in their place, then the special, apparently superstitious value attached to the preservation of human life will be questioned. This particular value will no longer be distinguished by an exceptionally solemn prohibition;

rather it will be assessed on a common scale alongside other desirable things. Yet it is not clear that the taking of lives can be marked and evaluated on a common scale on which increases of pleasure and diminutions of suffering are also measured. This is the suggested discontinuity which a utilitarian must deny.

Moral prohibitions in general, and particularly those that govern the taking of life, the celebration of the dead, and that govern sexual relations and family relations, are artifices that give human lives some distinctive, peculiar, even arbitrary human shape and pattern. They humanise the natural phases of experience, and lend them a distinguishing sense and direction, one among many possible ones. It is natural for men to expect these artificialities, without which their lives would seem to them inhuman. Largely for this reason a purely naturalistic and utilitarian interpretation of duties and obligations, permissions and prohibitions, in these areas, and particularly in the taking of human life, leaves uneasiness. The idea of morality is connected with the idea that taking human life is a terrible act, which has to be regulated by some set of overriding constraints that constitute a morality; and the connection of ideas alleged here is not a vague one. If there were a people who did not recoil from killing, and, what is a distinguishable matter, who seemed to attach no exceptional value to human life, they would be accounted a community of the subhuman; or, more probably, we would doubt whether their words and practices had been rightly interpreted and whether their way of life had been understood. Yet the taking of life does not have any exceptional importance in utilitarian ethics, that is, in an ethics that is founded exclusively on the actual, ascertained desires and sentiments of men (unlike J. S. Mill's); the taking of life is morally significant in so far as it brings other losses with it. For a strict utilitarian (which J. S. Mill was not) the horror of killing is only the horror of causing other losses, principally of possible happiness; in cases where there are evidently no such losses, the horror of killing becomes superstition. And such a conclusion of naturalism, pressed to its limits, does produce a certain vertigo after reflection. It seems that the mainspring of morality has been taken away.

This vertigo is not principally the result of looking across a century of cool political massacres, undertaken with rational aims; it is also a sentiment with a philosophical thought behind it. A consistent naturalism displaces the pre-reflective moral emphasis upon respect for life, and for the preservation of life, on to an exclusive concern for one or other of the expected future products of being alive—happiness, pleasure, the satisfaction of desires. Respect for human life, independent of the use made of it, may seem to utilitarians a survival of a sacramental consciousness, or at least a survival of a doctrine of the soul's destiny, or of the unique relation between God and man. It had been natural to speak of the moral prohibitions against the taking of life as being respect for the sacredness of an individual life; and this phrase has no proper place, it is very reasonably assumed, in the thought of anyone who has rejected belief in supernatural sanctions.

But the situation may be more complicated. The sacredness of life, so called, and the absolute prohibitions against the taking of life, except under strictly defined conditions, may be admitted to be human inventions. Once the human origin of the prohibitions has been recognised, the prohibition against the taking of life, and respect for human life as such, may still be reaffirmed as absolute. They are reaffirmed as complementary to a set of customs, habits and observances, which are understood by reference to their function, and which are sustained, partly because of, partly in spite of, this understanding: I mean sexual customs, family observances, ceremonial treatment of the dead, gentle treatment of those who are diseased and useless, and of the old and senile, customs of war and treatment of prisoners, treatment of convicted criminals, political and legal safeguards for the rights of individuals, and the customary rituals of respect and gentleness in personal dealings. This complex of habits, and the rituals associated with them, are carried over into a secular morality which makes no existential claims that a naturalist would dispute, and which still rejects the utilitarian morality associated with naturalism. The error of the optimistic utilitarian is that he carries the deritualisation of transactions between men to a point at which men not only can, but ought to, use and exploit each other as they use and exploit any other natural objects, as far as this is compatible with general happiness. And at this point, when the mere existence of an individual person by itself has no value, apart from the by-products and uses of the individual in producing and enjoying desirable states of mind, there is no theoretical barrier against social surgery of all kinds. Not only is there no such barrier in theory: but, more important, the non-existence of the barriers is explicitly recognised. The draining of moral significance from ceremonies, rituals, manners and observances, which imaginatively express moral attitudes and prohibitions, leaves morality incorporated only in a set of propositions and computations: thin and uninteresting propositions, when so isolated from their base in the observances, and manners, which govern ordinary relations with people, and which always manifest implicit moral attitudes and opinions. The computational morality, on which optimists rely, dismisses the non-propositional and unprogrammed elements in morality altogether, falsely confident that these elements can all be ticketed and brought into the computations. . . .

X

Are There Any Absolute Rights?

Alan Gewirth

It is a widely held opinion that there are no absolute rights. Consider what would be generally regarded as the most plausible candidate: the right to life. This right entails at least the negative duty to refrain from killing any human being. But it is contended that this duty may be overriden, that a person may be justifiably killed if this is the only way [illegible] from killing some other, innocent person, or if he is [illegible] bat in the army of an unjust aggressor nation with [illegible] n country is at war. It is also maintained that even an [illegible] may justifiably be killed if failure to do so will lead to [illegible] her such persons. Thus an innocent person's right to [illegible] overridden when a fat man stuck in the mouth of a [illegible] e exit of speleologists who will otherwise drown, or [illegible] some other guiltless person is strapped onto the front [illegible] tank, or when an explorer's choice to kill one among [illegible] ess natives about to be executed is the necessary and [illegible] on of the others' being spared, or when the driver of a runaway trolley can avoid killing five persons on one track only by killing one person on another track.[1] And topping all such tragic

[1] For the cave example, see Philippa Foot, "The Problem of Abortion and the Doctrine of Double Effect", *Oxford Review*, no. 5 (1967), p. 7. [See p. 149 this volume.—Ed.] For the "innocent shield" and the tank, see Robert Nozick, *Anarchy, State, and Utopia* (New York, 1974), p. 35, and Judith J. Thomson, *Self-Defense and Rights* (Lindley Lecture, University of Kansas, 1976), p. 11. For the explorer and the natives, see Bernard Williams, "A Critique of Utilitarianism", in J. J. C. Smart and B. Williams, *Utilitarianism For and Against* (Cambridge, 1973), pp. 98–9 [See p. 104 this volume.—Ed.]. For the trolley example, see Foot, *op. cit.*, p. 8 [See pp. 150–51 this volume.—Ed.], and Judith J. Thomson, "Killing, Letting Die, and the Trolley Problem", *The Monist*, 59 (1976), pp. 206 ff. I have

examples is the catastrophic situation where a nuclear war or some other unmitigated disaster can be avoided only by infringing some innocent person's right to life.

Despite such cases, I shall argue that certain rights can be shown to be absolute. But first the concept of an absolute right must be clarified.

I

1. I begin with the Hohfeldian point that the rights here in question are claim-rights (as against liberties, powers, and so forth) in that they are justified claims or entitlements to the carrying out of correlative duties, positive or negative. A duty is a requirement that some action be performed or not be performed; in the latter, negative case, the requirement constitutes a prohibition.

A right is *fulfilled* when the correlative duty is carried out, i.e., when the required action is performed or the prohibited action is not performed. A right is *infringed* when the correlative duty is not carried out, i.e., when the required action is not performed or the prohibited action is performed. Thus someone's right to life is infringed when the prohibited action of killing him is performed; someone's right to medical care is infringed when the required action of providing him with medical care is not performed. A right is *violated* when it is unjustifiably infringed, i.e., when the required action is unjustifiably not performed or the prohibited action is unjustifiably performed. And a right is *overriden* when it is justifiably infringed, so that there is sufficient justification for not carrying out the correlative duty, and the required action is justifiably not performed or the prohibited action is justifiably performed.

A right is *absolute* when it cannot be overriden in any circumstances, so that it can never be justifiably infringed and it must be fulfilled without any exceptions.

The idea of an absolute right is thus doubly normative: it includes not only the idea, common to all claim-rights, of a justified claim or entitlement to the performance or non-performance of certain actions, but also the idea of the exceptionless justifiability of performing or not performing those actions as required. These components show that the question whether there are any absolute rights demands for its adequate answer an explicit concern with criteria of justification. I shall here assume what I have elsewhere argued for in some detail: that these criteria, insofar as they are valid, are ultimately based on a

---

borrowed from Thomson's *Self-Defense and Rights*, p. 10, the terminological distinction used below between "infringing" and "violating" a right.

certain supreme principle of morality, the Principle of Generic Consistency (*PGC*).[2] This principle requires of every agent that he act in accord with the generic rights of his recipients as well as of himself, i.e., that he fulfil these rights. The generic rights are rights to the necessary conditions of action, freedom and well-being, where the latter is defined in terms of the various substantive abilities and conditions needed for action and for successful action in general. The *PGC* provides the ultimate justificatory basis for the validity of these rights by showing that they are equally had by all prospective purposive agents, and it also provides in general for the ordering of the rights in cases of conflict. Thus if two moral rights are so related that each can be fulfilled only by infringing the other, that right takes precedence whose fulfilment is more necessary for action. This criterion of degrees of necessity for action explains, for example, why one person's right not to be lied to must give way to another person's right not to be killed when these two rights are in conflict. In some cases the application of this criterion requires a context of institutional rules.

2. The general formula of a right is as follows: "A has a right to X against B by virtue of Y". In addition to the right itself, there are four elements here: the *subject* of the right, the right-holder (A); the *object* of the right (X); the *respondent* of the right, the person who has the correlative duty (B); and the *justificatory basis or ground* of the right (Y). I shall refer to these elements jointly as the *contents* of the right. Each of the elements may vary in generality. Various rights may conflict with one another as to one or another of these elements, so that not all rights can be absolute.

One aspect of these conflicts is especially important for understanding the question of absolute rights. Although, as noted above, the *objects* of moral rights are hierarchically ordered (according to the degree of their necessity for action), this is not true of the *subjects* of the rights. If one class or group of persons inherently had superior moral rights over another class or group (as was held to be the case throughout much of human history), any conflict between their respective rights would be readily resoluble: the rights of the former group would always take precedence, they would never be overriden (at least by the rights of members of other groups), and to this extent they would be absolute.[3] It is because (as is shown by the *PGC* as well as

[2] Alan Gewirth, *Reason and Morality* (Chicago, 1978), pp. 135 ff., 197–198, 343–44.

[3] Cf. Friedrich Nietzsche, *The Will to Power*, sec. 872: "The great majority of men have no right to existence, but are a misfortune to higher men" (trans. Walter Kaufmann (New York, 1967), p. 467). See also Nietzsche, *Beyond Good and Evil*, sec. 260 (trans. Kaufmann (New York, 1966), p. 206).

by other moral principles) moral rights are equally distributed among all human persons as prospective purposive agents that some of the main conflicts of rights arise. This is most obviously the case where one person's right to life conflicts with another person's, since in the absence of guilt on either side, it is assumed that the two persons have equal rights. Thus the difficulty of supporting the thesis that there are absolute rights derives much of its force from its connection with the principle that all persons are equal in their moral rights.

3. The differentiation of the elements of rights serves to explicate the various levels at which rights may be held to be absolute. We may distinguish three such levels. The first is that of *Principle Absolutism*. According to this, what is absolute, and thus always valid and never overridden, is only some moral principle of a very high degree of generality which, referring to the subjects, the respondents, and especially the objects of rights in a relatively undifferentiated way, presents a general formula for all the diverse duties of all respondents or agents toward all subjects or recipients. The *PGC* is such a principle; so too are the Golden Rule, the law of love, Kant's categorical imperative, and the principle of utility. Principle Absolutism, however, may leave open the question whether any specific rights are always absolute, and what is to be done in cases of conflict. Even act-utilitarianism might be an example of Principle Absolutism, for it may be interpreted as saying that those rights are absolute whose fulfilment would serve to maximize utility overall. These rights, whatever they may be, might of course vary in their specific contents from one situation to another.

At the opposite extreme is *Individual Absolutism*, according to which an individual person has an absolute right to some particular object at a particular time and place when all grounds for overriding the right in the particular case have been overcome. But this still leaves open the question of what are the general grounds or criteria for overriding any right, and what are the other specific relevant contents of such rights.

It is at the intermediate level, that of *Rule Absolutism*, that the question of absolute rights arises most directly. At this level, the rights whose absoluteness is in question are characterized in terms of specific objects with possible specification also of subjects and respondents, so that a specific rule can be stated describing the content of the right and the correlative duty. The description will not use proper names and other individual referring expressions, as in the case of Individual Absolutism, nor will it consist only in a general formula applicable to many specifically different kinds of rights and duties and hence of objects, subjects, and respondents, as in the case of Principle Absolutism. It is at this level that one asks whether the right to life of all persons or of all innocent persons is absolute; whether the rights to freedom of speech and of religion are absolute, and so forth.

The rights whose absoluteness is considered at the level of Rule Absolutism may vary in degree of generality, in that their objects, their subjects, and their respondents may be given with greater or lesser specificity. Thus there is greater specificity as we move along the following scale: the right of all persons to life, the right of all innocent persons to life, the right of all innocent persons to an economically secure life, the right of children to receive an economically secure and emotionally satisfying life from their parents, and so forth.

This variability raises the following problem. For a right to be absolute, it must be conclusively valid without any exceptions. But, as we have seen, rights may vary in generality, and all the resulting specifications of their objects, subjects, or respondents may constitute exceptions to the more general rights in which such specifications are not present. For example, the right of innocent persons to life may incorporate an exception to the right of all persons to life, for the rule embodying the former right may be stated thus: All persons have a right not to be killed except when the persons are not innocent, or except when such killing is directly required in order to prevent them from killing somebody else. Similarly, when it is said that all persons have a right to life, the specification of 'persons' may suggest (although it does not strictly entail) the exception-making rule that all animals (or even all organisms) have a right to life except when they are not persons (or not human). Hence, since an absolute right is one that is valid without any exceptions, it may be concluded either that no rights are absolute because all involve some specification, or that all rights are equally absolute because once their specifications are admitted they are entirely valid without any further exceptions.

The solution to this problem consists in seeing that not all specifications of the subjects, objects, or respondents of moral rights constitute the kinds of exception whose applicability to a right debars it from being absolute. I shall indicate three criteria for permissible specifications. First, when it is asked concerning some moral right whether it is absolute, the kind of specification that may be incorporated in the right can only be such as results in a concept that is recognizable to ordinary practical thinking. This excludes rights that are "overloaded with exceptions" as well as those whose application would require intricate utilitarian calculations.[4]

Second, the specifications must be justifiable through a valid moral principle. Since, as we saw above, the idea of an absolute right is

[4] See R. M. Hare, "Principles", *Proceedings of the Aristotelian Society*, 73 (1972–73), pp. 7 ff. This paper is also relevant to some of the other issues of "exceptions" discussed above. See also Marcus G. Singer, *Generalization in Ethics* (New York, 1961), pp. 100–103, 124–133, and David Lyons, "Mill's Theory of Morality", *Noûs*, 10 (1976), pp. 112–13.

doubly normative, a right with its specification would not even begin to be a candidate for absoluteness unless the specification were morally justified and could hence be admitted as a condition of the justifiability of the moral right. There is, for example, a good moral justification for incorporating the restriction of innocence on the subjects of the right not to be killed: but there is not a similarly good moral justification for incorporating racial, religious, and other such particularist specifications. It must be emphasized, however, that this moral specification guarantees only that the right thus specified is an appropriate candidate for being absolute; it is, of itself, not decisive as to whether the right *is* absolute.

A third criterion is that the permissible specification of a right must exclude any reference to the possibly disastrous consequences of fulfilling the right. Since a chief difficulty posed against absolute rights is that for any right there can be cases in which its fulfilment may have disastrous consequences, to put this reference into the very description of the right would remove one of the main grounds for raising the question of absoluteness.

The relation between rights and disasters is complicated by the fact that the latter, when caused by the actions of persons, are themselves infringements of rights. This point casts a new light on the consequentialist's thesis that there are no absolute rights. For when he says that every right may be overridden if this is required in order to avoid certain catastrophes—such as when torture alone will enable the authorities to ascertain where a terrorist has hidden a fused charge of dynamite—the consequentialist is appealing to basic rights. He is saying that in such a case one right—the right not to be tortured—is overridden by another right—the right to life of the many potential victims of the explosion. This raises the following question. Can the process of one right's overriding another continue indefinitely or does the process come to a stop with absolute rights?

In order to deal with this question, two points must be kept in mind. First, even when catastrophes threatening the infringement of basic rights are invoked to override other rights, at least part of the problem created by such conflict depends, as was noted above, on the assumption that all the persons involved have equal moral rights. There would be no serious conflict of rights and no problem about absolute rights if, for example, the rights of the persons threatened by the catastrophe were deemed inferior to those of persons not so threatened.

Second, despite the close connection between rights in general and the rights threatened by disastrous consequences, it is important to distinguish them. For if the appeal to avoidance of disastrous consequences were to be construed simply as an appeal for the fulfilment or protection of certain basic rights, then, on the assumption that certain disasters must always be avoided when they are threatened, the consequentialist would himself be an absolutist. We can escape this untoward result and render more coherent the opposition between absolutism and consequentialism if we recognize a further important assumption of the question whether there are any absolute rights. Amid the various possible specifications of Rule Absolutism, the rights in question are the normative property of *distinct individuals*.[5] In referring to some event as a "disaster" or a "catastrophe", on the other hand, what is often meant is that a large mass of individuals *taken collectively* loses some basic good to which they have a right. It is their *aggregate* loss that constitutes the catastrophe. (This, of course, accounts for the close connection between the appeal to disastrous consequences and utilitarianism.) Thus the question whether there are any absolute rights is to be construed as asking whether distinct individuals, each of whom has equal moral rights (and who are to be characterized, according to the conditions of Rule Absolutism, by specifications that are morally justifiable and recognizable to ordinary practical thinking), have any rights that may never be overriden by any other considerations, including even their catastrophic consequences for collective rights.

II

4. We must now examine the merits of the prime consequentialist argument against the possibility of absolute moral rights: that circumstances can always be imagined in which the consequences of fulfilling the rights would be so disastrous that their requirements would be overriden. The formal structure of the argument is as follows: (1) If R, then D. (2) O (~D). (3) Therefore, O(~R). For example, (1) if some person's right to life is fulfilled in certain circumstances, then some great disaster may or will occur. But (2) such disaster ought never to (be allowed to) occur. Hence, (3) in such circumstances the right ought not to be fulfilled so that it is not absolute.

Proponents of this argument have usually failed to notice that a parallel argument can be given in the opposite direction. If exceptions to the fulfilment of any moral right can be justified by imagining the possible disastrous consequences of fulfilling it, why cannot exceptionless moral rights be justified by giving them such contents that their infringement would be unspeakably evil? The argument to this effect may be put formally as follows: (1) If ~R, then E. (2) O(~E): (3) Therefore, O(R). For example, (1) if a mother's right not to be tortured

[5] Cf. H. L. A. Hart, "Are There Any Natural Rights?", *Philosophical Review*, 64 (1955), p. 182, and Hart, "Bentham on Legal Rights", in *Oxford Essays in Jurisprudence*, 2nd Series, ed. A. W. B. Simpson (Oxford, 1973), p. 193.

to death by her own son is not fulfilled, then there will be unspeakable evil. But (2) such evil ought never to (be allowed to) occur. Hence, (3) the right ought to be fulfilled without any exceptions, so that it is absolute.

Two preliminary points must be made about these arguments. First, despite their formal parallelism, there is an important difference in the meaning of 'then' in their respective first premises. In the first argument, 'then' signifies a consequential causal connection: if someone's right to life is fulfilled, there may or will ensue as a result the quite distinct phenomenon of a certain great disaster. But in the second argument, 'then' signifies a moral conceptual relation: the unspeakable evil is not a causal *consequence* of a mother's being tortured to death by her own son; it is rather a central moral constituent of it. Thus the second argument is not consequentialist, as the first one is, despite the fact that each of their respective first premises has the logical form of antecedent and consequent.

A related point bears on the second argument's specification of the right in question as a mother's right not to be tortured to death by her own son. This specification does not transgress the third requirement given above for permissible specifications: that reference to disastrous consequences must not be included in the formulation of the right. For the torturing to death is not a disastrous causal consequence of infringing the right; it is directly an infringement of the right itself, just as not being tortured to death by her own son is not a consequence of fulfilling the right but is the right. This distinction can perhaps be seen more clearly in such a less extreme case as the right not to be lied to. Being told a lie is not a causal *consequence* of infringing this right; rather, it just is an infringement of the right. In each case, moreover, the first two requirements for permissible specifications of moral rights are also satisfied: their contents are recognizable to ordinary practical thinking and they are justified by a valid moral principle.

5. Let us now consider the right mentioned above: a mother's right not to be tortured to death by her own son. Assume (although these specifications are here quite dispensable) that she is innocent of any crime and has no knowledge of any. What justifiable exception could there be to such a right? I shall construct an example which, though fanciful, has sufficient analogues in past and present thought and action to make it relevant to the status of rights in the real world.[6]

---

[6] Cf. Aristotle, *Nicomachean Ethics*, III. 1. 1110a5, 27, and H. V. Dicks, *Licensed Mass Murder: A Socio-Psychological Study of Some S. S. Killers* (London, 1972). For similar extreme examples, see I. M. Crombie, "Moral Principles", in *Christian Ethics and Contemporary Philosophy*, ed. Ian T. Ramsey (New York, 1966), p. 258; Paul Ramsey, "The Case of the Curious Exception", in *Norm and Context in Christian Ethics*, ed. Gene H. Outka and P. Ramsey (New York, 1968), pp. 101, 127 ff.; Donald Evans, "Paul Ramsey on Exceptionless Moral Rules",

Suppose a clandestine group of political extremists have obtained an arsenal of nuclear weapons; to prove that they have the weapons and know how to use them, they have kidnapped a leading scientist, shown him the weapons, and then released him to make a public corroborative statement. The terrorists have now announced that they will use the weapons against a designated large distant city unless a certain prominent resident of the city, a young politically active lawyer named Abrams, tortures his mother to death, this torturing to be carried out publicly in a certain way at a specified place and time in that city. Since the gang members have already murdered several other prominent residents of the city, their threat is quite credible. Their declared motive is to advance their cause by showing how powerful they are and by unmasking the moralistic pretensions of their political opponents.

Ought Abrams to torture his mother to death in order to prevent the threatened nuclear catastrophe? Might he not merely pretend to torture his mother, so that she could then be safely hidden while the hunt for the gang members continued? Entirely apart from the fact that the gang could easily pierce this deception, the main objection to the very raising of such questions is the moral one that they seem to hold open the possibility of acquiescing and participating in an unspeakably evil project. To inflict such extreme harm on one's mother would be an ultimate act of betrayal; in performing or even contemplating the performance of such an action the son would lose all self-respect and would regard his life as no longer worth living.[7] A mother's right not to be tortured to death by her own son is beyond any compromise. It is absolute.

This absoluteness may be analysed in several different interrelated dimensions, all stemming from the supreme principle of morality. The principle requires respect for the rights of all persons to the necessary conditions of human action, and this includes respect for the persons themselves as having the rational capacity to reflect on their purposes

---

American Journal of Jurisprudence, 16 (1971), pp. 204, 207; John M. Swomley, Jr., in *The Situation Ethics Debate*, ed. Harvey Cox (Philadelphia, 1968), p. 87. I have elsewhere argued for another absolute right: the right to the non-infliction of cancer. See Alan Gewirth, "Human Rights and the Prevention of Cancer", *American Philosophical Quarterly*, 17 (1980), pp. 117–25.

[7] This reference to the minimal moral conditions of a worthwhile life is, of course, an ancient theme; see Aristotle, *Nicomachean Ethics*, III. 1. 1110a 27; IV. 3. 1124b 7; IX. 8. 1169a 20 ff. For an excellent contemporary statement, see Alan Donagan, *The Theory of Morality* (Chicago, 1977), especially pp. 156–57, 183. For other recent discussions of the relation of the agent's character and intentions to moral absolutism, see John Casey, "Actions and Consequences", in *Morality and Moral Reasoning*, ed. J. Casey (London, 1971), pp. 155–7, 195 ff.; R. A. Duff, "Absolute Principles and Double Effect", *Analysis*, 36 (1976), pp. 73 ff.; P. T. Geach, *The Virtues* (Cambridge, 1977), pp. 113–17.

and to control their behaviour in the light of such reflection. The principle hence prohibits using any person merely as a means to the well-being of other persons. For a son to torture his mother to death even to protect the lives of others would be an extreme violation of this principle and hence of these rights, as would any attempt by others to force such an action. For this reason, the concept appropriate to it is not merely 'wrong' but such others as 'despicable', 'dishonourable', 'base', 'monstrous'. In the scale of moral modalities, such concepts function as the contrary extremes of concepts like the supererogatory. What is supererogatory is not merely good or right but goes beyond these in various ways; it includes saintly and heroic actions whose moral merit surpasses what is strictly required of agents. In parallel fashion, what is base, dishonourable, or despicable is not merely bad or wrong but goes beyond these in moral demerit since it subverts even the minimal worth or dignity both of its agent and of its recipient and hence, the basic presuppositions of morality itself. Just as the supererogatory is superlatively good, so the despicable is superlatively evil and diabolic, and its moral wrongness is so rotten that a morally decent person will not even consider doing it. This is but another way of saying that the rights it would violate must remain absolute.

6. There is, however, another side to this story. What of the thousands of innocent persons in the distant city whose lives are imperilled by the threatened nuclear explosion? Don't they too have rights to life which, because of their numbers, are far superior to the mother's right? May they not contend that while it is all very well for Abrams to preserve his moral purity by not killing his mother, he has no right to purchase this at the expense of their lives, thereby treating them as mere means to his ends and violating their own rights? Thus it may be argued that the morally correct description of the alternative confronting Abrams is not simply that it is one of not violating or violating an innocent person's right to life, but rather not violating one innocent person's right to life and thereby violating the right to life of thousands of other innocent persons through being partly responsible for their deaths, or violating one innocent person's right to life and thereby protecting or fulfilling the right to life of thousands of other innocent persons. We have here a tragic conflict of rights and an illustration of the heavy price exacted by moral absolutism. The aggregative consequentialist who holds that that action ought always to be performed which maximizes utility or minimizes disutility would maintain that in such a situation the lives of the thousands must be preferred.

An initial answer may be that terrorists who make such demands and issue such threats cannot be trusted to keep their word not to drop the bombs if the mother is tortured to death; and even if they now do keep their word, acceding in this case would only lead to further escalated demands and threats. It may also be argued that it is irrational to perpetrate a sure evil in order to forestall what is so far only a possible or threatened evil. Philippa Foot has sagely commented on cases of this sort that if it is the son's duty to kill his mother in order to save the lives of the many other innocent residents of the city, then "anyone who wants us to do something we think wrong has only to threaten that otherwise he himself will do something we think worse".[8] Much depends, however, on the nature of the "wrong" and the "worse". If someone threatens to commit suicide or to kill innocent hostages if we do not break our promise to do some relatively unimportant action, breaking the promise would be the obviously right course, by the criterion of degrees of necessity for action. The special difficulty of the present case stems from the fact that the conflicting rights are of the same supreme degree of importance.

It may be contended, however, that this whole answer, focusing on the probable outcome of obeying the terrorists' demands, is a consequentialist argument and, as such, is not available to the absolutist who insists that Abrams must not torture his mother to death whatever the consequences.[9] This contention imputes to the absolutist a kind of indifference or even callousness to the sufferings of others that is not warranted by a correct understanding of his position. He can be concerned about consequences so long as he does not regard them as possibly superseding or diminishing the right and duty he regards as absolute. It is a matter of priorities. So long as the mother's right not to be tortured to death by her son is unqualifiedly respected, the absolutist can seek ways to mitigate the threatened disastrous consequences and possibly to avert them altogether. A parallel case is found in the theory of legal punishment: the retributivist, while asserting that punishment must be meted out only to the persons who deserve it because of the crimes they have committed, may also uphold punishment for its deterrent effect so long as the latter, consequentialist consideration is subordinated to and limited by the conditions of the former, antecedentalist consideration.[10] Thus the absolutist can accommodate at least part of the consequentialist's substantive concerns within the limits of his own principle.

Is any other answer available to the absolutist, one that reflects the core of his position? Various lines of argument may be used to show that in refusing to torture his mother to death Abrams is not violating the rights of the multitudes of other residents who may die as a result, because he is not morally responsible for their deaths. Thus the

---

[8] "The Problem of Abortion and the Doctrine of Double Effect" (see n. 1), p. 10. [See p. 152 this volume.—Ed.]

[9] See Jonathan Bennett, "Whatever the Consequences", *Analysis*, 26 (1966), pp. 89–91. [See pp. 182–83 this volume.—Ed.]

[10] See Gewirth, *Reason and Morality*, pp. 294–9.

absolutist can maintain that even if these others die they still have an absolute right to life because the infringement of their right is not justified by the argument he upholds. At least three different distinctions may be adduced for this purpose. In the unqualified form in which they have hitherto been presented, however, they are not successful in establishing the envisaged conclusion.

One distinction is between direct and oblique intention. When Abrams refrains from torturing his mother to death, he does not directly intend the many ensuing deaths of the other inhabitants either as end or as means. These are only the foreseen but unintended side-effects of his action or, in this case, inaction. Hence, he is not morally responsible for those deaths.

Apart from other difficulties with the doctrine of double effect, this distinction as so far stated does not serve to exculpate Abrams. Consider some parallels. Industrialists who pollute the environment with poisonous chemicals and manufacturers who use carcinogenic food additives do not directly intend the resulting deaths; these are only the unintended but foreseen side-effects of what they do directly intend, namely, to provide profitable demand-fulfilling commodities. The entrepreneurs in question may even maintain that the enormous economic contributions they make to the gross national product outweigh in importance the relatively few deaths that regrettably occur. Still, since they have good reason to believe that deaths will occur from causes under their control, the fact that they do not directly intend the deaths does not remove their causal and moral responsibility for them. Isn't this also true of Abrams's relation to the deaths of the city's residents?

A second distinction drawn by some absolutists is between killing and letting die. This distinction is often merged with others with which it is not entirely identical, such as the distinctions between commission and omission, between harming and not helping, between strict duties and generosity or supererogation. For the present discussion, however, the subtle differences between these may be overlooked. The contention, then, is that in refraining from killing his mother, Abrams does not kill the many innocent persons who will die as a result; he only lets them die. But one does not have the same strict moral duty to help persons or to prevent their dying as one has not to kill them; one is responsible only for what one does, not for what one merely allows to happen. Hence, Abrams is not morally responsible for the deaths he fails to prevent by letting the many innocent persons die, so that he does not violate their rights to life.

The difficulty with this argument is that the duties bearing on the right to life include not only that one not kill innocent persons but also that one not let them die when one can prevent their dying at no comparable cost. If, for example, one can rescue a drowning man by throwing him a rope, one has a moral duty to throw him the rope. Failure to do so is morally culpable. Hence, to this extent the son who lets the many residents die when he can prevent this by means within his power is morally responsible for their deaths.

A third distinction is between respecting other persons and avoiding bad consequences. Respect for persons is an obligation so fundamental that it cannot be overridden even to prevent evil consequences from befalling some persons. If such prevention requires an action whereby respect is withheld from persons, then that action must not be performed, whatever the consequences.

One of the difficulties with this important distinction is that it is unclear. May not respect be withheld from a person by failing to avert from him some evil consequence? How can Abrams be held to respect the thousands of innocent persons or their rights if he lets them die when he could have prevented this? The distinction also fails to provide for degrees of moral urgency. One fails to respect a person if one lies to him or steals from him; but sometimes the only way to prevent the death of one innocent person may be by stealing from or telling a lie to some other innocent person. In such a case, respect for one person may lead to disrespect of a more serious kind for some other innocent person.

7. None of the above distinctions, then, serves its intended purpose of defending the absolutist against the consequentialist. They do not show that the son's refusal to torture his mother to death does not violate the other persons' rights to life and that he is not morally responsible for their deaths. Nevertheless, the distinctions can be supplemented in a way that does serve to establish these conclusions.

The required supplement is provided by the principle of the intervening action. According to this principle, when there is a causal connection between some person A's performing some action (or inaction) X and some other person C's incurring a certain harm Z, A's moral responsibility for Z is removed if, between X and Z, there intervenes some other action Y of some person B who knows the relevant circumstances of his action and who intends to produce Z or who produces Z through recklessness. The reason for this removal is that B's intervening action Y is the more direct or proximate cause of Z and, unlike A's action (or inaction), Y is the sufficient condition of Z as it actually occurs.[11]

An example of this principle may help to show its connection with the absolutist thesis. Martin Luther King Jr. was repeatedly told that because he led demonstrations in support of civil rights, he was

[11] Cf. H. L. A. Hart and A. M. Honoré, *Causation in the Law* (Oxford, 1959), pp. 69 ff., 127 ff., 292 ff. For an application of this principle in a related context, see Gewirth, "Human Rights and the Prevention of Cancer" (n. 6 above), pp. 118–9.

morally responsible for the disorders, riots, and deaths that ensued and that were shaking the American Republic to its foundations.[12] By the principle of the intervening action, however, it was King's opponents who were responsible because their intervention operated as the sufficient conditions of the riots and injuries. King might also have replied that the Republic would not be worth saving if the price that had to be paid was the violation of the civil rights of black Americans. As for the rights of the other Americans to peace and order, the reply would be that these rights cannot justifiably be secured at the price of the rights of blacks.

It follows from the principle of the intervening action that it is not the son but rather the terrorists who are morally as well as causally responsible for the many deaths that do or may ensue on his refusal to torture his mother to death. The important point is not that he lets these persons die rather than kills them, or that he does not harm them but only fails to help them, or that he intends their deaths only obliquely but not directly. The point is rather that it is only through the intervening lethal actions of the terrorists that his refusal eventuates in the many deaths. Since the moral responsibility is not the son's, it does not affect his moral duty not to torture his mother to death, so that her correlative right remains absolute.

This point also serves to answer some related questions about the rights of the many in relation to the mother's right. Since the son's refusal to torture his mother to death is justified, it may seem that the many deaths to which that refusal will lead are also justified, so that the rights to life of these many innocent persons are not absolute. But since they are innocent, why aren't their rights to life as absolute as the mother's? If, on the other hand, their deaths are unjustified, as seems obvious, then isn't the son's refusal to torture his mother to death also unjustified, since it leads to those deaths? But from this it would follow that the mother's right not to be tortured to death by her son is not absolute, for if the son's not infringing her right is unjustified, then his infringing it would presumably be justified.

The solution to this difficulty is that it is a fallacy to infer, from the two premises, (1) the son's refusal to kill his mother is justified and (2) many innocent persons die as a result of that refusal, to the conclusion (3) their deaths are justified. For, by the principle of the intervening action, the son's refusal is not causally or morally responsible for the deaths; rather, it is the terrorists who are responsible. Hence, the justification referred to in (1) does not carry through to (2). Since the terrorists' action in ordering the killings is unjustified, the resulting deaths are unjustified. Hence, the rights to life of the many innocent

---

[12] See, e.g., Charles E. Whittaker in Whittaker and William Sloane Coffin Jr., *Law, Order and Civil Disobedience* (Washington, D.C., 1967), pp. 11 ff.

victims remain absolute even if they are killed as a result of the son's justified refusal, and it is not he who violates their rights. He may be said to intend the many deaths obliquely, in that they are a foreseen but unwanted side-effect of his refusal. But he is not responsible for that side-effect because of the terrorists' intervening action.

It would be unjustified to violate the mother's right to life in order to protect the rights to life of the many other residents of the city. For rights cannot be justifiably protected by violating another right which, according to the criterion of degrees of necessity for action, is at least equally important. Hence, the many other residents do not have a right that the mother's right to life be violated for their sakes. To be sure, the mother also does not have a right that their equally important rights be violated in order to protect hers. But here too it must be emphasized that in protecting his mother's right the son does not violate the rights of the others; for by the principle of the intervening action, it is not he who is causally or morally responsible for their deaths. Hence too he is not treating them as mere means to his or his mother's ends.

8. Where, then, does this leave us? From the absoluteness of the mother's right not to be tortured to death by her son, does it follow that in the described circumstances a nuclear explosion should be permitted to occur over the city so that countless thousands of innocent persons may be killed, possibly including Abrams and his mother?

Properly to deal with this question, it is vitally important to distinguish between abstract and concrete absolutism. The abstract absolutist at no point takes account of consequences or of empirical or causal connections that may affect the subsequent outcomes of the two alternatives he considers. He views the alternatives as being both mutually exclusive and exhaustive. His sole concern is for the moral guiltlessness of the agent, as against the effects of the agent's choices for human weal or woe.

In contrast, as I suggested earlier, the concrete absolutist is concerned with consequences and empirical connections, but always within the limits of the right he upholds as absolute. His consequentialism is thus limited rather than unlimited. Because of his concern with empirical connections, he takes account of a broader range of possible alternatives than the simple dualism to which the abstract absolutist confines himself. His primary focus is not on the moral guiltlessness of the agent but rather on the basic rights of persons not to be subjected to unspeakable evils. Within this focus, however, the concrete absolutist is also deeply concerned with the effects of the fulfilment of these rights on the basic well-being of other persons.

The significance of this distinction can be seen by applying it to the case of Abrams. If he is an abstract absolutist, he deals with only two alternatives which he regards as mutually exclusive as well as exhaustive: (1) he tortures his mother to death; (2) the terrorists drop a nuclear bomb killing thousands of innocent persons. For the reasons indicated above, he rejects (1). He is thereby open to the accusation that he chooses (2) or at least that he allows (2) to happen, although the principle of the intervening action exempts him from moral guilt or responsibility.

If, however, Abrams is a concrete absolutist, then he does not regard himself as being confronted only by these two terrible alternatives, nor does he regard them or their negations as mutually exclusive. His thought-processes include the following additional considerations. In accordance with a point suggested above, he recognizes that his doing (1) will not *assure* the non-occurrence of (2). On the contrary, his doing (1) will probably lead to further threats of the occurrence of (2) unless he or someone else performs further unspeakably evil actions (3), (4), and so forth. (A parallel example may be found in Hitler's demand for Czechoslovakia at Munich after his taking over of Austria, his further demand for Poland after the capitulation regarding Czechoslovakia, and the ensuing tragedies.) Moreover, (2) may occur even if Abrams does (1). For persons who are prepared to threaten that they will do (2) cannot be trusted to keep their word.

On the other hand, Abrams further reasons, his not doing (1) may well not lead to (2). This may be so for several reasons. He or the authorities or both must try to engage the terrorists in a dialogue in which their grievances are publicized and seriously considered. Whatever elements of rationality may exist among the terrorists will thereby be reinforced, so that other alternatives may be presented. At the same time, a vigorous search and preventive action must be pursued so as to avert the threatened bombing and to avoid any recurrences of the threat.

It is such concrete absolutism, taking due account of consequences and of possible alternatives, that constitutes the preferred pattern of ethical reasoning. It serves to protect the rights presupposed in the very possibility of a moral community while at the same time it gives the greatest probability of averting the threatened catastrophe. In the remainder of this paper, I shall assume the background of concrete absolutism.

III

9. I have thus far argued that the right of a mother not to be tortured to death by her son is absolute. But the arguments would also ground an extension of the kind of right here at issue to many other subjects and respondents, including fathers, daughters, wives, husbands, grandparents, cousins, and friends. So there are many absolute rights, on the criterion of plurality supplied by Rule Absolutism.

It is sometimes held that moral obligations are "agent-relative" in that, at least in cases of conflict, one ought to give priority to the welfare of those persons with whom one has special ties of family or affection.[13] Applied to the present question, this view would suggest that the subjects having the absolute right that must be respected by respondents are limited to the kinds of relations listed above. It may also be thought that as we move away from familial and affectional relations, the proposed subjects of rights come to resemble more closely the anonymous masses of other persons who would be killed by a nuclear explosion, so that a quantitative measure of numbers of lives lost would become a more cogent consideration in allocating rights.

These conclusions, however, do not follow. Most of the arguments I have given above for the mother's absolute right not to be tortured to death apply to other possible human subjects without such specifications. My purpose in beginning with such an extreme case as the mother-son relation was to focus the issue as sharply as possible; but, this focus once gained, it may be widened in the ways just indicated. Although the mother has indeed a greater right to receive effective concern from her son than from other, unrelated persons, the unjustifiability of violating rights that are on the same level of necessity for action is not affected either by degrees of family relationship or by the numbers of persons affected. Abrams would not be justified in torturing to death some other innocent person in the described circumstances, and in failing to murder he would not be morally responsible for the deaths of other innocent persons who might be murdered by someone else as a consequence.

These considerations also apply to various progressively less extreme objects of rights than the not being tortured to death to which I have so far confined the discussion. The general content of these objects may be stated as follows: All innocent persons have an absolute right not to be made the intended victims of a homicidal project. This right, despite its increase in generality over the object, subject, and respondents of the previous right, still conforms to the requirements of Rule Absolutism. The word 'intended' here refers both to direct and to oblique intention, with the latter being subject to the principle of the intervening action. The word 'project' is meant to indicate a definite, deliberate design; hence, it excludes the kind of unforeseeable immediate crisis where, for example, the unfortunate driver of a trolley whose brakes have failed must choose between killing one person or five. The absolute right imposes a prohibition on any form of active participation in a homicidal project against innocent persons, whether

[13] See Derek Parfit, "Innumerate Ethics", *Philosophy and Public Affairs*, 7 No. 4 (1978), p. 287.

by the original designers or by those who would accept its conditions with a view to warding off what they would regard as worse consequences. The meaning of 'innocent' raises many questions of interpretation into which I have no space to enter here, but some of its main criteria may be gathered from the first paragraph of this paper. As for 'persons', this refers to all prospective purposive agents.

The right not to be made the intended victim of a homicidal project is not the only specific absolute right, but it is surely one of the most important. The general point underlying all absolute rights stems from the moral principle presented earlier. At the level of Principle Absolutism, it may be stated as follows: Agents and institutions are absolutely prohibited from degrading persons, treating them as if they had no rights or dignity. The benefit of this prohibition extends to all persons, innocent or guilty; for the latter, when they are justly punished, are still treated as responsible moral agents who are capable of understanding the principle of morality and acting accordingly, and the punishment must not be cruel or arbitrary. Other specific absolute rights may also be generated from this principle. Since the principle requires of every agent that he act in accord with the generic rights of his recipients as well as of himself, specific rights are absolute insofar as they serve to protect the basic presuppositions of the valid principle of morality in its equal application to all persons.

XI

The Problem of Abortion and the Doctrine of the Double Effect*

Philippa Foot

One of the reasons why most of us feel puzzled about the problem of abortion is that we want, and do not want, to allow to the unborn child the rights that belong to adults and children. When we think of a baby about to be born it seems absurd to think that the next few minutes or even hours could make so radical a difference to its status; yet as we go back in the life of the foetus we are more and more reluctant to say that this is a human being and must be treated as such. No doubt this is the deepest source of our dilemma, but it is not the only one. For we are also confused about the general question of what we may and may not do where the interests of human beings conflict. We have strong intuitions about certain cases; saying, for instance, that it is all right to raise the level of education in our country, though statistics allow us to predict that a rise in the suicide rate will follow, while it is not all right to kill the feeble-minded to aid cancer research. It is not easy, however, to see the principles involved, and one way of throwing light on the abortion issue will be by setting up parallels involving adults or children once born. So we will be able to isolate the 'equal rights' issue, and should be able to make some advance.

I shall not, of course, discuss all the principles that may be used in deciding what to do where the interests or rights of human beings conflict. What I want to do is to look at one particular theory, known as the 'doctrine of the double effect' which is invoked by Catholics in support of their views on abortion but supposed by them to apply

* 'The Problem of Abortion and the Doctrine of Double Effect' originally appeared in the *Oxford Review*, Number 5, 1967.

elsewhere. As used in the abortion argument this doctrine has often seemed to non-Catholics to be a piece of complete sophistry. In the last number of the *Oxford Review* it was given short shrift by Professor Hart.[1] And yet this principle has seemed to some non-Catholics as well as to Catholics to stand as the only defence against decisions on other issues that are quite unacceptable. It will help us in our difficulty about abortion if this conflict can be resolved.

The doctrine of the double effect is based on a distinction between what a man foresees as a result of his voluntary action and what, in the strict sense, he intends. He intends in the strictest sense both those things that he aims at as ends and those that he aims at as means to his ends. The latter may be regretted in themselves but nevertheless desired for the sake of the end, as we may intend to keep dangerous lunatics confined for the sake of our safety. By contrast a man is said not strictly, or directly, to intend the foreseen consequences of his voluntary actions where these are neither the end at which he is aiming nor the means to this end. Whether the word 'intention' should be applied in both cases is not of course what matters: Bentham spoke of '*oblique intention*', contrasting it with the '*direct intention*' of ends and means, and we may as well follow his terminology. Everyone must recognise that some such distinction can be made, though it may be made in a number of different ways, and it is the distinction that is crucial to the doctrine of the double effect. The words 'double effect' refer to the two effects that an action may produce: the one aimed at, and the one foreseen but in no way desired. By 'the doctrine of the double effect' I mean the thesis that it is sometimes permissible to bring about by oblique intention what one may not directly intend. Thus the distinction is held to be relevant to moral decision in certain difficult cases. It is said for instance that the operation of hysterectomy involves the death of the foetus as the foreseen but not strictly or directly intended consequence of the surgeon's act, while other operations kill the child and count as the direct intention of taking an innocent life, a distinction that has evoked particularly bitter reactions on the part of non-Catholics. If you are permitted to bring about the death of the child, what does it matter how it is done? The doctrine of the double effect is also used to show why in another case, where a woman in labour will die unless a craniotomy operation is performed, the intervention is not to be condoned. There, it is said, we may not operate but must let the mother die. We foresee her death but do not

[1] H. L. A. Hart, 'Intention and Punishment', *Oxford Review*, Number 4, Hilary 1967. Reprinted in Hart, *Punishment and Responsibility* (Oxford, 1968). I owe much to this article and to a conversation with Professor Hart, though I do not know whether he will approve of what follows.

directly intend it, whereas to crush the skull of the child would count as direct intention of its death.[2]

This last application of the doctrine has been queried by Professor Hart on the ground that the child's death is not strictly a means to saving the mother's life and should logically be treated as an unwanted but foreseen consequence by those who make use of the distinction between direct and oblique intention. To interpret the doctrine in this way is perfectly reasonable given the language that has been used; it would, however, make nonsense of it from the beginning. A certain event may be desired under one of its descriptions, unwanted under another, but we cannot treat these as two different events, one of which is aimed at and the other not. And even if it be argued that there are here two different events—the crushing of the child's skull and its death—the two are obviously much too close for an application of the doctrine of the double effect. To see how odd it would be to apply the principle like this we may consider the story, well known to philosophers, of the fat man stuck in the mouth of the cave. A party of potholers have imprudently allowed the fat man to lead them as they make their way out of the cave, and he gets stuck, trapping the others behind him. Obviously the right thing to do is to sit down and wait until the fat man grows thin; but philosophers have arranged that flood waters should be rising within the cave. Luckily (luckily?) the trapped party have with them a stick of dynamite with which they can blast the fat man out of the mouth of the cave. Either they use the dynamite or they drown. In one version the fat man, whose head is *in* the cave, will drown with them; in the other he will be rescued in due course.[3] Problem: may they use the dynamite or not? Later we will find parallels to this example. Here it is introduced for light relief and because it will serve to show how ridiculous one version of the doctrine of the double effect would be. For suppose that the trapped explorers were to argue that the death of the fat man might be taken as a merely foreseen consequence of the act of blowing him up. ('We didn't want to kill him . . . only to blow him into small pieces' or even '. . . only to blast him out of the cave.') I believe that those who use the doctrine of the double effect would rightly reject such a suggestion, though they will, of course, have considerable difficulty in explaining where the line is to be drawn. What is to be the criterion of 'closeness' if we say that anything very close to what we are literally aiming at counts as if part of our aim?

---

[2] For discussions of the Catholic doctrine on abortion see Glanville Williams, *The Sanctity of Life and the Criminal Law* (New York, 1957); also N. St. John Stevas, *The Right to Life* (London, 1963).

[3] It was Professor Hart who drew my attention to this distinction.

Let us leave this difficulty aside and return to the arguments for and against the doctrine, supposing it to be formulated in the way considered most effective by its supporters, and ourselves bypassing the trouble by taking what must on any reasonable definition be clear cases of 'direct' or 'oblique' intention.

The first point that should be made clear, in fairness to the theory, is that no one is suggesting that it does not matter what you bring about as long as you merely foresee and do not strictly intend the evil that follows. We might think, for instance, of the (actual) case of wicked merchants selling, for cooking, oil they knew to be poisonous and thereby killing a number of innocent people, comparing and contrasting it with that of some unemployed gravediggers, desperate for custom, who got hold of this same oil and sold it (or perhaps *they* secretly gave it away) in order to create orders for graves. They strictly (directly) intend the deaths they cause, while the merchants could say that it was not part of their *plan* that anyone should die. In morality, as in law, the merchants, like the gravediggers, would be considered as murderers; nor are the supporters of the doctrine of the double effect bound to say that there is the least difference between them in respect of moral turpitude. What they are committed to is the thesis that *sometimes* it makes a difference to the permissibility of an action involving harm to others that this harm, although foreseen, is not part of the agent's direct intention. An end such as earning one's living is clearly not such as to justify *either* the direct or oblique intention of the death of innocent people, but in certain cases one is justified in bringing about knowingly what one could not directly intend.

It is now time to say why this doctrine should be taken seriously in spite of the fact that it sounds rather odd, that there are difficulties about the distinction on which it depends, and that it seemed to yield one sophistical conclusion when applied to the problem of abortion. The reason for its appeal is that its opponents have often *seemed* to be committed to quite indefensible views. Thus the controversy has raged around examples such as the following. Suppose that a judge or magistrate is faced with rioters demanding that a culprit be found for a certain crime and threatening otherwise to take their own bloody revenge on a particular section of the community. The real culprit being unknown, the judge sees himself as able to prevent the bloodshed only by framing some innocent person and having him executed. Beside this example is placed another in which a pilot whose aeroplane is about to crash is deciding whether to steer from a more to a less inhabited area. To make the parallel as close as possible it may rather be supposed that he is the driver of a runaway tram which he can only steer from one narrow track on to another; five men are working on one track and one man on the other; anyone on the track he enters is bound to be killed. In the case of the riots the mob have five hostages, so that in both the exchange is supposed to be one man's life for the lives of five. The question is why we should say, without hesitation, that the driver should steer for the less occupied track, while most of us would be appalled at the idea that the innocent man could be framed. It may be suggested that the special feature of the latter case is that it involves the corruption of justice, and this is, of course, very important indeed. But if we remove that special feature, supposing that some private individual is to kill an innocent person and pass him off as the criminal we still find ourselves horrified by the idea. The doctrine of double effect offers us a way out of the difficulty, insisting that it is one thing to steer towards someone foreseeing that you will kill him and another to aim at his death as part of your plan. Moreover there is one very important element of good in what is here insisted. In real life it would hardly ever be certain that the man on the narrow track would be killed. Perhaps he might find a foothold on the side of the tunnel and cling on as the vehicle hurtled by. The driver of the tram does *not* then leap off and brain him with a crowbar. The judge, however, needs the death of the innocent man for his (good) purposes. If the victim proves hard to hang he must see to it that he dies another way. To choose to execute him is to choose that this evil *shall come about*, and this must therefore count as a *certainty* in weighing up the good and evil involved. The distinction between direct and oblique intention is crucial here, and is of great importance in an uncertain world. Nevertheless this is no way to defend the doctrine of double effect. For the question is whether the difference between aiming at something and obliquely intending it is *in itself* relevant to moral decisions; not whether it is important when correlated with a difference of certainty in the balance of good and evil. Moreover we are particularly interested in the application of the doctrine of the double effect to the question of abortion, and no one can deny that in medicine there are sometimes certainties so complete that it would be a mere quibble to speak of the 'probable outcome' of this course of action or that. It is not, therefore, with a merely philosophical interest that we should put aside the uncertainty and scrutinise the examples to test the doctrine of the double effect. Why can we not argue from the case of the steering driver to that of the judge?

Another pair of examples poses a similar problem. We are about to give a patient who needs it to save his life a massive dose of a certain drug in short supply. There arrive, however, five other patients each of whom could be saved by one-fifth of that dose. We say with regret that we cannot spare our whole supply of the drug for a single patient, just as we should say that we could not spare the whole resources of a ward for one dangerously ill individual when ambulances arrive bringing in victims of a multiple crash. We feel bound to let one man die rather than many if that is our only choice. Why then do we not feel justified in killing people in the interests of cancer research or to obtain, let us say, spare parts for grafting on to those who need them? We can suppose, similarly, that several dangerously ill people can be saved only if we kill a certain individual and make a serum from his dead body. (These examples are not over-fanciful considering present controversies about prolonging the life of mortally ill patients whose eyes or kidneys are to be used for others.) Why cannot we argue from the case of the scarce drug to that of the body needed for medical purposes? Once again the doctrine of the double effect comes up with an explanation. In one kind of case but not the other we aim at the death of an innocent man.

A further argument suggests that if the doctrine of the double effect is rejected this has the consequences of putting us hopelessly in the power of bad men. Suppose for example that some tyrant should threaten to torture five men if we ourselves would not torture one. Would it be our duty to do so, supposing we believed him, because this would be no different from choosing to rescue five men from his torturers rather than one? If so anyone who wants us to do something we think wrong has only to threaten that otherwise he himself will do something we think worse. A mad murderer, known to keep his promises, could thus make it our duty to kill some innocent citizen to prevent him from killing two. From this conclusion we are again rescued by the doctrine of the double effect. If we refuse, we foresee that the greater number will be killed but we do not intend it: it is he who intends (that is strictly or directly intends) the death of innocent persons; we do not.

At one time I thought that these arguments in favour of the doctrine of the double effect were conclusive, but I now believe that the conflict should be solved in another way. The clue that we should follow is that the strength of the doctrine seems to lie in the distinction it makes between what we *do* (equated with direct intention) and what we allow (thought of as obliquely intended). Indeed it is interesting that the disputants tend to argue about whether we are to be held responsible for what we allow as we are for what we do.[4] Yet it is not obvious that this is what they should be discussing, since the distinction between what one does and what one allows to happen is not the same as that between direct and oblique intention. To see this one has only to consider that it is possible *deliberately* to allow something to happen, aiming at it either for its own sake or as part of one's plan for obtaining something else. So one person might want another person dead and

[4] See, e.g., J. Bennett, 'Whatever the Consequences', *Analysis*, January 1966, and G. E. M. Anscombe's reply in *Analysis*, June 1966. [See pp. 178ff. and 197 this volume.—Ed.] See also Miss Anscombe's 'Modern Moral Philosophy' in *Philosophy*, January 1958.

deliberately allow him to die. And again one may be said to *do* things that one does not aim at, as the steering driver would kill the man on the track. Moreover there is a large class of things said to be brought about rather than either done or allowed and either kind of intention is possible. So it is possible to *bring about* a man's death by getting him to sea in a leaky boat, and the intention of his death may be either direct or oblique.

Whatever it may, or may not, have to do with the doctrine of the double effect, the idea of *allowing* is worth looking into in this context. I shall leave aside the special case of giving permission, which involves the idea of authority, and consider the two main divisions into which cases of allowing seem to fall. There is firstly the allowing which is forbearing to prevent. For this we need a sequence thought of as somehow already in train, and something that an agent could do to intervene. (The agent must be able to intervene, but does not do so.) So, for instance, he could warn someone, but *allows* him to walk into a trap. He could feed an animal but *allows* it to die for lack of food. He could stop a leaking tap but *allows* the water to go on flowing. This is the case of allowing with which we shall be concerned, but the other should be mentioned. It is the kind of allowing which is roughly equivalent to *enabling*; the root idea being the removal of some obstacle which is, as it were, holding back a train of events. So someone may remove a plug and *allow* water to flow; open a door and *allow* an animal to get out; or give someone money and *allow* him to get back on his feet.

The first kind of allowing requires an omission, but there is no other general correlation between omission and allowing, commission and bringing about or doing. An actor who fails to turn up for a performance will generally spoil it rather than allow it to be spoiled. I mention the distinction between omission and commission only to set it aside.

Thinking of the first kind of allowing (forbearing to prevent), we should ask whether there is any difference, from the moral point of view, between what one does or causes and what one merely allows. It seems clear that on occasions one is just as bad as the other, as is recognised in both morality and law. A man may murder his child or his aged relatives, by allowing them to die of starvation as well as by giving poison; he may also be convicted of murder on either account. In another case we would, however, make a distinction. Most of us allow people to die of starvation in India and Africa, and there is surely something wrong with us that we do; it would be nonsense, however, to pretend that it is only in law that we make the distinction between allowing people in the underdeveloped countries to die of starvation and sending them poisoned food. There is worked into our moral system a distinction between what we owe people in the form of aid and what we owe them in the way of non-interference. Salmond, in his *Jurisprudence*, expressed as follows the distinction between the two.

> A positive right corresponds to a positive duty, and is a right that he on whom the duty lies shall do some positive act on behalf of the person entitled. A negative right corresponds to a negative duty, and is a right that the person bound shall refrain from some act which would operate to the prejudice of the person entitled. The former is a right to be positively benefited; the latter is merely a right not to be harmed.[5]

As a general account of rights and duties this is defective, since not all are so closely connected with benefit and harm. Nevertheless for our purposes it will do well. Let us speak of negative duties when thinking of the obligation to refrain from such things as killing or robbing, and of the positive duty, e.g., to look after children or aged parents. It will be useful, however, to extend the notion of positive duty beyond the range of things that are strictly called duties, bringing acts of charity under this heading. These are owed only in a rather loose sense, and some acts of charity could hardly be said to be *owed* at all, so I am not following ordinary usage at this point.

Let us now see whether the distinction of negative and positive duties explains why we see differently the action of the steering driver and that of the judge, of the doctors who withhold the scarce drug and those who obtain a body for medical purposes, of those who choose to rescue five men rather than one man from torture and those who are ready to torture the one man themselves in order to save five. In each case we have a conflict of duties, but what kind of duties are they? Are we, in each case, weighing positive duties against positive, negative against negative, or one against the other? Is the duty to refrain from injury, or rather to bring aid?

The steering driver faces a conflict of negative duties, since it is his duty to avoid injuring five men and also his duty to avoid injuring one. In the circumstances he is not able to avoid both, and it seems clear that he should do the least injury he can. The judge, however, is weighing the duty of not inflicting injury against the duty of bringing aid. He wants to rescue the innocent people threatened with death but can do so only by inflicting injury himself. Since one does not *in general* have the same duty to help people as to refrain from injuring them, it is not possible to argue to a conclusion about what he should do from the steering driver case. It is interesting that, even where the strictest duty of positive aid exists, this still does not weigh as if a negative duty were involved. It is not, for instance, permissible to commit a murder to bring one's starving children food. If the choice is between inflicting injury on one or many there seems only one rational

[5] J. Salmond, *Jurisprudence*, 11th edition, p. 283.

course of action; if the choice is between aid to some at the cost of injury to others, and refusing to inflict the injury to bring the aid, the whole matter is open to dispute. So it is not inconsistent of us to think that the driver must steer for the road on which only one man stands while the judge (or his equivalent) may not kill the innocent person in order to stop the riots. Let us now consider the second pair of examples, which concern the scarce drug on the one hand and on the other the body needed to save lives. Once again we find a difference based on the distinction between the duty to avoid injury and the duty to provide aid. Where one man needs a massive dose of the drug and we withhold it from him in order to save five men, we are weighing aid against aid. But if we consider killing a man in order to use his body to save others, we are thinking of doing him an injury to bring others aid. In an interesting variant of the model, we may suppose that instead of killing someone we deliberately let him die. (Perhaps he is a beggar to whom we are thinking of giving food, but then we say 'No, they need bodies for medical research.') Here it does seem relevant that in allowing him to die we are aiming at his death, but presumably we are inclined to see this as a violation of negative rather than positive duty. If this is right, we see why we are unable in either case to argue to a conclusion from the case of the scarce drug.

In the examples involving the torturing of one man or five men, the principle seems to be the same as for the last pair. If we are bringing aid (rescuing people about to be tortured by the tyrant), we must obviously rescue the larger rather than the smaller group. It does not follow, however, that we would be justified in inflicting the injury, or getting a third person to do so, in order to save the five. We may therefore refuse to be forced into acting by the threats of bad men. To refrain from inflicting injury ourselves is a stricter duty than to prevent other people from inflicting injury, which is not to say that the other is not a very strict duty indeed.

So far the conclusions are the same as those at which we might arrive following the doctrine of the double effect, but in others they will be different, and the advantage seems to be all on the side of the alternative. Suppose, for instance, that there are five patients in a hospital whose lives could be saved by the manufacture of a certain gas, but that this inevitably releases lethal fumes into the room of another patient whom for some reason we are unable to move. His death, being of no use to us, is clearly a side effect, and not directly intended. Why then is the case different from that of the scarce drug, if the point about that is that we foresaw but did not strictly intend the death of the single patient? Yet it surely is different. The relatives of the gassed patient would presumably be successful if they sued the hospital and the whole story came out. We may find it particularly revolting that someone should be *used* as in the case where he is killed or allowed to die in the interest of medical research, and the fact of *using* may even determine what we would decide to do in some cases, but the principle seems unimportant compared with our reluctance to bring such injury for the sake of giving aid.

My conclusion is that the distinction between direct and oblique intention plays only a quite subsidiary role in determining what we say in these cases, while the distinction between avoiding injury and bringing aid is very important indeed. I have not, of course, argued that there are no other principles. For instance it clearly makes a difference whether our positive duty is a strict duty or rather an act of charity: feeding our own children or feeding those in faraway countries. It may also make a difference whether the person about to suffer is one thought of as uninvolved in the threatened disaster, and whether it is his presence that constitutes the threat to the others. In many cases we find it very hard to know what to say, and I have not been arguing for any general conclusion such as that we may never, whatever the balance of good and evil, bring injury to one for the sake of aid to others, even when this injury amounts to death. I have only tried to show that even if we reject the doctrine of the double effect we are not forced to the conclusion that the size of the evil must always be our guide.

Let us now return to the problem of abortion, carrying out our plan of finding parallels involving adults or children rather than the unborn. We must say something about the different cases in which abortion might be considered on medical grounds.

First of all there is the situation in which nothing that can be done will save the life of child and mother, but where the life of the mother can be saved by killing the child. This is parallel to the case of the fat man in the mouth of the cave who is bound to be drowned with the others if nothing is done. Given the certainty of the outcome, as it was postulated, there is no serious conflict of interests here, since the fat man will perish in either case, and it is reasonable that the action that will save someone should be done. It is a great objection to those who argue that the direct intention of the death of an innocent person is never justifiable that the edict will apply even in this case. The Catholic doctrine on abortion must here conflict with that of most reasonable men. Moreover we would be justified in performing the operation whatever the method used, and it is neither a necessary nor a good justification of the special case of hysterectomy that the child's death is not directly intended, being rather a foreseen consequence of what is done. What difference could it make as to how the death is brought about?

Secondly we have the case in which it is possible to perform an operation which will save the mother and kill the child or kill the mother and save the child. This is parallel to the famous case of shipwrecked mariners who believed that they must throw someone overboard if their boat was not to founder in a storm, and to the other famous case of the two sailors, Dudley and Stephens, who killed and ate the cabin boy when adrift on the sea without food. Here again there is no conflict of interests so far as the decision to act is concerned; only in deciding whom to save. Once again it would be reasonable to act, though one would respect someone who held back from the appalling action either because he preferred to perish rather than do such a thing or because he held on past the limits of reasonable hope. In real life the certainties postulated by philosophers hardly ever exist, and Dudley and Stephens were rescued not long after their ghastly meal. Nevertheless if the certainty were absolute, as it might be in the abortion case, it would seem better to save one than none. Probably we should decide in favour of the mother when weighing her life against that of the unborn child, but it is interesting that, a few years later, we might easily decide it the other way.

The worst dilemma comes in the third kind of example where to save the mother we must kill the child, say by crushing its skull, while if nothing is done the mother will perish but the child can be safely delivered after her death. Here the doctrine of the double effect has been invoked to show that we may not intervene, since the child's death would be directly intended while the mother's would not. On a strict parallel with cases not involving the unborn we might find the conclusion correct though the reason given was wrong. Suppose, for instance, that in later life the presence of a child was certain to bring death to the mother. We would surely not think ourselves justified in ridding her of it by a process that involved its death. For in general we do not think that we can kill one innocent person to rescue another, quite apart from the special care that we feel is due to children once they have prudently got themselves born. What we would be prepared to do when a great many people were involved is another matter, and this is probably the key to one quite common view of abortion on the part of those who take quite seriously the rights of the unborn child. They probably feel that if *enough* people were involved one must be sacrificed, and they think of the mother's life against the unborn child's life as if it were many against one. But of course many people do not view it like this at all, having no inclination to accord to the foetus or unborn child anything like ordinary human status in the matter of rights. I have not been arguing for or against these points of view but only trying to discern some of the currents that are pulling us back and forth. The levity of the examples is not meant to offend.

XII

Who Is Wronged?

G. E. M. Anscombe

Phillippa Foot on Double Effect: One Point

She says: "We are about to give to a patient who needs it to save his life, a massive dose of a certain drug in short supply. There arrive, however, five other patients each of whom could be saved by one fifth of that dose. We say with regret that we cannot spare our whole supply of the drug for a single patient, just as we should say that we could not spare the whole resources of a ward for one dangerously ill individual when ambulances arrive bringing in the victims of a multiple crash. We feel bound to let one man die rather than many if that is our only choice."* I feel a curious disagreement about this. There seems to me nothing wrong with giving the single patient the massive dose and letting the others die, or with refusing to deprive the single patient of care necessary to keep him alive because the hands needed for that care could help in saving the many victims of an accident. The latter care is vaguely sketched, and one pictures resources being lavishly used beyond necessity on one. But let it be made exact; let there be a machine which it takes three people to operate—it just will not work unless there are three on the job; and these three could be summoned away to help more than one person. It seems to me justifiable to say one can't spare those three people because of the job they are doing, if their work seems roughly as likely to save that one person as to save several to whose aid they could be called. Not that it seems (absolutely) *necessary* to keep them on the job they are doing; but either course, to leave the one to die or to keep them working his machine, seems O.K. Yet Mrs. Foot regards it as obvious that one must save the greater number.

* [See p. 151 this volume.—Ed.]

Why is this, and how could the disagreement be resolved? Suppose I am the doctor, and I don't use the drug at all. Whom do I wrong? None of them can say: "you owed it to *me*". For there might be nine, and if *one* can say that, all can; but if I used it, I let one at least go without and he can't say I owed it to *him*. Yet all can reproach me if I gave it to none. It was there, ready to supply human need, and human need was not supplied. So any one of them can say: you ought to have used it to help us who needed it; and so all are wronged. But if it was used for someone, as much as he needed it to keep him alive, no one has any ground for accusing me of having wronged *himself*.—Why, just because he was one of five who could have been saved, is he wronged in not being saved, if someone is supplied with it who needed it? What is *his* claim, except the claim that what was needed go to him rather than be wasted? But it was not wasted. So he was not wronged. So who was wronged? And if no one was wronged, what injury did I do?

Similarly if there are a lot of people stranded on a rock, and one person on another and someone goes with a boat to rescue the single one, what cause, so far, have any of the others for complaint? They are not injured unless help that was owing to them was withheld. There was the boat that could have helped them; but it was not left idle; no, it went to save that other one. What is the accusation that each of them can make? What wrong can he claim has been done him? None whatever: unless the preference signalizes some ignoble contempt.

I do not mean that 'because they are more' isn't a good reason for helping these and not that one, or these rather than those. It is a perfectly intelligible reason. But it doesn't follow from that that a man acts badly if he doesn't make it his reason. He acts badly if human need for what is in his power to give doesn't work in him as a reason. He acts badly if he chooses to rescue rich people rather than poor ones, having ill regard for the poor ones because they are poor. But he doesn't act badly if he uses his resources to save X, or X, Y and Z, *for no bad reason*, and is not affected by the consideration that he could save a larger number of people. For, once more: who can say he is wronged? And if no one is wronged, how does the rescuer commit any wrong?

In this connexion, the following observation is of some importance, as the contrary may be taken for granted by some: when I do action A for reasons R, it is not necessary or even usual for me to have any special reason for doing-action-A-rather-than-action-B, which may also be possible.

XIII

Against Moral Conservatism

Kai Nielsen

I

It is sometimes claimed that any consequentialist view of ethics has monstrous implications which make such a conception of morality untenable. What we must do—so the claim goes—is reject all forms of consequentialism and accept what has been labeled 'conservatism' or 'moral absolutism.' By 'conservatism' is meant, here, a normative ethical theory which maintains that there is a privileged moral principle or cluster of moral principles, prescribing determinate actions, with which it would always be wrong not to act in accordance no matter what the consequences. A key example of such a principle is the claim that it is always wrong to kill an innocent human, whatever the consequences of not doing so.

I will argue that such moral conservatism is itself unjustified and, indeed, has morally unacceptable consequences, while consequentialism does not have implications which are morally monstrous and does not contain evident moral mistakes.

A consequentialist maintains that actions, rules, policies, practices, and moral principles are ultimately to be judged by certain consequences: to wit (for a very influential kind of consequentialism), by whether doing them more than, or at least as much as doing anything else, or acting in accordance with them more than or at least as much as acting in accordance with alternative policies, practices, rules or principles, tends, on the whole, and for *everyone* involved, to maximize satisfaction and minimize dissatisfaction. The states of affairs to be sought are those which maximize these things to the greatest extent possible for all mankind. But while this all sounds very humane and humanitarian, when its implications are thought through, it has been forcefully argued, it will be seen actually to have inhumane and morally intolerable implications. Circumstances could arise in which one holding such a view would have to assert that one was justified in punishing, killing, torturing, or deliberately harming the innocent, and such a consequence is, morally speaking, unacceptable.[1] As Anscombe has put it, anyone who "really thinks, *in advance*, that it is open to question whether such an action as procuring the judicial execution of the innocent should be quite excluded from consideration—I do not want to argue with him; he shows a corrupt mind."[2]

At the risk of being thought to exhibit a corrupt mind and a shallow consequentialist morality, I should like to argue that things are not as simple and straightforward as Anscombe seems to believe.

Surely, every moral man must be appalled at the judicial execution of the innocent or at the punishment, torture, and killing of the innocent. Indeed, being appalled by such behavior partially defines what it is to be a moral agent. And a consequentialist has very good utilitarian grounds for being so appalled, namely, that it is always wrong to inflict pain for its own sake. But this does not get to the core considerations which divide a conservative position such as Anscombe's from a consequentialist view. There are a series of tough cases that need to be taken to heart and their implications thought through by any reflective person, be he a conservative or a consequentialist. By doing this, we can get to the heart of the issue between conservatism and consequentialism. Consider this clash between conservatism and consequentialism arising over the problem of a 'just war.'

> If we deliberately bomb civilian targets, we do not pretend that civilians are combatants in any simple fashion, but argue that this bombing will terminate hostilities more quickly, and will minimize all around suffering. It is hard to see how any brand of utilitarian will escape Miss Anscombe's objections. We are certainly killing the innocent . . . we are not killing them for the sake of killing them, but to save the lives of other innocent persons. Utilitarians, I think, grit their teeth and put up with this as part of the logic of total war; Miss Anscombe and anyone who thinks like her surely has to either redescribe the situation to ascribe guilt to the civilians or else she has to refuse to accept this sort of military tactics as simply wrong.[3]

---

[1] Alan Donagan, "Is There a Credible Form of Utilitarianism?" and H. J. McCloskey, "A Non-Utilitarian Approach to Punishment," both in *Contemporary Utilitarianism*, ed. Michael D. Bayles (Garden City, N.Y.: Doubleday & Co., 1968).

[2] Elizabeth Anscombe, "Modern Moral Philosophy," *Philosophy* 23 (January 1957): 16–17.

[3] Alan Ryan, "Review of Jan Narveson's *Morality and Utility*," *Philosophical Books* 9, no. 3 (October 1958): 14.

It is indeed true that we cannot but feel the force of Anscombe's objections here. But is it the case that anyone shows a corrupt mind if he defends such bombing when, horrible as it is, it will quite definitely lessen appreciably the total amount of suffering and death in the long run, and if he is sufficiently nonevasive not to rationalize such a bombing of civilians into a situation in which all the putatively innocent people—children and all—are somehow in some measure judged guilty? Must such a man exhibit a corrupt moral sense if he refuses to hold that such military tactics are never morally justified? Must this be the monstrous view of a fanatical man devoid of any proper moral awareness? It is difficult for me to believe that this must be so.

Consider the quite parallel actions of guerrilla fighters and terrorists in wars of national liberation. In certain almost unavoidable circumstances, they must deliberately kill the innocent. We need to see some cases in detail here to get the necessary contextual background, and for this reason the motion picture *The Battle of Algiers* can be taken as a convenient point of reference. There we saw Algerian women—gentle, kindly women with children of their own and plainly people of moral sensitivity—with evident heaviness of heart, plant bombs which they had every good reason to believe would kill innocent people, including children; and we also saw a French general, also a human being of moral fiber and integrity, order the torture of Arab terrorists and threaten the bombing of houses in which terrorists were concealed but which also contained innocent people, including children. There are indeed many people involved in such activities who are cruel, sadistic beasts, or simply morally indifferent or, in important ways, morally uncomprehending. But the characters I have referred to from *The Battle of Algiers* were not of that stamp. They were plainly moral agents of a high degree of sensitivity, and yet they deliberately killed or were prepared to kill the innocent. And, with inessential variations, this is a recurrent phenomenon of human living in extreme situations. Such cases are by no means desert-island or esoteric cases.

It is indeed arguable whether such actions are always morally wrong—whether anyone should ever act as the Arab women or French general acted. But what could not be reasonably maintained, *pace* Anscombe, by any stretch of the imagination, is that the characters I described from *The Battle of Algiers* exhibited corrupt minds. Possibly morally mistaken, yes; guilty of moral corruption, no.

Dropping the charge of moral corruption but sticking with the moral issue about what actions are right, is it not the case that my consequentialist position logically forces me to conclude that under some circumstances—where the good to be achieved is great enough—I must not only countenance but actually advocate such violence toward the innocent? But is it not always, no matter what the circumstances or consequences, wrong to countenance, advocate, or engage in such violence? To answer such a question affirmatively is to commit oneself to the kind of moral absolutism or conservatism which Anscombe advocates. But, given the alternatives, should not one be such a conservative or at least hold that certain deontological principles must never be overriden?

I will take, so to speak, the papal bull by the horns and answer that there are circumstances when such violence must be reluctantly assented to or even taken to be something that one, morally speaking, must do. But, *pace* Anscombe, this very much needs arguing, and I shall argue it; but first I would like to set out some further but simpler cases which have a similar bearing. They are, by contrast, artificial cases. I use them because, in their greater simplicity, by contrast with my above examples, there are fewer variables to control and I can more conveniently make the essential conceptual and moral points. But, if my argument is correct for these simpler cases, the line of reasoning employed is intended to be applicable to those more complex cases as well.

II

Consider the following cases embedded in their exemplary tales:

1. The Case of the Innocent Fat Man

Consider the story (well known to philosophers) of the fat man stuck in the mouth of a cave on a coast. He was leading a group of people out of the cave when he got stuck in the mouth of the cave and in a very short time high tide will be upon them, and unless he is promptly unstuck, they all will be drowned except the fat man, whose head is out of the cave. But, fortunately or unfortunately, someone has with him a stick of dynamite. The short of the matter is, either they use the dynamite and blast the poor innocent fat man out of the mouth of the cave or everyone else drowns. Either one life or many lives. Our conservative presumably would take the attitude that it is all in God's hands and say that he ought never to blast the fat man out, for it is always wrong to kill the innocent. Must or should a moral man come to that conclusion? I shall argue that he should not.

My first exemplary tale was designed to show that our normal, immediate, rather absolutistic, moral reactions need to be questioned along with such principles as 'The direct intention of the death of an innocent person is never justifiable.' I have hinted (and later shall argue) that we should *beware* of our moral outrage here—our naturally conservative and unreflective moral reactions—for here the consequentialist has a strong case for what I shall call 'moral radicalism.'

But, before turning to a defense of that, I want to tell another story taken from Phillipa Foot but used for my own purposes.[4] This tale, I shall argue, has a different import than our previous tale. Here our unrehearsed, commonsense moral reactions will stand up under moral scrutiny. But, I shall also argue when I consider them in Section III, that our commonsense moral reactions here, initial expectations to the contrary notwithstanding, can be shown to be justified on consequentialist grounds. The thrust of my argument for this case is that we are not justified in opting for a theistic and/or deontological absolutism or in rejecting consequentialism.

2. *The Magistrate and the Threatening Mob*

A magistrate or judge is faced with a very real threat from a large and uncontrollable mob of rioters demanding a culprit for a crime. Unless the criminal is produced, promptly tried, and executed, they will take their own bloody revenge on a much smaller and quite vulnerable section of the community (a kind of frenzied pogrom). The judge knows that the real culprit is unknown and that the authorities do not even have a good clue as to who he may be. But he also knows that there is within easy reach a disreputable, thoroughly disliked, and useless man, who, though innocent, could easily be framed so that the mob would be quite convinced that he was guilty and would be pacified if he were promptly executed. Recognizing that he can prevent the occurrence of extensive carnage only by framing some innocent person, the magistrate has him framed, goes through the mockery of a trial, and has him executed. Most of us regard such a framing and execution of such a man in such circumstances as totally unacceptable.[5] There are some who would say that it is categorically wrong—morally inexcusable—*whatever the circumstances*. Indeed, such a case remains a problem for the consequentialist, but here again, I shall argue, one can consistently remain a consequentialist and continue to accept commonsense moral convictions about such matters.

My storytelling is at an end. The job is to see what the stories imply. We must try to determine whether thinking through their implications should lead a clearheaded and morally sensitive man to abandon consequentialism and to adopt some form of theistic absolutism and/or deontological absolutism. I shall argue that it does not.

---

[4] Phillipa Foot, "The Problem of Abortion and the Doctrine of the Double Effect," *Oxford Review*, no. 5 (Trinity 1967), pp. 5–15. [See p. 150 this volume.—Ed.]

[5] Later, I shall show that there are desert-island circumstances—i.e., highly improbable situations—in which such judicial railroading might be a moral necessity. But I also shall show what little force desert-island cases have in the articulation and defense of a normative ethical theory.

III

I shall consider the last case first because there are good reasons why the consequentialist should stick with commonsense moral convictions for such cases. I shall start by giving my rationale for that claim. If the magistrate were a tough-minded but morally conscientious consequentialist, he could still, on straightforward consequentialist grounds, refuse to frame and execute the innocent man, even knowing that this would unleash the mob and cause much suffering and many deaths. The rationale for his particular moral stand would be that, by so framing and then executing such an innocent man, he would, in the long run, cause still more suffering through the resultant corrupting effect on the institution of justice. That is, in a case involving such extensive general interest in the issue—without that, there would be no problem about preventing the carnage or call for such extreme measures—knowledge that the man was framed, that the law had prostituted itself, would, surely, eventually leak out. This would encourage mob action in other circumstances, would lead to an increased skepticism about the incorruptibility or even the reliability of the judicial process, and would set a dangerous precedent for less clear-headed or less scrupulously humane magistrates. Given such a potential for the corruption of justice, a utilitarian or consequentialist judge or magistrate could, on good utilitarian or consequentialist grounds, argue that it was morally wrong to frame an innocent man. If the mob must rampage if such a sacrificial lamb is not provided, then the mob must rampage.

Must a utilitarian or consequentialist come to such a conclusion? The answer is no. It is the conclusion which is, as things stand, the most reasonable conclusion, but that he *must* come to it is far too strong a claim. A consequentialist could *consistently*—I did not say successfully—argue that, in taking the above tough-minded utilitarian position, we have overestimated the corrupting effects of such judicial railroading. His circumstance was an extreme one: a situation not often to be repeated even if, instead of acting as he did, he had set a precedent by such an act of judicial murder. A utilitarian rather more skeptical than most utilitarians about the claims of commonsense morality might reason that the lesser evil here is the judicial murder of an innocent man, vile as it is. He would persist in his moral iconoclasm by standing on the consequentialist rock that the lesser evil is always to be preferred to the greater evil.

The short of it is that utilitarians could disagree, as other consequentialists could disagree, about what is morally required of us in that case. The disagreement here between utilitarians or consequentialists of the same type is not one concerning fundamental moral principles but a disagreement about the empirical facts, about what course of action would in the long run produce the least suffering and the most happiness for *everyone* involved.[6]

However, considering the effect advocating the deliberate judicial killing of an innocent man would have on the reliance people put on commonsense moral beliefs of such a ubiquitous sort as the belief that the innocent must not be harmed, a utilitarian who defended the centrality of commonsense moral beliefs would indeed have a strong utilitarian case here. But the most crucial thing to recognize is that, to regard such judicial bowing to such a threatening mob as unqualifiedly wrong, as morally intolerable, one need not reject utilitarianism and accept some form of theistic or deontological absolutism.

It has been argued, however, that, in taking such a stance, I still have not squarely faced the moral conservative's central objection to the judicial railroading of the innocent. I allow, as a consequentialist, that there could be circumstances, at least as far as logical possibilities are concerned, in which such a railroading would be justified but that, as things actually go, it is not and probably never in fact will be justified. But the conservative's point is that in *no circumstances, either actual or conceivable, would it be justified*. No matter what the consequences, it is unqualifiedly unjustified. To say, as I do, that the situations in which it might be justified are desert-island, esoteric cases which do not occur in life, is not to the point, for, as Alan Donagan argues, "Moral theory is *a priori*, as clear-headed utilitarians like Henry Sidgwick recognized. It is, as Leibniz would say, 'true of all possible worlds.' "[7] Thus, to argue as I have and as others have that the counterexamples directed against the consequentialist's appeal to conditions which are never in fact fulfilled or are unlikely to be fulfilled is beside the point.[8] Whether "a moral theory is true or false depends on whether its implications for all possible worlds are true. Hence, whether utilitarianism (or consequentialism) is true or false cannot depend on how the actual world is."[9] It is possible to specify logically conceivable situations in which consequentialism would have implications which are monstrous—for example, certain beneficial judicial murders of the innocent (whether they are even remotely likely to obtain is irrelevant)—hence consequentialism must be false.

We should not take such a short way with consequentialists, for what is true in Donagan's claim about moral theory's being a priori

---

[6] 'Everyone' here is used distributively; i.e., I am talking about the interests of each and every one. In that sense, everyone's interests need to be considered.

[7] Alan Donagan (n. 1 above), p. 189.

[8] T. L. S. Sprigge argues in such a manner in his "A Utilitarian Reply to Dr. McCloskey," in *Contemporary Utilitarianism*, ed. Michael D. Bayles (Garden City, N.Y.: Doubleday & Co., 1968).

[9] Alan Donagan, p. 194.

will not refute or even render implausible consequentialism, and what would undermine it in such a claim about the a priori nature of moral theory and presumably moral claims is not true.

To say that moral theory is a priori is probably correct if that means that categorical moral claims—fundamental moral statements—cannot be deduced from empirical statements or nonmoral theological statements, such that it is a contradiction to assert the empirical and/or nonmoral theological statements and deny the categorical moral claims or vice versa.[10] In that fundamental sense, it is reasonable and, I believe, justifiable to maintain that moral theory is autonomous and a priori. It is also a priori in the sense that moral statements are not themselves a kind of empirical statement. That is, if I assert 'One ought never to torture any sentient creature' or 'One ought never to kill an innocent man,' I am not trying to predict or describe what people do or are likely to do but am asserting what they are *to do*. It is also true that, if a moral statement is true, it holds for all possible worlds *in which situations of exactly the sort characterized in the statement obtain*. If it is true for one, it is true for all. You cannot consistently say that *A* ought to do *B* in situation *Y* and deny that someone exactly like *A* in a situation exactly like *Y* ought to do *B*.

In these ways, moral claims and indeed moral theory are a priori. But it is also evident that none of these ways will touch the consequentialist or utilitarian arguments. After all, the consequentialist need not be, and typically has not been, an ethical naturalist—he need not think moral claims are derivable from factual claims or that moral claims are a subspecies of empirical statement and he could accept—indeed, he must accept—what is an important truism anyway, that you cannot consistently say that *A* ought to do *B* in situation *Y* and deny that someone exactly like *A* in a situation exactly like *Y* ought to do *B*. But he could and should deny that moral claims are a priori in the sense that rational men must or even will make them without regard for the context, the situation, in which they are made. We say people ought not to drive way over the speed limit, or speed on icy roads, or throw knives at each other. But, if human beings had a kind of metallic exoskeleton and would not be hurt, disfigured, or seriously inconvenienced by knives sticking in them or by automobile crashes, we would not—so evidently at least—have good grounds for saying such speeding or knife throwing is wrong. It would not be so obvious that it was unreasonable and immoral to do these things if these conditions obtained.

[10] There is considerable recent literature about whether it is possible to derive moral claims from nonmoral claims. See W. D. Hudson, ed., *The Is-Ought Question: A Collection of Papers on the Central Problem in Moral Philosophy* (New York: St. Martin's Press, 1969).

In the very way we choose to describe the situation when we make ethical remarks, it is important in making this choice that we know what the world is like and what human beings are like. Our understanding of the situation, our understanding of human nature and motivation cannot but effect our structuring of the moral case. The consequentialist is saying that, as the world goes, there are good grounds for holding that judicial killings are morally intolerable, though he would have to admit that if the world (including human beings) were very different, such killings could be something that ought to be done. But, in holding this, he is not committed to denying the universalizability of moral judgments, for, where he would reverse or qualify the moral judgment, the situation must be different. He is only committed to claiming that, where the situation is the same or relevantly similar and the persons are relevantly similar, they must, if they are to act morally, do the same thing. However, he is claiming both (1) that, as things stand, judicial killing of the innocent is always wrong and (2) that it is an irrational moral judgment to assert of reasonably determinate actions (e.g., killing an innocent man) that they are unjustifiable and morally unacceptable in all *possible* worlds, whatever the situation and whatever the consequences.

Donagan's claims about the a priori nature of moral theories do not show such a consequentialist claim to be mistaken or even give us the slightest reason for thinking that it is mistaken. What is brutal and vile, for example, throwing a knife at a human being just for the fun of it, would not be so, if human beings were invulnerable to harm from such a direction because they had a metallic exoskeleton. Similarly, what is, as things are, morally intolerable, for example, the judicial killing of the innocent, need not be morally intolerable in all conceivable circumstances.

Such considerations support the utilitarian or consequentialist skeptical of simply taking the claims of our commonsense morality as a rock-bottom ground of appeal for moral theorizing. Yet it may also well be the case—given our extensive cruelty anyway—that, if we ever start sanctioning such behavior, an even greater callousness toward life than the very extensive callousness extant now will, as a matter of fact, develop. Given a normative ethical theory which sanctions, *under certain circumstances*, such judicial murders, there may occur an undermining of our moral disapproval of killing and our absolutely essential moral principle that all human beings, great and small, are deserving of respect. This is surely enough, together with the not unimportant weight of even our unrehearsed moral feelings, to give strong utilitarian weight *here* to the dictates of our commonsense morality. Yet, I think I have also said enough to show that someone who questions their 'unquestionableness' in such a context does not thereby exhibit a 'corrupt mind' and that it is an open question whether he must be conceptually confused or morally mistaken over this matter.

IV

So far, I have tried to show with reference to the case of the magistrate and the threatening mob how consequentialists can reasonably square their normative ethical theories with an important range of commonsense moral convictions. Now, I wish by reference to the case of the innocent fat man to establish that there is at least a serious question concerning whether such fundamental commonsense moral convictions should always function as 'moral facts' or a kind of moral ground to test the adequacy of normative ethical theories or positions. I want to establish that careful attention to such cases shows that we are not justified in taking the principles embodied in our commonsense moral reasoning about such cases as normative for all moral decisions. That a normative ethical theory is incompatible with some of our 'moral institutions' (moral feelings or convictions) does not refute the normative ethical theory. What I will try to do here is to establish that this case, no more than the case examined in Section III, gives us adequate grounds for abandoning consequentialism and for adopting moral conservatism.

Forget the levity of the example and consider the case of the innocent fat man. If there really is no other way of unsticking our fat man and if plainly, without blasting him out, everyone in the cave will drown, then, innocent or not, he should be blasted out. This indeed overrides the principle that the innocent should never be deliberately killed, but it does not reveal a callousness toward life, for the people involved are caught in a desperate situation in which, if such extreme action is not taken, many lives will be lost and far greater misery will obtain. Moreover, the people who do such a horrible thing or acquiesce in the doing of it are not likely to be rendered more callous about human life and human suffering as a result. Its occurrence will haunt them for the rest of their lives and is as likely as not to make them more rather than less morally sensitive. It is not even correct to say that such a desperate act shows a lack of respect for persons. We are not treating the fat man merely as a means. The fat man's person—his interests and rights—are not ignored. Killing him is something which is undertaken with the greatest reluctance. It is only when it is quite certain that there is no other way to save the lives of the others that such a violent course of action is justifiably undertaken.

Alan Donagan, arguing rather as Anscombe argues, maintains that "to use any innocent man ill for the sake of some public good is directly to degrade him to being a mere means" and to do this is of course to violate a principle essential to morality, that is, that human beings should never merely be treated as means but should be treated as ends in themselves (as persons worthy of respect).[11] But, as my above remarks show, it need not be the case, and in the above situation it is not the case, that in killing such an innocent man we are treating him *merely* as a means. The action is universalizable, all alternative actions which would save his life are duly considered, the blasting out is done only as a last and desperate resort with the minimum of harshness and indifference to his suffering and the like. It indeed sounds ironical to talk this way, given what is done to him. But if such a terrible situation were to arise, there would always be more or less humane ways of going about one's grim task. And in acting in the more humane ways toward the fat man, as we do what we must do and would have done to ourselves were the roles reversed, we show a respect for his person.[12]

In so treating the fat man—not just to further the public good but to prevent the certain death of a whole group of people (that is to prevent an even greater evil than his being killed in this way)—the claims of justice are not overriden either, for each individual involved, if he is reasonably correct, should realize that if he were so stuck rather than the fat man, he should in such situations be blasted out. Thus, there is no question of being unfair. Surely we must choose between evils here, but is there anything more reasonable, more morally appropriate, than choosing the lesser evil when doing or allowing some evil cannot be avoided? That is, where there is no avoiding both and where our actions can determine whether a greater or lesser evil obtains, should we not plainly always opt for the lesser evil? And is it not obviously a greater evil that all those other innocent people should suffer and die than that the fat man should suffer and die? Blowing up the fat man is indeed monstrous. But letting him remain stuck while the whole group drowns is still more monstrous.

The consequentialist is on strong moral ground here, and, if his reflective moral convictions do not square either with certain unrehearsed or with certain reflective particular moral convictions of human beings, so much the worse for such commonsense moral convictions. One could even usefully and relevantly adapt here—though for a quite different purpose—an argument of Donagan's. Consequentialism of the kind I have been arguing for provides so persuasive "a theoretical basis for common morality that when it

---

[11] Alan Donagan (n. 1 above), pp. 199–200.

[12] Again, I am not asserting that we would have enough fortitude to assent to it were the roles actually reversed. I am making a conceptual remark about what as moral beings we must try to do and not a psychological observation about what we can do.

contradicts some moral intuition, it is natural to suspect that intuition, not theory, is corrupt."[13] Given the comprehensiveness, plausibility, and overall rationality of consequentialism, it is not unreasonable to override even a deeply felt moral conviction if it does not square with such a theory, though, if it made no sense or overrode the bulk of or even a great many of our considered moral convictions, that would be another matter indeed.

Anticonsequentialists often point to the inhumanity of people who will sanction such killing of the innocent, but cannot the compliment be returned by speaking of the even greater inhumanity, conjoined with evasiveness, of those who will allow even more death and far greater misery and then excuse themselves on the ground that they did not intend the death and misery but merely forbore to prevent it? In such a context, such reasoning and such forbearing to prevent seems to me to constitute a moral evasion. I say it is evasive because rather than steeling himself to do what in normal circumstances would be a horrible and vile act but in this circumstance is a harsh moral necessity, he allows, when he has the power to prevent it, a situation which is still many times worse. He tries to keep his 'moral purity' and avoid 'dirty hands' at the price of utter moral failure and what Kierkegaard called 'double-mindedness.' It is understandable that people should act in this morally evasive way but this does not make it right.

My consequentialist reasoning about such cases as the case of the innocent fat man is very often resisted on the grounds that it starts a very dangerous precedent. People rationalize wildly and irrationally in their own favor in such situations. To avoid such rationalization, we must stubbornly stick to our deontological principles and recognize as well that very frequently, if people will put their wits to work or just endure, such admittedly monstrous actions done to prevent still greater evils will turn out to be unnecessary.

The general moral principles surrounding bans on killing the innocent are strong and play such a crucial role in the ever-floundering effort to humanize the savage mind—savage as a primitive and savage again as a contemporary in industrial society—that it is of the utmost social utility, it can be argued, that such bans against killing the innocent not be called into question in any practical manner by consequentialist reasoning.

However, in arguing in this way, the moral conservative has plainly shifted his ground, and he is himself arguing on consequentialist grounds that we must treat certain nonconsequentialist moral principles as absolute (as principles which can never *in fact*, from a reasonable moral point of view, be overriden, for it would be just too disastrous to do so).[14] But now he is on my home court, and my reply

---

[13] Alan Donagan (n. 1 above), p. 198.

[14] Jonathan Bennett, "Whatever the Consequences," *Analysis*, vol. 26 (1966),

is that there is no good evidence at all that in the circumstances I characterized, overriding these deontological principles would have this disastrous effect. I am aware that a bad precedent could be set. Such judgments must not be made for more doubtful cases. But my telling my two stories in some detail, and my contrasting them, was done in order to make evident the type of situation, with its attendant rationale, in which the overriding of those deontological principles can be seen clearly to be justified and the situations in which this does not obtain and why. My point was to specify the situations in which we ought to override our commonsense moral convictions about those matters, and the contexts in which we are not so justified or at least in which it is not clear which course of action is justified.[15]

If people are able to be sufficiently clearheaded about these matters, they can see that there are relevant differences between the two sorts of cases. But I was also carefully guarding against extending such 'moral radicalism'—if such it should be called—to other and more doubtful cases. Unless solid empirical evidence can be given that such a 'moral radicalism' would—if it were to gain a toehold in the community—overflow destructively and inhumanely into the other doubtful and positively unjustifiable situations, nothing has been said to undermine the correctness of my consequentialist defense of 'moral radicalism' in the contexts in which I defended it.[16]

has shown that this is a very common equivocation for the conservative and makes, when unnoticed, his position seem more plausible than it actually is. [See pp. 182–83 this volume.—Ed.]

[15] I have spoken, conceding this to the Christian absolutist for the sake of the discussion, as if (1) it is fairly evident what our commonsense moral convictions are here and (2) that they are deontological principles taken to hold no matter what the consequences. But that either (1) or (2) is clearly so seems to me very much open to question.

[16] I do not mean to suggest that I am giving a blanket defense to our commonsense morality; that is one of the last things I would want to do. Much of what we or any other tribe take to be commonsense morality is little better than a set of magical charms to deal with our social environment. But I was defending the importance of such cross-culturally ubiquitous moral principles as that one ought not to harm the innocent or that promises ought to be kept. However, against Christian absolutists of the type I have been discussing, I take them to be prima facie obligations. This means that they always hold *ceteris paribus*; but the *ceteris paribus* qualification implies that they can be overridden on occasion. On my account, appeal to consequences and considerations about justice and respect for persons determines when they should on a given occasion be overridden.

XIV

Whatever the Consequences

Jonathan Bennett

The following kind of thing can occur.[1] A woman in labour will certainly die unless an operation is performed in which the head of her unborn child is crushed or dissected; while if it is not performed the child can be delivered, alive, by post-mortem Caesarian section. This presents a straight choice between the woman's life and the child's.

In a particular instance of this kind, some people would argue for securing the woman's survival on the basis of the special facts of the case: the woman's terror, or her place in an established network of affections and dependence, or the child's physical defects, and so on. For them, the argument could go the other way in another instance, even if only in a very special one—*e.g.* where the child is well formed and the woman has cancer which will kill her within a month anyway.

Others would favour the woman's survival in any instance of the kind presented in my opening paragraph, on the grounds that women are human while unborn children are not. This dubious argument does not need to be attacked here, and I shall ignore it.

Others again would say, just on the facts as stated in my first paragraph, that the *child* must be allowed to survive. Their objection to any operation in which an unborn child's head is crushed, whatever the special features of the case, goes like this:

> To do the operation would be to kill the child, while to refrain from doing it would not be to kill the woman but merely to conduct oneself in such a way that—as a foreseen but unwanted consequence—the woman died.

---

[1] J. K. Feeney and A. P. Barry in *Journal of Obstetrics and Gynaecology of the British Empire* (1954), p. 61. R. L. Cecil and H. F. Conn (eds.), *The Specialties in General Practice* (Philadelphia, 1957), p. 410.

> The question we should ask is not: 'The woman's life or the child's?', but rather: 'To kill, or not to kill, an innocent human?' The answer to *that* is that it is always absolutely wrong to kill an innocent human, even in such dismal circumstances as these.

This line of thought needs to be attacked. Some able people find it acceptable; it is presupposed by the Principle of Double Effect[2] which permeates Roman Catholic writing on morals; and I cannot find any published statement of the extremely strong philosophical case for its rejection.

I shall state that case as best I can. My presentation of it owes much to certain allies and opponents who have commented on earlier drafts. I gratefully acknowledge my debt to Miss G. E. M. Anscombe, A. G. N. Flew, A. Kenny and T. J. Smiley; and to a number of Cambridge research students, especially D. F. Wallace.

The Plan of Attack

There is no way of disproving the principle: 'It would always be wrong to kill an innocent human, whatever the consequences of not doing so.' The principle is consistent and reasonably clear; it can be fed into moral syllogisms to yield practical conclusions; and although its application to borderline cases may raise disturbing problems, this is true of any moral principle. Someone who thinks that the principle is laid down by a moral authority whose deliverances are to be accepted without question, without *any* testing against the dictates of the individual conscience, is vulnerable only to arguments about the credentials of his alleged authority; and these are not my present concern. So I have no reply to make to anyone who is prepared to say: 'I shall obey God's command never to kill an innocent human. I shall make no independent moral assessment of this command—whether to test the reasonableness of obeying it, or to test my belief that it *is* God's command, or for any other purpose.' My concern is solely with those who accept the principle: 'It would always be wrong to kill an innocent human, whatever the consequences of not doing so', not just because it occurs in some received list of moral principles but also because they think that it can in some degree be recommended to the normal conscience. Against this, I shall argue that a normal person who accepts the principle must either have failed to see what it involves or be passively and unquestioningly obedient to an authority.

---

[2] See G. Kelly, *Medico-Moral Problems* (Dublin, 1955), p. 20; C. J. McFadden, *Medical Ethics* (London, 1962), pp. 27–33; T. J. O'Donnell, *Morals in Medicine* (London, 1959), pp. 39–44; N. St. John-Stevas, *The Right to Life* (London, 1963), p. 71.

I do not equate 'the normal conscience' with 'the "liberal" conscience'. Of course, the principle *is* rejected by the 'liberal' majority; but I shall argue for the stronger and less obvious thesis that the principle is in the last resort on a par with 'It would always be wrong to shout, whatever the consequences of not doing so', or 'It would always be wrong to leave a bucket in a hall-way, whatever *etc.*'. It is sometimes said that we 'should not understand' someone who claimed to accept such wild eccentricities as these as fundamental moral truths—that he would be making a logical mistake, perhaps about what it is for something to be a 'moral' principle. I need not claim so much. It is enough to say that such a person, if he was sincere and in his right mind, could safely be assumed to have delivered himself over to a moral authority and to have opted out of moral thinking altogether. The same could be said of anyone who accepted *and really understood* the principle: 'It would always be wrong to kill an innocent human, whatever the consequences of not doing so.' This principle is accepted by reasonable people who, though many of them give weight to some moral authority, have not abdicated from independent moral thinking. Clearly, they regard the principle as one which others might be led to accept, or at least to take seriously, on grounds other than subservience to an authority. From this fact, together with the thesis for which I shall argue, it follows that those who accept the principle (like others who at least treat it with respect) have not thought it through, have not seen what it comes to in concrete cases where it yields a different practical conclusion from that yielded by 'It is wrong to kill an innocent human unless there are very powerful reasons for doing so'. I aim to show what the principle comes to in these cases, and so to expose it for what it is.

My arguments will tell equally against any principle of the form 'It would always be wrong to . . . , whatever the consequences of not doing so'; but I shall concentrate on the one principle about killing, and indeed on its application to the kind of obstetrical situation described in my opening paragraph.

I need a label for someone who accepts principles of the form: 'It would always be wrong to . . . , whatever the consequences of not doing so.' 'Roman Catholic' is at once too wide and too narrow; 'intrinsicalist' is nasty; 'absolutist' is misleading; 'deontologist' means too many other things as well. Reluctantly, I settle for 'conservative'. This use has precedents, but I offer it as a stipulative definition—an expository convenience and not a claim about 'conservatism' in any ordinary sense.

Well then: When the conservative condemns the operation described in my opening paragraph, he does so *partly* because the operation involves the death of an innocent human. So does its nonperformance; but for the conservative the dilemma is asymmetrical because the two alternatives involve human deaths in different ways: in one case the death is part of a killing, in the other there is no killing and a death occurs only as a consequence of what is done. From the premiss that operating would be killing an innocent human, together with the principle: 'It would always be wrong to kill an innocent human, whatever *etc.*', it does follow that it would be wrong to operate. But the usual conservative—the one I plan to attack—thinks that his principle has *some* measure of acceptability on grounds other than unquestioning obedience to an authority. He must therefore think that the premiss: 'In this case, operating would be killing an innocent human while not-operating would involve the death of an innocent human only as a consequence' gives *some* reason for the conclusion: 'In this case, operating would be wrong'. I shall argue that it gives no reason at all: once the muddles have been cleared away, it is just not humanly possible to see the premiss as supporting the conclusion, however weakly, except by accepting the principle 'It would always be wrong *etc.*' as an unquestionable *donnée*.

The Action/Consequence Distinction

When James killed Henry, what happened was this: James contracted his fingers round the handle of a knife, and moved his hand in such a way that the knife penetrated Henry's body and severed an artery; blood escaped from the wound, the rate of oxygen-transfer to Henry's body-cells fell drastically, and Henry died. In general, someone's performing a physical action includes his moving some part or parts of his body. (The difference between 'He moved his hand' and 'His hand moved' is not in question here: I am referring to movements which he *makes*.) He does this in a physical environment, and other things happen in consequence. A description of what he *did* will ordinarily entail something not only about his movements but also, *inter alia*, about some of their upshots. Other upshots will not ordinarily be covered by any description of 'what he did', but will be counted amongst 'the consequences of what he did'. There are various criteria for drawing the line between what someone did and the consequences of what he did; and there can be several proper ways of drawing it in a given case.

This last point notwithstanding, there are wrong ways of dividing a set of happenings into action and consequences. Even where it is not positively wrong to give a very parsimonious account of 'what he did', it may be preferable to be more inclusive. If in my chosen example the obstetrician does the operation, it is true that he crushes the child's head with the consequence that the child dies, but a better account, perhaps, would say that he *kills* the child by crushing its head. There can certainly be outright wrongness at the other end of the scale: we cannot be as inclusive as we like in our account of 'what he did'. If at the last time when the operation could save the woman's life the obstetrician is resignedly writing up his notes, it is just not true that, as he sits at his desk, he is killing the woman; nor, indeed, is he killing her at any other time.

The use of the action/consequence distinction in the conservative premiss is, therefore, perfectly correct. Operating *is* killing; not-operating is not. What are we saying when we say this? By what criteria is the action/consequence distinction drawn in the present case? I shall try, by answering this, to show that in this case one cannot attach moral significance to the fact that the line drawn by the distinction falls where it does. Briefly, the criteria for the action/consequence distinction fall into two groups: those which could support a moral conclusion but which do not apply to every instance of the obstetrical example; and those which do apply to the example but which it would be wildly eccentric to think relevant to the moral assessment of courses of action. There is no overlap between the two groups.

Aspects of the Distinction: First Group

Some differences which tend to go with the action/consequence distinction, and are perhaps to be counted amongst the criteria for it, clearly do have moral significance. None of them, however, is generally present in the obstetrical example.

Given a question about whether some particular upshot of a movement I made is to be covered by the description of what I *did*:

(a) The answer may depend in part upon whether in making the movement I was entirely confident that that upshot would ensue; and this could reasonably be thought relevant to the moral assessment of my conduct. This aspect of the action/consequence distinction, however, is absent from most instances of the obstetrical example. The classification of not-operating as something other than killing does not imply that the obstetrician rates the woman's chance of survival (if the operation is not performed) higher than the child's chance of survival (if it is performed). If it did imply this then, by contraposition, not-operating would in many such cases have to be classified as killing after all.

(b) The answer may depend in part upon how certain or inevitable it was that that upshot would ensue from my movement, or upon how confidently I ought to have expected it to ensue; and that too may have a strong bearing on the moral assessment of my conduct. But it gets no grip on the obstetrical example, for in many cases of that kind there is moral certainty on both sides of the dilemma. If the conservative says that the action/consequence distinction, when correctly drawn, is always associated with morally significant differences in the inevitability of upshots of movements, then he is vulnerable to an argument by contraposition like the one in (a). He is vulnerable in other ways as well, which I shall discuss in my next section.

(c) The answer may depend in part upon whether I made the movement partly or wholly for the sake of achieving that upshot; and this is a morally significant matter. But the obstetrical example is symmetrical in that respect also: if the obstetrician crushes the child's head he does so not because this will lead to the child's death or because it constitutes killing the child, but because that is his only way of removing the child's body from the woman's.

To summarize: moral conclusions may be supported by facts (a) about what is expected, but in the example each upshot is confidently expected; (b) about what is inevitable, but in the example each upshot is inevitable; or (c) about what is ultimately aimed at, but in the example neither upshot is aimed at.

An Aside: Degrees of Inevitability

I have suggested that a conservative might say: 'The action-consequence distinction is always associated with a morally significant difference in the degree to which upshots are certain or inevitable.' This is false; but let us grant it in order to see whether it can help the conservative on the obstetrical example. I concede, for purposes of argument, that if the operation is not performed the woman will pretty certainly die, while if it is performed the child will even more certainly die.

What use can the conservative make of this concession? Will he say that the practical decision is to be based on a weighing of the comparative desirability of upshots against the comparative certainty of their achievement? If so, then he must allow that there *could* be a case in which it was right to kill the child—perhaps a case where a healthy young widow with four children is bearing a hydrocephalic child, and where her chance of survival if the operation is not performed is *nearly* as bad as the child's chance of survival if it is performed. If a professed 'conservative' allows that there could, however improbably, be such a case, then he is not a conservative but a consequentialist; he does after all base his final judgment on the special features of the case; and he has misrepresented his position by using the language of action and consequence to express his implausible views about the comparative inevitability of upshots. On the other hand, if the conservative still absolutely rules out the killing of the child, whatever the details of the particular case, then what could be his point in claiming that there is a difference in degree of inevitability? The moral significance of this supposed difference would, at best, have to be conceded to be an obscure one which threw no light on why anyone should adopt the conservative view.

A certain conservative tactic is at issue here. Miss G. E. M. Anscombe has said:

> If someone really thinks, *in advance*, that it is open to question whether such an action as procuring the judicial execution of the innocent should be quite excluded from consideration—I do not want to argue with him; he shows a corrupt mind.[3]

The phrase 'quite excluded from consideration' clearly places Miss Anscombe as what I am calling a 'conservative'. (The phrase 'a corrupt mind', incidentally, tends to confirm my view that conservatives think their position can stand the light of day, *i.e.* that they do not see it as tenable only by those who passively obey some moral authority.) Now, in the course of a footnote to this passage Miss Anscombe remarks:

> In discussion when this paper was read, as was perhaps to be expected, this case was produced: a government is required to have an innocent man tried, sentenced and executed under threat of a 'hydrogen bomb war'. It would seem strange to me to have much hope of averting a war threatened by such men as made this demand. But the most important thing about the way in which cases like this are invented in discussions, is the assumption that only two courses are open: here, compliance and open defiance. No one can say in advance of such a situation what the possibilities are going to be—*e.g.* that there is none of stalling by a feigned willingness to comply, accompanied by a skilfully arranged 'escape' of the victim.

This makes two points about the case as described: there might be nothing we could do which would have a good chance of averting a war; and if there were one such thing we could do there might be several. The consequentialist might meet this by trying yet again to describe a case in which judicially executing an innocent man *is* the only thing we could do which would have a good chance of averting a war. When he has added the details which block off the other alternatives, his invented case may well be far removed from present political likelihood; it may even be quite fantastic. Still, what does the conservative say about it?

[3] G. E. M. Anscombe, 'Modern Moral Philosophy', *Philosophy*, vol. 33 (1958), p. 17.

Here is Miss Anscombe, at her most gamesome, on the subject of 'fantastic' examples:

> A point of method I would recommend to the corrupter of the youth would be this: concentrate on examples which are either banal: you have promised to return a book, but . . . and so on, or fantastic: what you ought to do if you had to move forward, and stepping with your right foot meant killing twenty-five young men, while stepping with your left foot would kill fifty drooling old ones. (Obviously the right thing to do would be to jump and polish off the lot.)[4]

The cards are now well stacked; but this is a game in which a conservative should not be taking a hand at all. Someone may say (i): 'In no situation could it be right to procure the judicial execution of the innocent: political probability aside, the judicial execution of the innocent is absolutely impermissible in any possible circumstances.' Or someone may say (ii): 'It is never right to procure the judicial execution of the innocent: a situation in which this would be right has never arisen, isn't going to arise, and cannot even be described without entering into the realm of political fantasy.' These are different. The former is conservatism, according to which 'the judicial execution of the innocent should be quite excluded from consideration'. The latter is not conservatism: according to it, the judicial execution of the innocent is taken into consideration, assessed in the light of the political probabilities of the world we live in, and excluded on that basis. The former is Miss Anscombe's large type; the latter, apparently, is her footnote. The difference between (i) 'In no situation could it be right . . .' and (ii) 'No situation is even remotely likely to occur in which it would be right . . .' can be masked by dismissing what is relevant but unlikely as 'fantastic' and therefore negligible. But the difference between the two positions is crucial, even if in the first instance it can be brought out only by considering 'fantastic' possibilities. The two may yield the same real-life practical conclusions, but (ii) can be understood and argued with in a way in which (i) cannot. If someone accepts (ii), and is not afraid to discuss a 'fantastic' but possible situation in which he would approve the judicial execution of an innocent man, he can be challenged to square this with his contrary judgment in regard to some less fantastic situation. Whether he could meet the challenge would depend on the details of his moral position and of the situations in question. The point is that we should know where we stood with him: for example, we should know that it was

[4] G. E. M. Anscombe, 'Does Oxford Moral Philosophy Corrupt the Youth?', *The Listener*, February 14, 1957, p. 267. See also the correspondence in ensuing numbers, and Michael Tanner, 'Examples in Moral Philosophy', *Proceedings of the Aristotelian Society*, vol. 65 (1964–5).

relevant to adduce evidence about how good the chances would be of averting war in this way in this situation, or in that way in that. It is just this sort of thing which the unwavering conservative must regard as irrelevant; and that is what is wrong with his position. Miss Anscombe says: 'No one can say in advance of such a situation what the possibilities are going to be'; but the central objection to conservatism is, precisely, that it says in advance that for the judging of the proposed course of action *it does not matter* what the possibilities are going to be. Why, then, go on about them—if not to disguise conservatism as something else when the going gets tough?

I have based this paper on the obstetrical example in the hope that, without being jeered at for having 'invented' an example which is 'fantastic', I could present a kind of case in which a conservative principle would yield a practical conclusion different from any likely to be arrived at by consequentialist arguments. The claim that in these cases there would always be a morally significant difference between the woman's chance of survival and the child's could only be another attempt to get the spotlight off conservatism altogether—to get the consequentialist to accept the conservative's conclusion and forget about his principle. In the obstetrical example, the attempt is pretty desperate (though, with the aid of judiciously selected statistics, it is made often enough); with other kinds of example, used to examine this or other conservative principles, it might be easier for the conservative to make a show of insisting on the addition of details which render the examples 'fantastic'. But this does not mean that the case against conservatism is stronger here than elsewhere. It means only that the obstetrical example gives less scope than most for the 'there-might-be-another-way-out' move, or protective-coloration gambit, which some conservatives sometimes use when they shelter their position by giving the impression that it does not really exist.

A conservative might invoke inevitability, without comparing degrees of it in the consequentialist manner, by saying that if the operation is not performed the woman still has *some* chance of survival while if it is performed the child has *none*. Barring miracles, this is wrong about the woman; not barring miracles, it is wrong about the child. It could seem plausible only to someone who did not bar miracles but took a peculiar view of how they operate. Some people do attach importance in this regard to the fact that if the operation is not performed the woman may take some time to die: they seem to think—perhaps encouraged by an eccentric view of God as powerful but *slow*—that the longer an upshot is delayed the more room there is for a miraculous intervention. This belief, whatever the assumptions which underlie it, gives no help to the conservative position. For suppose the obstetrician decides to try, after operating and delivering the child, to repair its head by microsurgery. The woman's supposed 'some chance' of survival if the child's head is not crushed is of the same kind as the obstetrician's 'some chance' of saving the child after crushing its head: in each case there is what the well-informed plain man would call 'no chance', but in each case it will take a little time for the matter to be finally settled by the events themselves—for the woman to die or the obstetrician to admit failure. Would the conservative say that the obstetrician's intention to try to save the child in this way, though hopeless, completely alters the shape of the problem and perhaps makes it all right for the obstetrician to crush the child's head? If so, then what we have here is a morality of gestures and poses.

Aspects of the Distinction: Second Group

I return to the main thread of my argument. Of the remaining three aspects of the action/consequence distinction, it was not quite true to say that all are present in (every instance of) the obstetrical example; for the first of them has not even that merit. The main point, however, is that even if it were always present it would not help the conservative—though it might help us to diagnose his trouble.

(d) Someone's decision whether an upshot of a movement of mine is to be covered by his description of what I *did* may depend partly on his moral assessment of my role in the total situation. Your condemnation of me, or perhaps your approval, may be reflected in your putting on the 'action' side of the line an upshot which an indifferent onlooker would count as merely a 'consequence'. This aspect of the action/consequence distinction—if indeed it is one independently of those already discussed—cannot help the conservative who believes that a premiss using the distinction tends to *support* a moral conclusion. That belief demands a relevance relation which slopes the other way.

There seem to be two remaining aspects to the action/consequence distinction. Certainly, there are only two which do appear in all instances of the obstetrical example. These two must be the sole justification for saying that operating would be killing while not-operating would not be killing; and so they must bear the whole weight of any conservative but non-authoritarian case against killing the child.

(e) Operating is killing-the-child because if the obstetrician operates there is a high degree of *immediacy* between what he does with his hands and the child's dying. This immediacy consists in the brevity or absence of time-lag, spatial nearness, simplicity of causal connexions, and paucity of intervening physical objects. The relations amongst these are complex; but they are severally relevant to the action/consequence distinction, and in the obstetrical example they all pull together, creating an overwhelming case for calling the performance of the operation the *killing* of the child.

(f) Not-operating is not killing-the-woman because it is not *doing* anything at all but is merely *refraining* from doing something.

Since (e) and (f) are so central to the action/consequence distinction generally, it is appropriate that they should sometimes bear its whole weight, as they do in the conservative's (correct) application of the distinction to the obstetrical example. But if (e) and (f) are all there is to the premiss: 'In this case, operating would be killing an innocent human while not-operating would involve the death of an innocent human only as a consequence', then this premiss offers no support at all to the conclusion: 'In this case, operating would be wrong.'

The matters which I group under 'immediacy' in (e) may borrow moral significance from their loose association with facts about whether and in what degree upshots are (a) expected, (b) inevitable or (c) aimed at. In none of these respects, however, is there a relevant asymmetry in the obstetrical example. The question is: why should a difference in degree of immediacy, unaccompanied by other relevant differences, be taken to support a moral discrimination? I cannot think of a remotely plausible answer which does not consist solely in an appeal to an authority.[5]

Suggestions come to mind about 'not getting one's hands dirty'; and the notion of what I call 'immediacy' does help to show how the literal and the metaphorical are mingled in some uses of that phrase. In so doing, however, it exposes the desire to 'keep one's hands clean', in cases like the obstetrical example, as a symptom of muddle or primness or, worst of all, a moral egoism like Pilate's. (To be fair: I do not think that many conservatives would answer in this way. If they used similar words it would probably not be to express the nasty sentiment I have mentioned but rather to say something like: 'I must obey God's law; and the rest is up to God.' Because this suggests a purely authoritarian basis, and because it certainly has nothing to do with immediacy, it lies beyond my present scope.)

Similarly with the acting/refraining distinction in (f). I shall argue in my next section that our criteria for this distinction do not invest it with any moral significance whatever—except when the distinction is drawn on the basis of independently formed moral judgments, and then it cannot help the conservative case for the reason given in (d). And if

[5] Conservatives use words like 'direct' to cover a jumble of factors of which immediacy is the most prominent. Pius XII has said that a pain-killing, life-shortening drug may be used 'if there exists no direct causal link, either through the will of interested parties or by the nature of things, between the induced 'consciousness' [*sic*] and the shortening of life . . .' (Quoted in St. John-Stevas, *op. cit.*, p. 61.)

neither (e) immediacy nor (f) acting/refraining separately has moral significance, then clearly they cannot acquire any by being taken together.

Acting and Refraining

Suppose the obstetrician does not operate, and the woman dies. He does not kill her, but he *lets her die*. The reproach suggested by these words is just an unavoidable nuisance, and I shall not argue from it. When I say 'he lets her die', I mean only that he knowingly refrains from preventing her death which he alone could prevent, and he cannot say that her survival is in a general way 'none of my business' or 'not [even *prima facie*] my concern'. If my arguments so far are correct, then this one fact—the fact that the non-operating obstetrician *lets the woman die* but does not *kill her*—is the only remaining feature of the situation which the conservative can hope to adduce as supporting his judgment about what ought to be done in every instance of the obstetrical example.[6] Let us examine the difference between 'X killed Y' and 'X let Y die'.

Some cases of letting-die are also cases of killing. If on a dark night X knows that Y's next step will take him over the edge of a high cliff, and he refrains from uttering a simple word of warning because he doesn't care or because he wants Y dead, then it is natural to say not only that X lets Y die but also that he kills him—even if it was not X who suggested the route, removed the fence from the cliff-top, *etc*. Cases like this, where a failure-to-prevent is described as a doing partly *because* it is judged to be wicked or indefensible, are beside my present point; for I want to see what difference there is between killing and letting-die which might be a *basis for* a moral judgment. Anyway, the letting-die which is also killing must involve malice or wanton indifference, and there is nothing like that in the obstetrical example. In short, to count these cases as relevant to the obstetrical example would be to suggest that not-operating would after all be killing the woman—a plainly false suggestion which I have disavowed. I wish to criticise the conservative's argument, not to deny his premiss. So from now on I shall ignore cases of letting-die which are also cases of killing; and it will make for brevity to pretend that they do not exist. For example, I shall say that killing involves moving one's body—which is false of some of these cases, but true of all others.

One more preliminary point: the purposes of the present enquiry do

[6] In a case where the child cannot survive anyway: 'It is a question of the *direct taking* of one innocent life or merely *permitting* two deaths. In other words, there is question of one *murder* against two deaths . . .' Kelly, *op. cit.*, p. 181.

not demand that a full analysis be given either of 'X killed Y' or of 'X let Y die'. We can ignore any implications either may have about what X (a) expected, (b) should have expected, or (c) was aiming at; for the obstetrical example is symmetrical in all those respects. We can also ignore the fact that 'X killed Y' loosely implies something about (e) immediacy which is not implied by 'X let Y die', for immediacy in itself has no moral significance.

Consider the statement that *Joe killed the calf*. A certain aspect of the analysis of this will help us to see how it relates to *Joe let the calf die*. To say that Joe killed the calf is to say that

(1) Joe moved his body

and

(2) the calf died;

but it is also to say something about how Joe's moving was connected with the calf's dying—something to the effect that

(3) if Joe had not moved as he did, the calf would not have died.

How is (3) to be interpreted? We might take it, rather strictly, as saying

(3′): If Joe had moved in *any* other way, the calf would not have died.

This, however, is too strong to be a necessary condition of Joe's having killed the calf. Joe may have killed the calf even if he could have moved in other ways which would equally have involved the calf's dying. Suppose that Joe cut the calf's throat, but could have shot it instead: in that case he clearly killed it; but (3′) denies that he killed it, because the calf might still have died even if Joe had not moved in just the way he did.

We might adopt a weaker reading of (3), namely as saying

(3″): Joe could have moved in *some* other way without the calf's dying.

But where (3′) was too strong to be necessary, (3″) is too weak to express a sufficient connexion between Joe's moving and the calf's dying. It counts Joe as having killed the calf not only in cases where we should ordinarily say that he killed it but also in cases where the most we should say is that he let it die.

The truth lies somewhere between (3′), which is appropriate to 'Joe killed the calf in the only way open to him', and (3″), which is appropriate to 'Joe killed the calf or let it die'. Specifically, the connexion between Joe's moving and the calf's dying which is appropriate to 'Joe killed the calf' but not to 'Joe let the calf die' is expressed by

> (3‴): Of all the other ways in which Joe might have moved, *relatively few* satisfy the condition: if Joe had moved like that, the calf would have died.

And the connexion which is appropriate to 'Joe let the calf die' but not to 'Joe killed the calf' is expressed by

> (4): Of all the other ways in which Joe might have moved, *almost all* satisfy the condition: if Joe had moved like that, the calf would have died.

This brings me to the main thesis of the present section: apart from the factors I have excluded as already dealt with, the difference between 'X killed Y' and 'X let Y die' *is* the difference between (3‴) and (4). When the killing/letting-die distinction is stripped off its implications regarding immediacy, intention *etc.*—which lack moral significance or don't apply to the example—all that remains is a distinction having to do with where a set of movements lies on the scale which has 'the only set of movements which would have produced that upshot' at one end and 'movements other than the only set which would have produced that upshot' at the other.

This, then, is the conservative's residual basis for a moral discrimination between operating and not-operating. Operating would be killing: if the obstetrician makes movements which constitute operating, then the child will die; and there are very few other movements he could make which would also involve the child's dying. Not-operating would only be letting-die: if throughout the time when he could be operating the obstetrician makes movements which constitute not-operating, then the woman will die; but the vast majority of alternative movements he could make during that time would equally involve the woman's dying. I do not see how anyone doing his own moral thinking about the matter could find the least shred of moral significance in *this* difference between operating and not-operating.

Suppose you are told that X killed Y in the only way possible in the circumstances; and this, perhaps together with certain other details of the case, leads you to judge X's conduct adversely. Then you are told: 'You have been misled: there is another way in which X could have killed Y.' Then a third informant says: 'That is wrong too: there are two other ways . . . *etc.*' Then a fourth: 'No: there are three other ways . . . *etc.*' Clearly, these successive corrections put no pressure at all on your original judgment: you will not think it relevant to your judgment on X's killing of Y that it could have been carried out in any one of *n* different ways. But the move from 'X killed Y in the only possible way' to 'X killed Y in one of the only five possible ways' is of the same *kind* as the move from 'X killed Y' to 'X let Y die' (except for the latter's implications about immediacy); and the moral insignificance of the former move is evidence for the moral insignificance of the latter move also.

The difference between 'X killed Y' and 'X let Y die' is the sum-total of a vast number of differences such as that between 'X killed Y in one of the only *n* possible ways' and 'X killed Y in one of the only *n* + 1 possible ways'. If the difference between '. . . *n* . . .' and '. . . *n* + 1 . . .' were morally insignificant only because it was *too small* for any moral discrimination to be based upon it, then the sum-total of millions of such differences might still have moral significance. But in fact the differences in question, whatever their size, are of the *wrong kind* for any moral discrimination to be based upon them. Suppose you have judged X adversely, on the basis of the misinformation: 'X killed Y is the only way possible in the circumstances'; and this is then replaced, in one swoop, by the true report: 'X did not kill Y at all, though he did knowingly let Y die'. Other things being equal, would this give you the slightest reason to retract your adverse judgment? Not a bit of it! It would be perfectly reasonable for you to reply: 'The fact remains that X chose to conduct himself in a way which he knew would involve Y's death. At first I thought his choice could encompass Y's death only by being the choice of some rather specific course of conduct; whereas the revised report shows me that X's choice could have encompassed Y's death while committing X to very little. At first I thought it had to be a choice to act; I now realize that it could have been a choice to refrain. What of it?'

There are several things a conservative is likely to say at this point—all equivalent. 'When we know that the crucial choice could have been a choice to refrain from something, we can begin to allow for the possibility that it may have been a choice to refrain from doing something wrong, such as killing an innocent human.' Or: 'You say "other things being equal", but in the obstetrical example they aren't equal. By representing letting-die as a kind of wide-optioned killing you suppress the fact that the alternative to letting the woman die is killing the child.'

Replies like these are available to the conservative only if he does not need them and can break through at some other point; for they assume the very point which is at issue, namely that in every instance of the obstetrical example it would be wrong to kill the child. I think that in some cases it would indeed be wrong—(I do not press for a blanket judgment on all instances of the example—quite the contrary); and in such a case the obstetrician, if he rightly let the woman die, could defend his doing so on the basis of the details of the particular case. Furthermore, he might wish to begin his defence by explaining:

'I let the woman die, but I did not kill her'; for letting-die is in general likely to be more defensible than killing. My analysis incidentally shows one reason why: the alternatives to killing are always very numerous, and the odds are that at least one of them provides an acceptable way out of the impasse; whereas the alternative to letting-die is always some fairly specific course of conduct, and if there are conclusive objections to *that* then there's an end of the matter. All this, though, is a matter of likelihoods. It is no help in the rare cases where the alternatives to killing, numerous as they are, arguably do *not* include an acceptable way out of the impasse because they all involve something of the same order of gravity as a killing, namely a letting-die. The conservative may say: 'Where innocent humans are in question, letting-die is not of the same order of gravity as killing: for one of them is not, and the other is, absolutely wrong in all possible circumstances.' But this, like the rejoinders out of which this paragraph grew, assumes the very point which is at issue. All these conservative moves come down to just one thing: 'At this point your argument fails; for the wrongness of killing the child, in any instance of the obstetrical example, *can* be defended on the basis of your own analysis of the acting/refraining distinction—plus the extra premiss that it would always be wrong to kill the child.'

The Stress on the Specific

My argument is finished; but its strategy might be thought to be open to a certain criticism which I want to discuss.

The obstetrical example is a *kind* of situation, on every instance of which the conservative makes a certain judgment. I have argued that this judgment, as applied to many instances of the example, cannot be defended except by the unquestioning invocation of authority. This would have been damaging to the conservative position even if I had appealed only to 'fantastic' kinds of instance such as seldom or never occur; but in fact my claims have been true of many real-life instances of the obstetrical example. Still, a conservative might resist my drive towards the relatively specific, my insistence upon asking: 'What is there about *this* kind of instance which justifies your judgment upon it?' He might claim that even my opening paragraph presents so special a kind of situation that he cannot fairly be asked to find in *it* something which supports his judgment other than by a blanket appeal to his general principle that it would always be wrong to kill an innocent human. There are two ways in which he might defend this stand: they look alike, but their fatal defects are very different.

The first is by the use of a sub-Wittgensteinian argument from the nature of language. Although I have never encountered it, it is a possible and plausible objection to my strategy of argument. The conservative might say: 'Granted that facts about (a) expectation, (b) inevitability and (c) intention are irrelevant to the way the action/consequence distinction applies to the obstetrical example; it does not follow that when we apply the distinction to the example *all* we are doing—apart from (d) reflecting our already-formed moral judgments—is to report facts about (e) immediacy and (f) acting/refraining. Language and thought don't work like this. When we say: "Operating would be killing; not-operating would not be killing though it would have death as a consequence", we are not *just* talking about immediacy and specificity of options. We are using words which, *qua* words in the language, are laden with associations having to do with (a)–(d); and these associations of the words cannot simply be ignored or forgotten in a particular case. Language is not atomic in that way, and it would be at best a clumsy instrument if it were.'

I agree that we often do, and perhaps must sometimes, decide our conduct in one situation partly through verbal carry-overs from others in which similar conduct could be justified more directly. But I think that everyone will agree that the more serious a practical problem is, the greater is our obligation to resist such verbal carry-overs and scrutinize the particular problem in order to see what there is about *it* which would justify this or that solution to it. A practical problem in which human lives are at stake is a deeply serious one, and it would be an abdication from all moral seriousness to settle it by verbal carry-overs. I am not saying: 'Take pity on the poor woman, and never mind what the correct description of the situation is.' I am opposing someone who says: 'This is the correct description of the situation—never mind what its force is in this particular case.'

The second objection to my stress on the particular case, or the specific kind of case, is one which conservatives do sometimes use; and it connects with a muddle which is not special to conservatives. It goes like this: 'We must have rules. If every practical problem had to be solved on the spot, on the basis of the fine details of the particular case, the results would be disastrous. Take a situation which falls under some rule which I know to be justified in most situations. There may not be time or means for me to learn much more about the present situation than just that it does fall under the rule; the details of the case, even if I can discover them, may be too complex for me to handle; my handling of them, even if intellectually efficient, may without my knowing it be self-interested or corrupt; by deciding, however uncorruptly, not to follow the rule on this occasion, I may weaken its hold on me in other situations where it clearly ought to be followed; and even if I could be sure that I was in no such danger, I might help others into it by publicly breaking the rule.[7]

This is all true, but it does not help the conservative. Notice first that it tells against undue attention to individual cases rather than against undue attention to limited kinds of case: its target is not the specific but the particular. Still, it could be developed into an attack on over-stressing very specifically detailed kinds of case: its opening words would then have to be replaced by: 'We must have rather general rules.' This is true too, but it is still no help to the conservative.

This argument for our bringing practical problems under rather general rules is based on the consequences of our not doing so: it points to the dangers attendant on suspending a general rule and considering whether one's practical problem might be better resolved by applying a less general one. But sometimes these dangers will be far too slight to justify doing what a given general rule enjoins in a particular situation. If the thesis under discussion is to have any practical upshot which is not ludicrous ('Never break any general rule which would enjoin the right action in more cases than not'), or vague to the point of vacuity ('Always apply some fairly general rule'), or merely question-begging ('Never break a rule forbidding an action which really is absolutely impermissible'), then it must allow us to raise questions of the form: 'Need we be deterred by the dangers attendant on suspending *this* rule in favour of *this* more specific rule in *this* kind of situation?' The answer will depend upon what the challenged general rule is, what the proposed substitute for it is, the intelligence and character of the agent, and the likelihood that his breaking the rule (if it comes to that) would become generally known and, if known, demoralizing to others. These matters need not be so complex as to defeat finite intelligence, or so primrose-strewn that fallen man dare not venture among them. Furthermore, they can themselves be embodied in rules carefully formulated in advance—meta-rules about the kinds of situation in which this or that ground-level general rule may be suspended in favour of this or that more specific one.

Here is a possible case. A certain obstetrician accepts the rule, 'Do not kill innocent humans', as applicable in every kind of situation he has thought of except the kind described in my opening paragraph. He wants a rule for this kind too, as a shield against the confusions, temptations and pressures of the concrete situation; and after reflection he adopts the following: 'If the child is not hydrocephalic it is not to be killed. If it is hydrocephalic it is to be killed unless either (a) the woman is bound to die within a month anyway, or (b) the woman has

---

[7] For a gesture in this direction, see St. John-Stevas, *op. cit.*, pp. 14–16. See also McFadden, *op. cit.*, p. 133.

no other children under eighteen and she is known to be a chronic acute depressive. If (a) or (b) or both are true, the child is not to be killed.'

By preferring this rule to the more general one for instances of the obstetrical example, the obstetrician is not rendering it likely that in some situations he will flounder around not knowing what rule about killing to apply. For he has a clear enough meta-rule: 'If the only way to save a woman's life is to kill the child she is bearing, apply this rule . . . ; otherwise apply the rule: Do not kill innocent humans.'

The obstetrician is not satisfied with his ground-level rule for instances of the obstetrical example, and he hopes to be able to improve it. Still, he is resigned to his rule's ignoring various matters which, though they are relevant to what the ideally right action would be, would involve him in the dangers of over-specificity mentioned above. 'Is the woman a potential murderess or the child a mongol?'—the answers are probably unobtainable. 'In what ways would the woman's death represent a real loss to others?'—the answer, even if discoverable, could be so complex as to elude any manageable rule. 'Would either course of action bring the medical profession into undeserved but seriously damaging disrepute?'—it would be too easy for that to be unconsciously conflated with the question of which course would best further the obstetrician's own career. 'Would the child, if delivered alive, be especially helpful to students of hydrocephalus?'—asking that could be the first step on a downward path: by allowing one woman to die partly because her child will be medically interesting if alive, even an uncorrupt man may ease the way towards allowing some other woman to die partly because *she* will be medically interesting when dead.

Although he pays heed—neurotically pays far too much heed—to the conservative's warnings against over-specificity, this obstetrician arrives at a conclusion quite different from the conservative's. That is the crux. The conservative who warns against the dangers of over-specificity is trying to find a consequentialist basis for his whole position. Unlike the 'protective-coloration gambit' discussed earlier, this is legitimate enough in itself; but it simply does not yield the conservative position on the matter under discussion. For it to do so, the conservative would have to show that our obstetrician's more specific rule is *too* dangerous in the ways mentioned above; and he would have to do this without applying danger-inflating standards which would commit him also to condemning as too dangerous the suspension of the general rule: 'Never leave a bucket in a hall-way.' He may object: 'Buckets in hall-ways are not important enough to provide a fair analogy. Where something as grave as killing is in question, we should be especially sensitive to the dangers of suspending a general rule.' But then when something as grave as letting someone die is involved in applying the rule, we should be especially reluctant to accept, without good empirical evidence, popular clichés about the dangers of suspending general rules. The two points cancel out.

Of course, there are these dangers, and we should guard against them. To assess them at all precisely, though, would require more than we know of sociology, psychology and the philosophy of mind; and so our guarding against them can consist only in our keeping the urge towards specificity under some restraint, our remembering that in this matter it is not always true that the sky is the limit. The conservative who hopes to secure his position by pointing out these dangers must claim that he *can* assess them, and can discover in them a simple, sweeping pattern which picks out a certain list of general rules as the ones which ought never to be suspended by anyone in any circumstances. No-one would explicitly make so preposterous a claim.

'So you do at any rate retreat from act- to rule-utilitarianism?' No. Rule-utilitarianism can be presented (1) as a quasi-mystical doctrine about the importance of rule-following '*per se*', or (2) as a doctrine about the importance of rule-following because of what rule-following empirically *is*, because of what happens when people follow rules and what happens when they don't. In version (1), rule-utilitarianism is a distinct doctrine which has nothing to recommend it. In version (2), it is just part of a thorough act-utilitarianism. (In most actual presentations, there is a cloudy attempt to combine (2)'s reasonableness with (1)'s rejection of act-utilitarianism.) In this section I have been discussing what the consequences might be, for myself or others, of my suspending or breaking a given general rule. These are among, not additional to, the consequential factors whose relevance I have been urging all through the paper. There has been no retreat.

Conclusion

Principles of the form: 'It would always be wrong to . . . , whatever the consequences of not doing so' seem defensible because the action/consequence distinction does often have a certain kind of moral significance. But in proportion as a situation gives real work to the rider '. . . whatever the consequences of not doing so', in proportion as it puts pressure on this rider, in proportion as the 'consequences of not doing so' give some moral reason for 'doing so'—to that extent the action/consequence distinction lacks moral significance in that situation. The obstetrical example is just an extreme case: there the rider serves to dismiss the entire moral case against applying the principle; and, proportionately, the action/consequence distinction carries no moral weight at all.

The phenomenon of conservatism, then, can be explained as follows. The conservative naturally thinks that the action/consequence distinction has great moral significance because of its frequent connexion with differences concerning (a) expectation, (b) inevitability, (c) intention and (d) independently formed moral judgments. He then encounters cases like the obstetrical example, where (a)–(d) are irrelevant but where the distinction can still be applied because of facts about (e) immediacy and (f) acting/refraining. Failing to see that in these cases the distinction has lost absolutely all its moral bite, and perhaps encouraged by a mistake about 'rule-following *per se*', he still applies his principle in the usual way. Those who do not follow him in this he finds lax or opportunist or corrupt; and many of them half agree, by conceding to his position a certain hard and unfeeling uprightness. Both are wrong. Conservatism, when it is not mere obedience, is mere muddle.

XV

A Note on Mr. Bennett

G. E. M. Anscombe

The nerve of Mr. Bennett's argument is that if A results from your not doing B, then A results from whatever you do instead of doing B.[1] While there may be much to be said for this view, still it does not seem right on the face of it.

[1] ' "Whatever the Consequences" ', *Analysis*, January 1966, p. 96. [See pp. 175ff. this volume.—Ed.]

XVI

On Moral Absolutism

James Rachels

I

Most philosophers would reject out of hand the notion of an inviolable moral rule, for, it would be said, every rule has its exceptions. Generally speaking, one ought not to lie; but circumstances might arise in which lying is justified. Generally speaking, one ought not to kill another human being; but circumstances might arise in which even killing is justified. And so on. The worse the action in question, the rarer the circumstances in which it would be justified. Some actions might be so bad that in fact no such desperate circumstances ever arise; however, even in these extreme cases such circumstances could be imagined.

The circumstances in which generally bad actions are nevertheless justified, it is said, are those in which the consequences of not doing the action are worse than the evil involved in the action itself; or, alternatively, in which the consequences are so good as to outweigh the evil of the action. Then we are justified in doing the bad act—in violating the moral rule prohibiting actions of that sort—by the expectation of redeeming consequences. Now Miss Anscombe protests that philosophers who defend this sort of view—'every single English academic moral philosopher since Sidgwick,' she says—are assuming a great deal more than they ought:

> It is noticeable that none of these philosophers displays any consciousness that there is such an ethic, which he is contradicting: it is pretty well taken for obvious among them that a prohibition such as that on murder does not operate in the face of some consequences. But of course the strictness of the prohibition has as its point *that you are not to be tempted by fear or hope of consequences.*[1]

[1] G. E. M. Anscombe, 'Modern Moral Philosophy,' *Philosophy*, vol. 33 (1958), p. 10.

She approves of such prohibitions: there are 'certain things' that should be prohibited 'simply in virtue of their description as such-and-such identifiable kinds of action, regardless of any further consequences.' I shall call this kind of view *moral absolutism*.

Moral absolutists might disagree on which actions are sufficiently bad so that they should be prohibited altogether. Miss Anscombe, in the passage just quoted, mentions murder as an example. However, someone might agree that *some* kinds of actions should be absolutely prohibited, but disagree that murder is one of them. He might say that the evil must be greater than that of simple murder, and offer as an alternative example genocide. Others might think that the standard of evil could be set much lower, and that the absolute prohibitions could be extended to such lesser sins as lying, breaking one's promises, and so forth. Thus absolutists may disagree among themselves as to which prohibitions are to be taken as inviolable; and the plausibility of the absolutist position may vary considerably according to which version we are considering.

The most extreme form of moral absolutism would be the view that *every* sort of bad action—i.e., every sort of action that is *prima facie* objectionable just in virtue of the kind of action is—should be utterly prohibited. On this view, *no* general prohibition could ever be set aside by considerations as to consequences. If an act, considered merely as the kind of action it is, is a bad sort of thing to do, then it should never be done, and that's that. A good man, recognizing that his action would be an act of a bad type, will deliberate no further; he will not allow himself 'to be tempted by fear or hope of consequences.'

It is not clear whether Miss Anscombe would advocate this strongest possible version of the absolutist position. There is, however, at least one philosopher who is unequivocal in its advocacy, namely P. T. Geach.[2] Geach argues for the principle 'We must not do evil that good may come' as applicable to all actions that are, considered in themselves, evil; 'that good may come,' he says, is never a justification for doing them (p. 120). Lying, for example, is usually considered bad, but not so bad that on occasion it is not justified. But in saying this, we are admitting that lying is a bad sort of action; so, for Geach, lying is out: it is not even to be considered, no matter how extreme the circumstances and no matter what the results of lying would be in the particular case at hand. The moral decision of what to do will be settled when the action has been seen to fall under the prohibition against lying—'That would be lying, so I can't do it'—and no further deliberation is necessary or even proper. The same could be said for

---

[2] P. T. Geach, *God and the Soul* (London, 1969). All parenthetical references in the text will be to the ninth essay in this book, 'The Moral Law and the Law of God.' [See pp. 63ff. this volume.—Ed.]

any sort of objectionable act. In this paper I shall concentrate on Geach's brand of absolutism, not because it is the most plausible (it is not), but because it is the most interesting and because it puts the issues in sharpest focus.

In order to state more precisely what is at issue here, we need an example. An unabashedly maudlin example will put the question most clearly: Marigold Smith, a sweet and innocent young girl, asks us how we like her new dress, which seems to us perfectly awful. But we know that she is very sensitive and that, being poor, this is the only new dress she will have for some time to come. Do we lie and say we like the dress, making her happy, or do we tell the truth and make her miserable? The Geachean absolutist would say that the right thing to do is obviously to tell the truth, because we mustn't lie—do that sort of thing—under any circumstances. Others might say that the right thing to do is to lie, on the grounds that sparing Marigold's feelings is simply more important than telling the truth. Now if we make a list of the reasons for and against telling this particular lie, it will look like this:

A. Reasons for the action
   1. *Reasons having to do with the intrinsic character of the action*: in this case there are none.
   2. *Reasons having to do with the consequences of the action*: it would save the girl from misery and make her happy.

B. Reasons against the action
   1. *Reasons having to do with the intrinsic character of the action*: it would be an act of lying.
   2. *Reasons having to do with the consequences of the action*: in this case there are none.

A similar list could be made for any action, and I take it that every reason which anyone would want to urge for or against the action could be classified under one of these four headings.

We can distinguish at least five possible views here.[3]

(*1*) It might be held that, in assessing an action, only its consequences are of any importance; the intrinsic character of the action itself counts for nothing at all. Therefore, every reason for or against an action will be classified under either A2 or B2. This view has the consequence, which many philosophers have found objectionable, that if there is a situation in which the effects of lying are exactly the same as the effects of truthfulness, then there is nothing to choose between the two options—one is equally as good as the other. This would be the most extreme form of consequentialism.

[3] This classification presupposes a clear distinction between actions and consequences; whether this supposition is justified is taken up in the final section below.

(*2*) A less extreme form of consequentialism would be the view that the intrinsic character of the act has some importance, but not enough to overcome any contrary considerations as to consequences. In other words, reasons of type A2 will always outweigh reasons of type B1, and reasons of type B2 will always outweigh reasons of type A1. If there are reasons of types A2 and B2 present in a single case, then the decision of what to do will depend on which of these are stronger. Only if these considerations are of equal weight should we bring reasons of types A1 or B1 into our deliberations. On this view, in the case where the effects of lying are just the same as the effects of telling the truth, we can conclude that we should tell the truth.

(*3*) On the other side, it could be said that only the intrinsic character of the action has any importance, and that consequences never matter at all; i.e., that the only reasons for or against any action are those found under A1 or B1. On this view, if an action considered in itself is not bad, but a consequence of the action would be the destruction of the world, there would nonetheless be no reason to avoid doing it!

(*4*) A second anti-consequentialist position would be the view that the consequences of an act have some importance, but not enough to justify doing the act when there are reasons against it having to do with its intrinsic character. That is, reasons of type B1 always override reasons of type A2; and similarly, reasons of type A1 always override reasons of type B2.

(*5*) Finally, there is what we might call the 'compromise' view, the view that both the intrinsic character of the action and its consequences are important for determining whether it ought to be done; and that the decision of which overrides which is a matter for judicious assessment in each case. On this view, no general formula such as those proposed in (*1*)–(*4*) is possible—each case must be judged on its own merits.

Now both (*1*) and (*2*) are versions of consequentialism that have been defended by utilitarians; indeed, it seems to me necessary to interpret utilitarianism along these lines if utilitarianism is not to lose its *raison d'être* and collapse into some version of the compromise view. (*3*) is an utterly insane view which no one has ever defended, so far as I know; I include it only to preserve the symmetry of the classification. (*4*) seems to be Geach's view, and also Kant's view; and (*5*) is the view of e.g. Sir David Ross. As crude as this classification may be, I think it shows the usual distinction between utilitarians and deontologists to be even cruder: to lump e.g. Kant and Ross together as 'deontologists' is to conceal the really crucial difference between them, that Ross was willing to allow an importance to consequences which Kant was not willing to allow.

II

Geach's defense of absolutism is embedded in his discussion of the relevance of religious belief to ethics. Geach rejects the widely-held view that belief in God has no logical consequences for one's moral code; the argument of Plato's *Euthyphro*, he says, is only a piece of sophistry. For the religious believer, an absolutist code is mandatory; whereas the nonbeliever will have no reason to adopt such a code. The non-believer will be at best a compromiser, or if he is especially misguided, a consequentialist. But belief in God does make a difference: the believer will be an absolutist. To prove this Geach offers an argument with premises taken from natural theology. He does not argue whether these premises are true (though he clearly believes them to be true); the point is only that *if* one accepts these premises, then it is reasonable to adopt the view of moral absolutism. The argument goes as follows (p. 124):

Unlike other creatures he has made, God has created men to be voluntary agents. Given this, it is reasonable to think that God will 'direct men to his own ends' by 'command and counsel' as well as foisting his will on them 'willy-nilly'. Now all rational men know that some sorts of actions are generally undesirable, e.g., lying. Following the principles of natural theology, such knowledge is to be regarded as knowledge of divine prohibitions. The question is then whether these divine commands are to be taken as absolute rules, holding without exception, or only as guidelines to be applied at man's discretion. If the latter, then it is puzzling that God has left men incompetent to judge when they should follow the rules and when they should not. Geach asks rhetorically, 'But what man is competent judge in his own cause, to make exception in a particular case? Even apart from bias, our knowledge of the present relevant circumstances is grossly fallible; still more, our foresight of the future'. This incompetence would not matter so much if God were to provide individual guidance for each man in each case—a kind of continual personal revelation—but obviously this does not happen for all of us. But if we do not know when a rule applies and when it does not, then we might as well not have the rule. Therefore, if God's commands are not absolute, then he has in fact left us without any directions whatever. 'So unless the rational knowledge that these practices are *generally undesirable* is itself a promulgation of the Divine law *absolutely forbidding* such practices, God has left most men without any promulgation of commands to them on these matters at all: which, on the theological premises I am assuming, is absurd.' The situation, then, is this: although everyone can know that some practices are generally undesirable, only the believer can know that these practices are absolutely forbidden. It is in this way that knowledge of God makes a difference to one's moral code.

The first thing to notice about this argument is that it does have the exceedingly strong conclusion which I have already described: if it is valid, it shows the *every* practice which is correctly thought to be generally undesirable is in fact absolutely forbidden—thus, there *are no* practices that are merely 'generally undesirable'.

The second thing to notice is that the theological premises are in fact unnecessary to the argument. They do no work in generating the conclusion. As I read the argument, these are the steps involved (here retaining the theological references):

(*1*) We do in fact possess knowledge that certain sorts of actions are generally undesirable. According to natural theology, this knowledge is understood as a promulgation of divine commands.

(*2*) Either God forbids us to do these actions in all cases, or he permits exceptions in some special cases.

(*3*) Since the actions in question are known to be generally undesirable, we would be justified in doing them in special cases only if we knew that a greater good would be accomplished.

(*4*) However, due to our incorrigible ignorance and prejudice, we cannot judge in particular cases whether a greater good would be accomplished. Moreover, this deficiency is not made good by divine revelation.

(*5*) Therefore, we are never justified in doing these acts. God's commands are absolute prohibitions.

Now the argument may be secularized as follows, deleting the theological trappings, without the loss of anything important:

(*6*) We do in fact possess knowledge that certain sorts of actions are generally undesirable.

(*7*) Generally undesirable actions should either be avoided in all cases, or done in some special cases only as circumstances require.

(*8*) Since the actions in question are known to be generally undesirable, we would be justified in doing them in special cases only if we knew that a greater good would be accomplished.

(*9*) However, due to our incorrigible ignorance and prejudice, we cannot judge in particular cases whether a greater good would be accomplished.

(*10*) Therefore, we are never justified in doing these acts.[4]

[4] This form of the argument is unnecessarily cumbersome; I give it in this form only to retain the parallel with Geach's version. A simpler formulation would be: If

If I am right, then Geach is mistaken in thinking that this argument provides the believer with reasons unavailable to the nonbeliever for accepting an absolutist code. If the argument *(1)*–*(5)* is conclusive for the believer, then the argument *(6)*–*(10)* is equally conclusive for the nonbeliever. There is then no difference in their respective situations; if one should be an absolutist on these grounds, so should the other. And in assessing the argument, there is no need to consider the merits (or demerits) of the theological trappings, since they are logically idle.

The crucial move in this argument is the appeal to people's incompetence in judging when to make exceptions to moral rules. This is not an unfamiliar move in the dispute between absolutists and consequentialists. The absolutist argues that in making actual choices we do not know for certain exactly what our circumstances are or what the effects of our action will be; we are condemned to act in situations which at best we only partially understand. Kant, for example, in arguing that one ought never to lie, emphasizes that even the well-intentioned liar cannot be certain of the consequences which he seeks. He proposes the case of a man being asked directions by a scoundrel intent on murder:

> After you have honestly answered the murderer's question as to whether his intended victim is at home, it may be that he has slipped out so that he does not come in the way of the murderer, and thus that the murder may not be committed. But if you had lied and said he was not at home when he had really gone out without your knowing it, and if the murderer had then met him as he went away and murdered him, you might justly be accused as the cause of his death. For if you had told the truth as far as you knew it, perhaps the murderer might have been apprehended by the neighbors while he searched the house and thus the deed might have been prevented. . . .
>
> To be truthful (honest) in all deliberations, therefore, is a sacred and absolutely commanding decree of reason, limited by no expediency.[5]

Add to this fallibility the fact that men are inescapably prejudiced to their own interests, and the situation is made even worse. The upshot

---

an action is a generally bad sort of thing to do, then we would be justified in doing it only if we know that a greater good would be accomplished. But, due to ignorance and prejudice, we can never know that a greater good will be accomplished; therefore, if an action is a generally bad sort of thing to do, we are never justified in doing it.

[5] Immanuel Kant, 'On a Supposed Right to Lie from Altruistic Motives,' translated by Lewis White Beck in *Kant's Critique of Practical Reason and Other Writings in Moral Philosophy* (Chicago, 1949), p. 348. [See p. 17 this volume.—Ed.] Compare Kant's remarks in *The Metaphysical Principles of Morals*, Part II of *The Metaphysics of Morals*, translated by James Ellington (Indianapolis, 1964), pp. 92–93. Sartre presents a case very much like the one described by Kant in his short story 'The Wall,' translated by Lloyd Alexander, in Jean-Paul Sartre, *Intimacy and Other Stories* (New York, 1948).

is that consequentialism (and *a fortiori* the compromise view) is unworkable because we cannot accurately gauge in advance the actual results of any act. The alternative, it is said, is an arrangement in which we do not even try to judge individual cases, but only 'do our duty' according to a set of predetermined rules.

I want to reject this argument, but not too hastily, for even though it is ultimately unsatisfactory it contains the germ of an important truth. In order to uncover this truth, it will be helpful to examine the relation between acting from a consideration of reasons and acting on principles.

It is a widely-held view, propounded by Kant and popularized more recently by Hare, that every rational decision of what to do must be based on principles. In *The Language of Morals*[6] Hare argues that giving reasons for a choice is the same thing as appealing to principles. Reasons are, by their very nature, universal; if some consideration is a reason in one case, it follows logically that it is also a reason in all relevantly similar cases. It would be inconsistent for someone to say in one case 'I won't do that because it would be lying' and in another case to put no special weight on the fact that a contemplated action would involve lying. Therefore, the argument goes, to accept 'It would be lying' as a reason for not doing an action on a particular occasion is to commit oneself to the principle 'Do not lie' as valid for all such occasions.

This argument, I think, is the source of a highly misleading view of the role of principles in practical decision-making. It is one thing to accept a reason, and quite another to accept a principle. To accept 'It would be lying' as a reason against doing a certain action does not rule out the possibility that one might do the action anyway, since there might be weightier reasons in its favor. But if we accept the principle 'Do not lie' as applicable in this situation, then we are bound not to do the action. This is because reasons are things that are to be *taken into account*, given weight in one's deliberations, etc., whereas principles are things that are to be *acted on*. When we make an exception to a principle, we say that the principle *does not apply* in that case—it is set aside, abandoned, not acted on, for the sake of a supposedly greater good. But the abandonment of the principle does not necessarily mean that the agent has not given the corresponding reason due consideration; he may have abandoned the principle which would forbid the action, but without ignoring any of the reasons against it.

Hare denies that principles are abandoned in these cases. Rather, he says, they are *modified*. 'Suppose then that we find ourselves in

[6] R. M. Hare, *The Language of Morals* (Oxford, 1952), I.4.2. For a similar identification of reasons and principles, see William K. Frankena, *Ethics* (Englewood Cliffs, 1963), pp. 22–23.

circumstances which fall under the principle, but which have certain other peculiar features, not met before, which make us ask 'Is the principle really intended to cover cases like this, or is it incompletely specified—is there here a case belonging to a class which should be treated as exceptional?' . . . If we decide that this should be an exception, we thereby modify the principle by laying down an exception to it.'[7] Thus, if I subscribe to the principle 'Do not lie', and I encounter circumstances ϕ in which lying seems the thing to do, then I must conclude that I had not formulated the principle correctly. The improved formulation would, presumably, be 'Do not lie except in circumstances ϕ'.

There are serious difficulties with this. If we meet circumstances ψ, in which lying also seems the thing to do, the principle would become 'Do not lie except in circumstances ϕ and ψ'. Then if we meet circumstances χ in which lying again seems the thing to do, the principle becomes 'Do not lie except in circumstances ϕ, ψ, and χ'—and so on, and so on. The original principle, which seemed to give clear-cut instructions for what to do, now begins to look suspiciously like 'Do not lie except when it's all right to lie'. It may well be asked whether having such an open-ended principle is any different than having no principle at all—since we can never be sure if the amendments are all in, we must make a fresh choice in each case about whether the principle 'applies' as it stands or whether yet another qualification is to be attached. What we are actually doing is judging each case on its own merits, and then modifying the 'principle' to bring it into line.

In *Freedom and Reason*[8] Hare makes a somewhat different suggestion. There he says that, in making a rational choice, the only principle to which one is committing oneself is the principle that *In all cases precisely like the one at hand the same sort of action is to be done.* Thus the foregoing difficulty is circumvented; there will be no question of whether the principle 'applies' in other cases unless they are exactly like the original case, and then, of course, it does apply. But it could be argued that 'principles' this specific really don't deserve the name. If someone proposed to give us his principles about lying, and proceeded to give us a catalogue of very definite sorts of situations in which he would lie, and equally definite sorts of situations in which he would be truthful, we would probably conclude that he does not know what the word means. On this understanding of 'principles' we are not in the business of applying fixed standards to new cases as we meet them; rather, we are making new decisions for each case. Therefore, when we invoke principles to justify such decisions, it is mere ration-

[7] *The Language of Morals*, I.4.3.

[8] R. M. Hare, *Freedom and Reason* (Oxford, 1963), II.7.6.

alization; for we are first deciding on the merits of each case what is to be done, and then we are formulating the principle *ad hoc*. This is certainly not what is ordinarily meant by 'acting on principle'.

In light of these rather obvious difficulties, why should anyone want to insist that every rational decision is necessarily made on the basis of a principle? The only motive, so far as I can see, is to preserve the universal applicability of reasons. But surely we can do that simply by insisting that whatever considerations are given weight in one case must also be given weight in other cases. We need not bring in (and inevitably distort) the concept of a *principle* at all.

The difference between considering reasons and having principles is at bottom a difference between sharply contrasting styles of decision-making. The 'man of principle' is the man who insists that some things are to be done (or not done) come what may. Geach, not Hare, is right about this. Where his principles are concerned, this man tends to be stern and inflexible, as Geach says he should be: for to say 'It's a matter of principle' is a prelude to closing off debate and to closing one's mind to contrary considerations. We sometimes admire such men if they 'stick to their principles' when it means personal sacrifice on their part; but, contrary to Geach, we feel differently when such inflexibility leads to an unfeeling disregard for other people, e.g. when the 'man of principle' will not lie on a trivial matter even to spare someone otherwise needless misery, as when Marigold asks how we like her new dress. And sometimes such men are admired because they are deeply 'committed' on moral issues; the 'man of principle' is equated with the man of integrity. But this, I think, is a mistake. Integrity does not necessarily involve the acceptance of inviolable rules; it only means being true to one's own sense of right. Similarly, moral seriousness does not entail inflexibility.

The alternative style of decision-making—acting from a consideration of reasons as opposed to acting on fixed principles—is represented by the man who makes his decisions by considering the reasons in each case, by weighing off one consideration against another, and deciding what action seems required in the particular case at hand. Such a man must be consistent, of course, i.e., he must not give considerations weight in one case that he will not give them in other cases; and he must avoid prejudice and self-deception as best he can. He may have principles, to be sure, but he will be ready to abandon them if the situation demands it. And if my arguments have been sound, he will be doing just that—*abandoning* the principle; he may not abandon it lightly, but he will be abandoning it rather than modifying it or what-have-you.

On Geach's view this sort of deliberation is impossible, because no one has the mental resources to judge the merits of individual cases.

Therefore, the wise man, recognizing his own limitations, will be a 'man of principle'. I said that Geach's argument, though unsatisfactory in the end, contains the germ of an important truth. Now I can state what that truth is: it is that there *is* a connection between the need for principles and uncertainty as to the effects of one's action. In making practical decisions about what to do, we need principles most in just those cases in which the likely effects of our action are least clear. If I must reply to a question put to me in circumstances in which I cannot judge what will come of my answer, I may have to say to myself 'Well, honesty is the best policy' and tell the truth because that principle is the only guide I have. Even if I am no absolutist, I have no alternative but to 'act on principle' in such cases where I am in the dark as to the likely outcome of my action. And, as a practical matter, we simply don't have the time or opportunity to investigate the likely outcome of every action we perform; so we need habits of action—'principles'—to guide our everyday conduct when we cannot stop to calculate the effects of our every move. These are the cases of relative ignorance in which the need for principles is most clearly felt. But contrast the cases in which I know very well what the effects of my action will be: Marigold asks how I like her new dress, and if I tell the truth she will be miserable whereas if I lie she will be happy. Here the situation is very different; since I know what my truth-telling will bring, I do not have to rely on my 'principles' for guidance.

The point is that the role of principles in practical decision-making has been emphasized far too much. Principles are often merely things that we *fall back on* when we have no other guidance, i.e., when we cannot evaluate a particular action on its own terms due to ignorance or lack of time. These are precisely the cases in which it is reasonable to make decisions 'on principle'. So we might very well expect someone to claim that people are always incompetent to evaluate particular actions, if he wished to defend the absolutist view that moral decisions are always to be made like this. And this is just what Geach does. But there is the rub; contrary to what Geach says, it is simply false that we are always incompetent to judge particular cases. It may be that we are inevitably biased when our own interests are involved (although I see no reason to think this is so), but very often our own interests are not involved. Where is the 'interest' that warps my judgment in telling the girl that I like her new dress? If anything, it is interest in her happiness, not mine. Moreover, our 'knowledge of present circumstances' and our 'foresight of the future', while they are by no means perfect, are certainly not always 'grossly fallible' in the sense required by Geach's argument. This seems too obvious to belabor, and those inclined to scepticism will probably not be brought around by my insistence that I *do* know that the girl is poor, that this is her only new dress, and so forth.

Therefore, it seems that we are at an impasse: the absolutist must regard Marigold's misery as less important than his own truthfulness; and those who oppose him think that this is a morally unacceptable assessment of the situation. We may have reached a rock-bottom moral disagreement which is not resolvable by mere argument. The absolutist, if he is wrong, may be guilty of an unfeeling heart rather than a muddled intellect.

III

However, it may be possible to convict the absolutist not merely of lack of human feeling but of arguing from a logically incoherent position as well. The most obvious objection to moral absolutism, which I have so far not mentioned, has to do with the possibility of conflict-cases. If it is held to be absolutely wrong to do *A* in any circumstances, and also wrong to do *B* in any circumstances, then what of the case in which an agent is faced with the choice between doing *A* and *B*, when he must do something, and when there are no other alternatives open? If we can produce any convincing cases of this sort, then the absolutist view will be shown to be logically untenable.

Geach tries to close off this possibility by appealing to God's power to prevent such cases from arising:

> 'But suppose circumstances are such that observance of one Divine law, say the law against lying, involves breach of some other absolute Divine prohibition?'—If God is rational, he does not command the impossible; if God governs all events by his providence, he can see to it that circumstances in which a man is inculpably faced by a choice between forbidden acts do not occur. Of course such circumstances (with the clause 'and there is no way out' written into their description) are consistently describable; but God's providence could ensure that they do not in fact arise. Contrary to what unbelievers often say, belief in the existence of God does make a difference to what one expects to happen. (p. 128)[9]

I must admit that my Marigold Smith example is fictitious; but it will not be difficult to substitute a real-life example in its place. During the Second World War Dutch fishermen regularly smuggled Jewish refugees to England in their fishing-boats, and the following sort of situation sometimes arose. A Dutch boat, with refugees in the hold, would be stopped by a Nazi patrol-boat. The Nazi captain would call out and

[9] If Geach's previous argument were accepted, along with this, it would follow that the occurrence of such circumstances would be sufficient grounds for concluding that God does not exist (!).

ask the Dutch captain where he was bound, who was on board, and so forth. The fishermen would lie and be allowed to pass. Now it is clear that the fishermen had only two alternatives, to lie or to allow their passengers (and themselves) to be taken and shot. No third alternative was available; they could not, for example, remain silent or outrun the Nazis. This seems just the sort of case that Geachean absolutism could not handle, and it is a real case, God's power notwithstanding. However, we must not be too quick here. There are at least two rejoinders that might be attempted.

(*1*) It might be said that the fishermen's choice was not between lying and murdering, both of which are prohibited, but only between lying and not lying, only one of which is prohibited. For it would not be the fishermen who murdered the refugees, but the Nazis—and the fishermen would be responsible for having lied. So there is no conflict: the fishermen should tell the truth.

The question here is whether there is a morally relevant difference between murder and failing to save a life. Murdering and refraining from saving life are certainly different sorts of actions; in fact, it might be said that whereas murdering someone is an action, refraining from saving his life is not an action at all but only an omission of action. But surely no moral conclusion can be drawn from *this* difference; for if any action is morally required in any situation, then at least some omission is morally blameworthy, namely the omission of that required action. So we cannot say that only actions, as opposed to omissions, are blameworthy.

Again, it might be said that murder is much worse than omitting to save a life. This may be so; if Smith murders Brown while Jones watches and does nothing to stop him, it is Smith who will be taken to trial and punished, not Jones; and surely this is as it should be, for it is Smith, not Jones, who did the evil deed. But even if this is true, it does not matter here. Even if murder is worse than omitting life-saving, it does not follow that omitting life-saving is not bad and that we do not have a duty to save life whenever we can. And, while we may not think as badly of Jones as we do of Smith, we may still think quite badly of Jones.

Another retort would be that we cannot assert a general duty to save life in the same way that we can assert a general duty not to murder, because it would result in the requirement of supererogatory actions. For example, if I hear of a terrible natural disaster—say, an earthquake or flood—in some distant place, I might be able to save a life by going there and working with the relief forces. But this does not mean that I have a *duty* to do that; to do that would be 'above and beyond' the call of mere duty. I should be praised if I do it; but I cannot reasonably be damned for not doing it. However, as an argument to show that we never have an obligation to save life, this clearly will not do. While I may not be blameworthy for failing to perform actions requiring exceptional effort and sacrifice, it does not follow that I will not be blameworthy for failing to save a life when doing so would *not* require exceptional effort. A man who watches a child drown in a bathtub, and does nothing, is, if not the moral equivalent of a murderer, at least very close.

Therefore, I see no difference between the duty to save life and the duty not to murder that would aid the absolutist in explaining away the conflict-case. So this rejoinder must be judged a failure.

(*2*) The second absolutist rejoinder would go like this. If the fishermen lie, they will be doing a bad sort of action (lying) in order to achieve an admittedly good result (lives will be saved). If they tell the truth, they will be doing a good sort of action (telling the truth) but unfortunately there will be bad consequences (people will be killed). Now on absolutist grounds there is no conflict here, because it is not necessary for the fishermen to do one bad action in order to avoid doing another bad action. To be sure, there would be bad *consequences* of the good action, but that is beside the point; for the absolutist admits that sometimes there will be bad consequences of good actions—his view is simply that in these cases the good actions should be done anyway. The point is that in so far as the *actions* are concerned, the choice is simply between a good action and a bad action, between a permitted action and a forbidden action. So even though this might be a conflict-case for the compromiser, it would not be a conflict-case for the absolutist (nor, we might observe, would it be a conflict-case for the consequentialist). Therefore, even if the absolutist is charged with moral obtuseness, he cannot be charged with *logical* failings.

The question here is whether the distinction between actions and consequences can bear the burden required of it. Just why is 'lying' the name of an action while 'saving a life' is not? Certainly, if we describe the action as lying, then *under that description* it is a consequence of the action, rather than a part of the action itself, that a life is saved. But we could always describe the act to begin with as an act of saving life. Then we could say that the fishermen's choice is between truth-telling and life-saving, both of which are actions and both of which cannot be done; and then this case *would* be a conflict-case of the sort which Geach says cannot arise. In order to avoid this, and say that this is not a genuine conflict-case, the Geachean absolutist must maintain that 'saving a life', contrary to appearances, cannot be the name of an action.

In maintaining this, the absolutist would be going against one of the most universally accepted tenets of modern action-theory, *viz.*, that an action can be given many different descriptions, none of which captures the 'essence' of the action any more than the others. For example, a single action might be described in any of the following ways:

Jones moved his finger,
Jones pulled the trigger,
Jones fired the gun,
Jones shot Smith,
Jones killed Smith,
Jones started a riot,

and so on. This list illustrates what Joel Feinberg[10] felicitously calls the 'accordian effect': the description of an action can be expanded or contracted so that what was a consequence of the action under the old description becomes a part of the action itself under the new description, or vice versa. Thus, Smith's being shot is a consequence of what Jones did under the second description listed, but not under the fourth. Clearly, the absolutist cannot accept such a view of act-descriptions, because it would vitiate the whole point of 'not doing evil that good may come'—the 'good to come' could simply be written into the description of the action, making it a good sort of action rather than an evil one, and thus reversing the original judgment.[11]

What the absolutist needs is a way to freeze the accordian, so that we can firmly distinguish between actions and consequences at least for the limited purpose at hand. We might try to do this by appealing to Arthur Danto's conception of a 'basic action'.[12] An action *A* is a *basic action* of an agent *X* if and only if *A* is an action performed by *X* and there is no action *B* such that *X* does *B* and *B* causes *A*. In other words, basic actions are those that are not done by way of doing something else; they are done 'directly'. Jones' shooting Smith is not a basic action because there is another action, pulling the trigger, such that Jones does the latter action and that 'causes' (Danto's word) the former. Similarly, in the case of the fishermen confronting the Nazis, saving life is not a basic action because there is another action, lying, such that the lie causes the life to be saved. Utilizing this concept, we can interpret Geachean absolutism as the doctrine that if the performance of a basic action is, considered in itself, a bad thing to do, then that action must not be done no matter what other nonbasic actions

[10] Joel Feinberg, 'Action and Responsibility,' *Philosophy in America*, edited by Max Black (London, 1965), pp. 134–160.

[11] Cf. Andrew Oldenquist, 'Rules and Consequences,' *Mind*, vol. 75 (1966), pp. 180–192. As Oldenquist points out, if this line of criticism is correct, then *no* ethical theory which depends on the act-consequence distinction is sound.

[12] Arthur Danto, 'What We Can Do,' *The Journal of Philosophy*, vol. 60 (1963), pp. 435–445; and 'Basic Actions,' *American Philosophical Quarterly*, vol. 2 (1965), pp. 141–148.

may be done by way of it. This interpretation would at least have the advantage of extricating the absolutist from the pinch of Feinberg's accordian.

But unfortunately, this move creates other, equally serious, difficulties for the absolutist. The only really clear examples of basic actions are simple bodily movements—blinking one's eyes, moving one's arms, kicking one's legs, and things like that. Obviously none of these are in themselves good or evil sorts of things to do, and it would be absurd to make them the objects of absolute prohibitions. On the other hand, the actions which the absolutists are most anxious to prohibit are clearly not basic actions, e.g. 'procuring the judicial execution of the innocent,' which is a favorite example of both Geach and Anscombe. So, on this interpretation, absolutism would be such a clearly absurd view that it would attract no serious proponents.

There are, of course, other arbitrary points at which we might try to freeze the accordian, but none of them is sufficient to salvage the absolutist's position. It might be suggested, for example, that the act-consequence distinction is to be made in terms of the agent's *expectations*: the description of the act proper will include the upshots which he expects to bring about, while the consequences will consist in the unexpected upshots. Not only is this completely counter-intuitive (this is not so important in itself, for now the distinction is a purely technical one that is purported to be important for moral philosophy even if it is not reflected by our ordinary understanding of 'actions' and 'consequences'); it gives no assistance to the absolutist. For since the fishermen do expect their lying to save life (that is why they do it), their lying should on this reading of the distinction be described as an act of saving life.

Again, it might be suggested that the distinction be marked in terms of the agent's *aims, wants*, or *intentions*. The action is to be described by reference to what the agent aims, wants, or intends to accomplish, while other results, even though they are expected, are to be put down as consequences. This is somewhat more plausible than the previous suggestion, but it is clearly of no more help to the absolutist. For on this way of drawing the distinction, the fishermen's lying should also be described as an act of saving life, since that is what they aim at, want, or intend.[13]

The upshot of all this is that we have found no way for the absolutist to accommodate the conflict-cases. And, failing a way of treating these

---

[13] For a much more detailed treatment of various ways of marking the act-consequence distinction, which also supports the conclusion that none of the available ways is sufficient for absolutist purposes, see Jonathan Bennett, ' "Whatever the Consequences",' *Analysis*, vol. 26 (1966), pp. 83–102. [See pp. 175ff. this volume.—Ed.]

cases, absolutism stands convicted of logical as well as moral shortcomings.

The conflict-cases inevitably push us toward what I have called the compromise view. I do not particularly like the label—I have used it only because I could think of none that I liked any better—because it suggests that this is a position to which we retreat only after the other positions have been found untenable. But I do not think this is so: the 'compromise' view strikes me as *prima facie* the most plausible from the outset. On this view, both the intrinsic character of the act and its consequences are important, so that the difficulty of making a firm act-consequence distinction is no embarrassment. Making a moral decision is seen as a matter of weighing the relevant considerations, balancing off the pros and cons, and, in the words of Bishop Butler, seeing what course of action 'sits most easy on the mind'. Moral judgments will have to be made one at a time as the cases arise, for one of the results of abandoning absolutism is that we are deprived of any easy mechanical way of making such decisions. But this seems to me to accurately reflect the moral intuitions of most thoughtful people, including 'every single English academic moral philosopher since Sidgwick,' and to be a virtue, not a vice, of the compromise view.

XVII

War and Massacre

Thomas Nagel

From the apathetic reaction to atrocities committed in Vietnam by the United States and its allies, one may conclude that moral restrictions on the conduct of war command almost as little sympathy among the general public as they do among those charged with the formations of U.S. military policy.[1] Even when restrictions on the conduct of warfare are defended, it is usually on legal grounds alone: their moral basis is often poorly understood. I wish to argue that certain restrictions are neither arbitrary nor merely conventional, and that their validity does not depend simply on their usefulness. There is, in other words, a moral basis for the rules of war, even though the conventions now officially in force are far from giving it perfect expression.

I

No elaborate moral theory is required to account for what is wrong in cases like the Mylai massacre, since it did not serve, and was not intended to serve, any strategic purpose. Moreover, if the participation of the United States in the Indo-Chinese war is entirely wrong to begin with, then that engagement is incapable of providing a justification for *any* measures taken in its pursuit—not only for the measures which are atrocities in every war, however just its aims.

But this war has revealed attitudes of a more general kind, which influenced the conduct of earlier wars as well. After it has ended, we shall still be faced with the problem of how warfare may be conducted,

[1] This essay was completed in 1971. Direct U.S. military involvement in the Vietnam War lasted from 1961 to 1973. Hence the present tense.

and the attitudes that have resulted in the specific conduct of this war will not have disappeared. Moreover, similar problems can arise in wars or rebellions fought for very different reasons, and against very different opponents. It is not easy to keep a firm grip on the idea of what is not permissible in warfare, because while some military actions are obvious atrocities, other cases are more difficult to assess, and the general principles underlying these judgments remain obscure. Such obscurity can lead to the abandonment of sound intuitions in favor of criteria whose rationale may be more obvious. If such a tendency is to be resisted, it will require a better understanding of the restrictions than we now have.

I propose to discuss the most general moral problem raised by the conduct of warfare: the problem of means and ends. In one view, there are limits on what may be done even in the service of an end worth pursuing—and even when adherence to the restriction may be very costly. A person who acknowledges the force of such restrictions can find himself in acute moral dilemmas. He may believe, for example, that by torturing a prisoner he can obtain information necessary to prevent a disaster, or that by obliterating one village with bombs he can halt a campaign of terrorism. If he believes that the gains from a certain measure will clearly outweigh its costs, yet still suspects that he ought not to adopt it, then he is in a dilemma produced by the conflict between two disparate categories of moral reason: categories that may be called *utilitarian* and *absolutist*.

Utilitarianism gives primacy to a concern with what will *happen*. Absolutism gives primacy to a concern with what one is *doing*. The conflict between them arises because the alternatives we face are rarely just choices between *total outcomes*: they are also choices between alternative pathways or measures to be taken. When one of the choices is to do terrible things to another person, the problem is altered fundamentally; it is no longer merely a question of which outcome would be worse.

Few of us are completely immune to either of these types of moral intuition, though in some people, either naturally or for doctrinal reasons, one type will be dominant and the other suppressed or weak. But it is perfectly possible to feel the force of both types of reason very strongly; in that case the moral dilemma in certain situations of crisis will be acute, and it may appear that every possible course of action or inaction is unacceptable for one reason or another.

II

Although it is this dilemma that I propose to explore, most of the discussion will be devoted to its absolutist component. The utilitarian component is straightforward by comparison, and has a natural appeal to anyone who is not a complete skeptic about ethics. Utilitarianism says that one should try, either individually or through institutions, to maximize good and minimize evil (the definition of these categories need not enter into the schematic formulation of the view), and that if faced with the possibility of preventing a great evil by producing a lesser, one should choose the lesser evil. There are certainly problems with the formulation of utilitarianism, and much has been written about it, but its intent is morally transparent. Nevertheless, despite the additions and refinements, it continues to leave large portions of ethics unaccounted for. I do not suggest that some form of absolutism can account for them all, only that an examination of absolutism will lead us to see the complexity, and perhaps the incoherence, of our moral ideas.

Utilitarianism certainly justifies *some* restrictions on the conduct of warfare. There are strong utilitarian reasons for adhering to any limitation which seems natural to most people—particularly if the limitation is widely accepted already. An exceptional measure which seems to be justified by its results in a particular conflict may create a precedent with disastrous long-term effects.[2] It may even be argued that war involves violence on such a scale that it is never justified on utilitarian grounds—the consequences of refusing to go to war will never be as bad as the war itself would be, even if atrocities were not committed. Or in a *more* sophisticated vein it might be claimed that a uniform policy of never resorting to military force would do less harm in the long run, if followed consistently, than a policy of deciding each case on utilitarian grounds (even though on occasion particular applications of the pacifist policy might have worse results than a specific utilitarian decision). But I shall not consider these arguments, for my concern is with reasons of a different kind, which may remain when reasons of utility and interest fail.[3]

In the final analysis, I believe that the dilemma cannot always be resolved. While not every conflict between absolutism and utilitarianism creates an insoluble dilemma, and while it seems to me certainly right to adhere to absolutist restrictions unless the utilitarian considerations favoring violation are overpoweringly weighty and extremely

[2] Straightforward considerations of national interest often tend in the same direction: the inadvisability of using nuclear weapons seems to be overdetermined in this way.

[3] These reasons, moreover, have special importance in that they are available even to one who denies the appropriateness of utilitarian considerations in international matters. He may acknowledge limitations on what may be done to the soldiers and civilians of other countries in pursuit of his nation's military objectives, while denying that one country should in general consider the interests of nationals of other countries in determining its policies.

certain—nevertheless, when that special condition is met, it may become impossible to adhere to an absolutist position. What I shall offer, therefore, is a somewhat qualified defense of absolutism. I believe it underlies a valid and fundamental type of moral judgment—which cannot be reduced to or overridden by other principles. And while there may be other principles just as fundamental, it is particularly important not to lose confidence in our absolutist intuitions, for they are often the only barrier before the abyss of utilitarian apologetics for large-scale murder.

III

One absolutist position that creates no problems of interpretation is pacifism: the view that one may not kill another person under any circumstances, no matter what good would be achieved or evil averted thereby. The type of absolutist position that I am going to discuss is different. Pacifism draws the conflict with utilitarian considerations very starkly. But there are other views according to which violence may be undertaken, even on a large scale, in a clearly just cause, so long as certain absolute restrictions on the character and direction of that violence are observed. The line is drawn somewhat closer to the bone, but it exists.

The philosopher who has done most to advance contemporary philosophical discussion of such a view, and to explain it to those unfamiliar with its extensive treatment in Roman Catholic moral theology, is G. E. M. Anscombe. In 1958 Miss Anscombe published a pamphlet entitled *Mr. Truman's Degree*,[4] on the occasion of the award by Oxford University of an honorary doctorate to Harry Truman. The pamphlet explained why she had opposed the decision to award that degree, recounted the story of her unsuccessful opposition, and offered some reflections on the history of Truman's decision to drop atom bombs on Hiroshima and Nagasaki, and on the difference between murder and allowable killing in warfare. She pointed out that the policy

---

[4] (Privately printed.) See also her essay 'War and Murder', in *Nuclear Weapons and Christian Conscience*, ed. Walter Stein (London: The Merlin Press, 1961). [See pp. 29ff. this volume.—Ed.] The present paper is much indebted to these two essays throughout. These and related subjects are extensively treated by Paul Ramsey in *The Just War* (New York: Scribners, 1968). Among recent writings that bear on the moral problem are Jonathan Bennett, 'Whatever the Consequences', *Analysis*, XXVI, no. 3 (1966), 83–102 [See pp. 175ff. this volume.—Ed.]; and Philippa Foot, 'The Problem of Abortion and the Doctrine of the Double Effect', *Oxford Review*, V (1967), 5–15 [See pp. 147ff. this volume.—Ed.], Miss Anscombe's replies are 'A Note on Mr. Bennett', *Analysis*, XXVI, no. 3 (1966) [See p. 197 this volume.—Ed.], 208 and 'Who is Wronged?', *Oxford Review*, V (1967), 16–17 [See pp. 159ff. this volume.—Ed.]

of deliberately killing large numbers of civilians either as a means or as an end in itself did not originate with Truman, and was common practice among all parties during World War II for some time before Hiroshima. The Allied area bombings of German cities by conventional explosives included raids which killed more civilians than did the atomic attacks; the same is true of certain fire-bomb raids on Japan.

The policy of attacking the civilian population in order to induce an enemy to surrender, or to damage his morale, seems to have been widely accepted in the civilized world, and seems to be accepted still, at least if the stakes are high enough. It gives evidence of a moral conviction that the deliberate killing of noncombatants—women, children, old people—is permissible if enough can be gained by it. This follows from the more general position that any means can in principle be justified if it leads to a sufficiently worthy end. Such an attitude is evident not only in the more spectacular current weapons systems but also in the day-to-day conduct of the nonglobal war in Indo-China: the indiscriminate destructiveness of antipersonnel weapons, napalm, and aerial bombardment; cruelty to prisoners; massive relocation of civilians; destruction of crops; and so forth. An absolutist position opposes to this the view that certain acts cannot be justified no matter what the consequences. Among those acts is murder—the deliberate killing of the harmless: civilians, prisoners of war, and medical personnel.

In the present war such measures are sometimes said to be regrettable, but they are generally defended by reference to military necessity and the importance of the long-term consequences of success or failure in the war. I shall pass over the inadequacy of this consequentialist defense in its own terms. (That is the dominant form of moral criticism of the war, for it is part of what people mean when they ask, 'Is it worth it?') I am concerned rather to account for the inappropriateness of offering any defense of that kind for such actions.

Many people feel, without being able to say much more about it, that something has gone seriously wrong when certain measures are admitted into consideration in the first place. The fundamental mistake is made there, rather than at the point where the overall benefit of some monstrous measure is judged to outweigh its disadvantages, and it is adopted. An account of absolutism might help us to understand this. If it is not allowable to *do* certain things, such as killing unarmed prisoners or civilians, then no argument about what will happen if one does not do them can show that doing them would be all right.

Absolutism does not, of course, require one to ignore the consequences of one's acts. It operates as a limitation on utilitarian reasoning, not as a substitute for it. An absolutist can be expected to try to maximize good and minimize evil, so long as this does not require him to transgress an absolute prohibition like that against murder. But when such a conflict occurs, the prohibition takes complete precedence over any consideration of consequences. Some of the results of this view are clear enough. It requires us to forgo certain potentially useful military measures, such as the slaughter of hostages and prisoners or indiscriminate attempts to reduce the enemy civilian population by starvation, epidemic infectious diseases like anthrax and bubonic plague, or mass incineration. It means that we cannot deliberate on whether such measures are justified by the fact that they will avert still greater evils, for as intentional measures they cannot be justified in terms of any consequences whatever.

Someone unfamiliar with the events of this century might imagine that utilitarian arguments, or arguments of national interest, would suffice to deter measures of this sort. But it has become evident that such considerations are insufficient to prevent the adoption and employment of enormous antipopulation weapons once their use is considered a serious moral possibility. The same is true of the piecemeal wiping out of rural civilian populations in airborne antiguerrilla warfare. Once the door is opened to calculations of utility and national interest, the usual speculations about the future of freedom, peace, and economic prosperity can be brought to bear to ease the consciences of those responsible for a certain number of charred babies.

For this reason alone it is important to decide what is wrong with the frame of mind which allows such arguments to begin. But it is also important to understand absolutism in the cases where it genuinely conflicts with utility. Despite its appeal, it is a paradoxical position, for it can require that one refrain from choosing the lesser of two evils when that is the only choice one has. And it is additionally paradoxical because, unlike pacifism, it permits one to do horrible things to people in some circumstances but not in others.

IV

Before going on to say what, if anything, lies behind the position, there remain a few relatively technical matters which are best discussed at this point.

First, it is important to specify as clearly as possible the kind of thing to which absolutist prohibitions can apply. We must take seriously the proviso that they concern what we deliberately do to people. There could not, for example, without incoherence, be an absolute prohibition against *bringing about* the death of an innocent person. For one may find oneself in a situation in which, no matter what one does, some innocent people will die as a result. I do not mean just that there are cases in which someone will die no matter what one does, because one is not in a position to affect the outcome one way or the other. That, it is to be hoped, is one's relation to the deaths of most innocent people. I have in mind, rather, a case in which someone is bound to die, but who it is will depend on what one does. Sometimes these situations have natural causes, as when too few resources (medicine, lifeboats) are available to rescue everyone threatened with a certain catastrophe. Sometimes the situations are manmade, as when the only way to control a campaign of terrorism is to employ terrorist tactics against the community from which it has arisen. Whatever one does in cases such as these, some innocent people will die as a result. If the absolutist prohibition forbade doing what would result in the deaths of innocent people, it would have the consequence that in such cases nothing one could do would be morally permissible.

This problem is avoided, however, because what absolutism forbids is *doing* certain things to people, rather than bringing about certain *results*. Not everything that happens to others as a result of what one does is something that one has *done* to them. Catholic moral theology seeks to make this distinction precise in a doctrine known as the law of double effect, which asserts that there is a morally relevant distinction between bringing about or permitting the death of an innocent person deliberately, either as an end in itself or as a means, and bringing it about or permitting it as a side effect of something else one does deliberately. In the latter case, even if the outcome is foreseen, it is not murder, and does not fall under the absolute prohibition, though of course it may still be wrong for other reasons (reasons of utility, for example). Briefly, the principle states that one is sometimes permitted knowingly to bring about or permit as a side-effect of one's actions something which it would be absolutely impermissible to bring about or permit deliberately as an end or as a means. In application to war or revolution, the law of double effect permits a certain amount of civilian carnage as a side-effect of bombing munitions plants or attacking enemy soldiers. And even this is permissible only if the cost is not too great to be justified by one's objectives.

However, despite its importance and its usefulness in accounting for certain plausible moral judgments, I do not believe that the law of double effect is a generally applicable test for the consequences of an absolutist position. Its own application is not always clear, so that it introduces uncertainty where there need not be uncertainty.

In Indo-China, for example, there is a great deal of aerial bombardment, strafing, spraying of napalm, and employment of pellet- or needle-spraying antipersonnel weapons against rural villages in which guerrillas are suspected to be hiding, or from which small-arms fire has been received. The majority of those killed and wounded in these aerial attacks are reported to be women and children, even when some combatants are caught as well. However, the government regards these civilian casualties as a regrettable side-effect of what is a legitimate attack against an armed enemy.

It might be thought easy to dismiss this as sophistry: if one bombs, burns, or strafes a village containing a hundred people, twenty of whom one believes to be guerrillas, so that by killing most of them one will be statistically likely to kill most of the guerrillas, then is not one's attack on the group of one hundred a *means* of destroying the guerrillas, pure and simple? If one makes no attempt to discriminate between guerrillas and civilians, as is impossible in an aerial attack on a small village, then one cannot regard as a mere side-effect the deaths of those in the group that one would not have bothered to kill if more selective means had been available.

The difficulty is that this argument depends on one particular description of the act, and the reply might be that the means used against the guerrillas is not: killing everybody in the village—but rather: obliteration bombing of the *area* in which the twenty guerrillas are known to be located. If there are civilians in the area as well, they will be killed as a side-effect of such action.[5]

Because of casuistical problems like this, I prefer to stay with the original, unanalyzed distinction between what one does to people and what merely happens to them as a result of what one does. The law of double effect provides an approximation to that distinction in many cases, and perhaps it can be sharpened to the point where it does better than that. Certainly the original distinction itself needs clarification, particularly since some of the things we do to people involve things happening to them as a result of other things we do. In a case like the one discussed, however, it is clear that by bombing the village one slaughters and maims the civilians in it. Whereas by giving the only available medicine to one of two sufferers from a disease, one does not kill the other or deliberately allow him to die, even if he dies as a result.

The second technical point is this. The absolutist focus on actions rather than outcomes does not merely introduce a new, outstanding item into the catalogue of evils. That is, it does not say that the worst thing in the world is the deliberate murder of an innocent person. For if that were all, then one could presumably justify one such murder on the ground that it would prevent several others, or ten thousand on the ground that they would prevent a hundred thousand more. That is a familiar argument. But if this is allowable, then there is no absolute prohibition against murder after all. Absolutism requires that we *avoid* murder at all costs, not that we *prevent* it at all costs.

It would also be possible to adopt a deontological position less stringent than absolutism, without falling into utilitarianism. There are two ways in which someone might acknowledge the moral relevance of the distinction between deliberate and nondeliberate killing, without

---

[5] This counter-argument was suggested by Rogers Albritton.

being an absolutist. One would be to count murder as a specially bad item in the catalogue of evils, much worse than accidental death or nondeliberate killing. But the other would be to say that deliberately killing an innocent is impermissible unless it is the only way to prevent some very large evil (say the deaths of fifty innocent people). Call this the *threshold* at which the prohibition against murder is overridden. The position is not absolutist, obviously, but it is also not equivalent to an assignment of utilitarian disvalue to murder equal to the disvalue of the threshold. This is easily seen. If a murder had the disvalue of fifty accidental deaths, it would still be permissible on utilitarian grounds to commit a murder to prevent one other murder, plus some lesser evil like a broken arm. Worse still, we would be required on utilitarian grounds to prevent one murder even at the cost of forty-nine accidental deaths that we could otherwise have prevented. These are not in fact consequences of a deontological prohibition against murder with a threshold, because it does not say that the occurrence of a certain kind of act is a bad thing, and therefore to be prevented, but rather tells everyone to *refrain* from such acts, except under certain conditions. In fact, it is perfectly compatible with a deontological prohibition against murder to hold that, considered as an outcome, a murder has *no* more disvalue than an accidental death. While the admission of thresholds would reduce the starkness of the conflicts discussed here, I do not think it would make them disappear, or change their basic character. They would persist in the clash between any deontological requirement and utilitarian values somewhat lower than its threshold.

Finally, let me remark on a frequent criticism of absolutism that depends on a misunderstanding. It is sometimes suggested that such prohibitions depend on a kind of moral self-interest, a primary obligation to preserve one's own moral purity, to keep one's hands clean no matter what happens to the rest of the world. If this were the position, it might be exposed to the charge of self-indulgence. After all, what gives one man a right to put the purity of his soul or the cleanness of his hands above the lives or welfare of large numbers of other people? It might be argued that a public servant like Truman has no right to put himself first in that way; therefore if he is convinced that the alternatives would be worse, he must give the order to drop the bombs, and take the burden of those deaths on himself, as he must do other distasteful things for the general good.

But there are two confusions behind the view that moral self-interest underlies moral absolutism. First, it is a confusion to suggest that the need to preserve one's moral purity might be the *source* of an obligation. For if by committing murder one sacrifices one's moral purity or integrity, that can only be because there is *already* something wrong with murder. The general reason against committing murder cannot therefore be merely that it makes one an immoral person. Secondly, the notion that one might sacrifice one's moral integrity justifiably, in the service of a sufficiently worthy end, is an incoherent notion. For if one were justified in making such a sacrifice (or even morally required to make it), then one would not be sacrificing one's moral integrity by adopting that course: one would be preserving it.

Moral absolutism is not unique among moral theories in requiring each person to do what will preserve his own moral purity in all circumstances. This is equally true of utilitarianism, or of any other theory which distinguishes between right and wrong. Any theory which defines the right course of action in various circumstances and asserts that one should adopt that course, *ipso facto*, asserts that one should do what will preserve one's moral purity, simply because the right course of action *is* what will preserve one's moral purity in those circumstances. Of course utilitarianism does not assert that this is *why* one should adopt that course, but we have seen that the same is true of absolutism.

V

It is easier to dispose of false explanations of absolutism than to produce a true one. A positive account of the matter must begin with the observation that war, conflict, and aggression are relations between persons. The view that it can be wrong to consider merely the overall effect of one's action on the general welfare comes into prominence when those actions involve relations with others. A man's acts usually affect more people than he deals with directly, and those effects must naturally be considered in his decisions. But if there are special principles governing the manner in which he should *treat* people, that will require special attention to the particular persons toward whom the act is directed, rather than just to its total effect.

Absolutist restrictions in warfare appear to be of two types: restrictions on the class of persons at whom aggression or violence may be directed and restrictions on the manner of attack, given that the object falls within that class. These can be combined, however, under the principle that hostile treatment of any person must be justified in terms of something *about that person* which makes the treatment appropriate. Hostility is a personal relation, and it must be suited to its target. One consequence of this condition will be that certain persons may not be subjected to hostile treatment in war at all, since nothing about them justifies such treatment. Others will be proper objects of hostility only in certain circumstances, or when they are engaged in certain pursuits. And the appropriate manner and extent of hostile treatment will depend on what is justified by the particular case.

A coherent view of this type will hold that extremely hostile behavior toward another is compatible with treating him as a person—even perhaps as an end in himself. This is possible only if one has not automatically stopped treating him as a person as soon as one starts to fight with him. If hostile, aggressive, or combative treatment of others always violated the condition that they be treated as human beings, it would be difficult to make further distinctions on that score *within* the class of hostile actions. That point of view, on the level of international relations, leads to the position that if complete pacifism is not accepted, no holds need be barred at all, and we may slaughter and massacre to our hearts' content, if it seems advisable. Such a position is often expressed in discussions of war crimes.

But the fact is that ordinary people do not believe this about conflicts, physical or otherwise, between individuals, and there is no more reason why it should be true of conflicts between nations. There seems to be a perfectly natural conception of the distinction between fighting clean and fighting dirty. To fight dirty is to direct one's hostility or aggression not at its proper object, but at a peripheral target which may be more vulnerable, and through which the proper object can be attacked indirectly. This applies in a fist fight, an election campaign, a duel, or a philosophical argument. If the concept is general enough to apply to all these matters, it should apply to war—both to the conduct of individual soldiers and to the conduct of nations.

Suppose that you are a candidate for public office, convinced that the election of your opponent would be a disaster, that he is an unscrupulous demagogue who will serve a narrow range of interests and seriously infringe the rights of those who disagree with him; and suppose you are convinced that you cannot defeat him by conventional means. Now imagine that various unconventional means present themselves as possibilities: you possess information about his sex life which would scandalize the electorate if made public; or you learn that his wife is an alcoholic or that in his youth he was associated for a brief period with a proscribed political party, and you believe that this information could be used to blackmail him into withdrawing his candidacy; or you can have a team of your supporters flatten the tires of a crucial subset of his supporters on election day; or you are in a position to stuff the ballot boxes; or, more simply, you can have him assassinated. What is wrong with these methods, given that they will achieve an overwhelmingly desirable result?

There are, of course, many things wrong with them: some are against the law; some infringe the procedures of an electoral process to which you are presumably committed by taking part in it; very importantly, some may backfire, and it is in the interest of all political candidates to adhere to an unspoken agreement not to allow certain personal matters to intrude into a campaign. But that is not all. We have in addition the feeling that these measures, these methods of attack, are *irrelevant* to the issue between you and your opponent, that in taking them up you would not be directing yourself to that which makes him an object of your opposition. You would be directing your attack not at the true target of your hostility, but at peripheral targets that happen to be vulnerable.

The same is true of a fight or argument outside the framework of any system of regulations or law. In an altercation with a taxi driver over an excessive fare, it is inappropriate to taunt him about his accent, flatten one of his tires, or smear chewing gum on his windshield; and it remains inappropriate even if he casts aspersions on your race, politics, or religion, or dumps the contents of your suitcase into the street.[6]

The importance of such restrictions may vary with the seriousness of the case; and what is unjustifiable in one case may be justified in a more extreme one. But they all derive from a single principle: that hostility or aggression should be directed at its true object. This means both that it should be directed at the person or persons who provoke it and that it should aim more specifically at what is provocative about them. The second condition will determine what form the hostility may appropriately take.

It is evident that some idea of the relation in which one should stand to other people underlies this principle, but the idea is difficult to state. I believe it is roughly this: whatever one does to another person intentionally must be aimed at him as a subject, with the intention that he receive it as a subject. It should manifest an attitude to *him* rather than just to the situation, and he should be able to recognize it and identify himself as its object. The procedures by which such an attitude is manifested need not be addressed to the person directly. Surgery, for example, is not a form of personal confrontation but part of a medical treatment that can be offered to a patient face to face and received by him as a response to his needs and the natural outcome of an attitude toward *him*.

Hostile treatment, unlike surgery, is already addressed *to* a person, and does not take its interpersonal meaning from a wider context. But hostile acts can serve as the expression or implementation of only a limited range of attitudes to the person who is attacked. Those attitudes in turn have as objects certain real or presumed characteristics or activities of the person which are thought to justify them. When this background is absent, hostile or aggressive behavior can no longer be

---

[6] Why, on the other hand, does it seem appropriate, rather than irrelevant, to punch someone in the mouth if he insults you? The answer is that in our culture it is an insult to punch someone in the mouth, and not just an injury. This reveals, by the way, a perfectly unobjectionable sense in which convention may play a part in determining exactly what falls under an absolutist restriction and what does not. I am indebted to Robert Fogelin for this point.

intended for the reception of the victim as a subject. Instead it takes on the character of a purely bureaucratic operation. This occurs when one attacks someone who is not the true object of one's hostility—the true object may be someone else, who can be attacked through the victim; or one may not be manifesting a hostile attitude toward anyone, but merely using the easiest available path to some desired goal. One finds oneself not facing or addressing the victim at all, but operating on him—without the larger context of personal interaction that surrounds a surgical operation.

If absolutism is to defend its claim to priority over considerations of utility, it must hold that the maintenance of a direct interpersonal response to the people one deals with is a requirement which no advantages can justify one in abandoning. The requirement is absolute only if it rules out any calculation of what would justify its violation. I have said earlier that there may be circumstances so extreme that they render an absolutist position untenable. One may find then that one has no choice but to do something terrible. Nevertheless, even in such cases absolutism retains its force in that one cannot claim *justification* for the violation. It does not become *all right*.

As a tentative effort to explain this, let me try to connect absolutist limitations with the possibility of justifying *to the victim* what is being done to him. If one abandons a person in the course of rescuing several others from a fire or a sinking ship, one *could* say to him, 'You understand, I have to leave you to save the others.' Similarly, if one subjects an unwilling child to a painful surgical procedure, one can say to him, 'If you could understand, you would realize that I am doing this to help you.' One could *even* say, as one bayonets an enemy soldier, 'It's either you or me.' But one cannot really say while torturing a prisoner, 'You understand, I have to pull out your fingernails because it is absolutely essential that we have the names of your confederates'; nor can one say to the victims of Hiroshima, 'You understand, we have to incinerate you to provide the Japanese government with an incentive to surrender.'

This does not take us very far, of course, since a utilitarian would presumably be willing to offer justifications of the latter sort to his victims, in cases where he thought they were sufficient. They are really justifications to the world at large, which the victim, as a reasonable man, would be expected to appreciate. However, there seems to me something wrong with this view, for it ignores the possibility that to treat someone else horribly puts you in a special relation to him, which may have to be defended in terms of other features of your relation to him. The suggestion needs much more development; but it may help us to understand how there may be requirements which are absolute in the sense that there can be no justification for violating them. If the justification for what one did to another person had to be such that it could be offered to him specifically, rather than just to the world at large, that would be a significant source of restraint.

If the account is to be deepened, I would hope for some results along the following lines. Absolutism is associated with a view of oneself as a small being interacting with others in a large world. The justifications it requires are primarily interpersonal. Utilitarianism is associated with a view of oneself as a benevolent bureaucrat distributing such benefits as one can control to countless other beings, with whom one may have various relations or none. The justifications it requires are primarily administrative. The argument between the two moral attitudes may depend on the relative priority of these two conceptions.[7]

VI

Some of the restrictions on methods of warfare which have been adhered to from time to time are to be explained by the mutual interests of the involved parties: restrictions on weaponry, treatment of prisoners, etc. But that is not all there is to it. The conditions of directness and relevance which I have argued apply to relations of conflict and aggression apply to war as well. I have said that there are two types of absolutist restrictions on the conduct of war: those that limit the legitimate targets of hostility and those that limit its character, even when the target is acceptable. I shall say something about each of these. As will become clear, the principle I have sketched does not yield an unambiguous answer in every case.

First let us see how it implies that attacks on some people are allowed, but not attacks on others. It may seem paradoxical to assert that to fire a machine gun at someone who is throwing hand grenades at your emplacement is to treat him as a human being. Yet the relation with him is direct and straightforward.[8] The attack is aimed specifically against the threat presented by a dangerous adversary, and not against a peripheral target through which he happens to be vulnerable but which has nothing to do with that threat. For example, you might stop him by machine-gunning his wife and children, who are standing nearby, thus distracting him from his aim of blowing you up and enabling you to capture him. But if his wife and children are not

[7] Finally, I should mention a different possibility, suggested by Robert Nozick: that there is a strong general presumption against benefiting from the calamity of another, whether or not it has been deliberately inflicted for that or any other reason. This broader principle may well lend its force to the absolutist position.

[8] Marshall Cohen once remarked that, according to my view, shooting at someone establishes an I–thou relationship.

threatening your life, that would be to treat them as means with a vengeance.

This, however, is just Hiroshima on a smaller scale. One objection to weapons of mass annihilation—nuclear, thermonuclear, biological, or chemical—is that their indiscriminateness disqualifies them as direct instruments for the expression of hostile relations. In attacking the civilian population, one treats neither the military enemy nor the civilians with that minimal respect which is owed to them as human beings. This is clearly true of the direct attack on people who present no threat at all. But it is also true of the character of the attack on those who *are* threatening you, i.e., the government and military forces of the enemy. Your aggression is directed against an area of vulnerability quite distinct from any threat presented by them which you may be justified in meeting. You are taking aim at them through the mundane life and survival of their countrymen, instead of aiming at the destruction of their military capacity. And of course it does not require hydrogen bombs to commit such crimes.

This way of looking at the matter also helps us to understand the importance of the distinction between combatants and noncombatants, and the irrelevance of much of the criticism offered against its intelligibility and moral significance. According to an absolutist position, deliberate killing of the innocent is murder, and in warfare the role of the innocent is filled by noncombatants. This has been thought to raise two sorts of problems: first, the widely imagined difficulty of making a division, in modern warfare, between combatants and noncombatants; second, problems deriving from the connotation of the word 'innocence'.

Let me take up the latter question first.[9] In the absolutist position, the operative notion of innocence is not moral innocence, and it is not opposed to moral guilt. If it were, then we would be justified in killing a wicked but noncombatant hairdresser in an enemy city who supported the evil policies of his government, and unjustified in killing a morally pure conscript who was driving a tank toward us with the profoundest regrets and nothing but love in his heart. But moral innocence has very little to do with it, for in the definition of murder 'innocent' means 'currently harmless', and it is opposed not to 'guilty' but to 'doing harm'. It should be noted that such an analysis has the consequence that in war we may often be justified in killing people who do not deserve to die, and unjustified in killing people who do deserve to die, if anyone does.

So we must distinguish combatants from noncombatants on the basis of their immediate threat or harmfulness. I do not claim that the line is a sharp one, but it is not so difficult as is often supposed to place

[9] What I say on this subject derives from Anscombe.

individuals on one side of it or the other. Children are not combatants even though they may join the armed forces if they are allowed to grow up. Women are not combatants just because they bear children or offer comfort to the soldiers. More problematic are the supporting personnel, whether in or out of uniform, from drivers of munitions trucks and army cooks to civilian munitions workers and farmers. I believe they can be plausibly classified applying the condition that the prosecution of conflict must direct itself to the cause of danger, and not to what is peripheral. The threat presented by an army and its members does not consist merely in the fact that they are men, but in the fact that they are armed and are using their arms in the pursuit of certain objectives. Contributions to their arms and logistics are contributions to this threat; contributions to their mere existence as men are not. It is therefore wrong to direct an attack against those who merely serve the combatants' needs as human beings, such as farmers and food suppliers, even though survival as a human being is a necessary condition of efficient functioning as a soldier.

This brings us to the second group of restrictions: those that limit what may be done even to combatants. These limits are harder to explain clearly. Some of them may be arbitrary or conventional, and some may have to be derived from other sources; but I believe that the condition of directness and relevance in hostile relations accounts for them to a considerable extent.

Consider first a case which involves both a protected class of noncombatants and a restriction on the measures that may be used against combatants. One provision of the rules of war which is universally recognized, though it seems to be turning into a dead letter in Vietnam, is the special status of medical personnel and the wounded in warfare. It might be more efficient to shoot medical officers on sight and to let the enemy wounded die rather than be patched up to fight another day. But someone with medical insignia is supposed to be left alone and permitted to tend and retrieve the wounded. I believe this is because medical attention is a species of attention to completely general human needs, not specifically the needs of a combat soldier, and our conflict with the soldier is not with his existence as a human being.

By extending the application of this idea, one can justify prohibitions against certain particularly cruel weapons: starvation, poisoning, infectious diseases (supposing they could be inflicted on combatants only), weapons designed to maim or disfigure or torture the opponent rather than merely to stop him. It is not, I think, mere casuistry to claim that such weapons attack the men, not the soldiers. The effect of dum-dum bullets, for example, is much more extended than necessary to cope with the combat situation in which they are used. They abandon any attempt to discriminate in their effects between the combatant and the human being. For this reason the use of flamethrowers and napalm is an atrocity in all circumstances that I can imagine, whoever the target may be. Burns are both extremely painful and extremely disfiguring—far more than any other category of wound. That this well-known fact plays no (inhibiting) part in the determination of U.S. weapons policy suggests that moral sensitivity among public officials has not increased markedly since the Spanish Inquisition.[10]

Finally, the same condition of appropriateness to the true object of hostility should limit the scope of attacks on an enemy country: its economy, agriculture, transportation system, and so forth. Even if the parties to a military conflict are considered to be not armies or governments but entire nations (which is usually a grave error), that does not justify one nation in warring against every aspect or element of another nation. That is not justified in a conflict between individuals, and nations are even more complex than individuals, so the same reasons apply. Like a human being, a nation is engaged in countless other pursuits while waging war, and it is not in those respects that it is an enemy.

The burden of the argument has been that absolutism about murder has a foundation in principles governing all one's relations to other persons, whether aggressive or amiable, and that these principles and that absolutism, apply to warfare as well, with the result that certain measures are impermissible no matter what the consequences.[11] I do not mean to romanticize war. It is sufficiently utopian to suggest that when nations conflict they might rise to the level of limited barbarity that typically characterizes violent conflict between individuals, rather

---

[10] Beyond this I feel uncertain. Ordinary bullets, after all, can cause death, and nothing is more permanent than that. I am not at all sure why we are justified in trying to kill those who are trying to kill us (rather than merely in trying to stop them with force which may also result in their deaths). It is often argued that incapacitating gases are a relatively humane weapon (when not used, as in Vietnam, merely to make people easier to shoot). Perhaps the legitimacy of restrictions against them must depend on the dangers of escalation, and the great utility of maintaining *any* conventional category of restriction so long as nations are willing to adhere to it.

Let me make clear that I do not regard my argument as a defense of the moral immutability of the Hague and Geneva Conventions. Rather, I believe that they rest partly on a moral foundation, and that modifications of them should also be assessed on moral grounds.

[11] It is possible to draw a more radical conclusion, which I shall not pursue here. Perhaps the technology and organization of modern war are such as to make it impossible to wage as an acceptable form of interpersonal or even international hostility. Perhaps it is too impersonal and large-scale for that. If so, then absolutism would in practice imply pacifism, given the present state of things. On the other hand, I am skeptical about the unstated assumption that a technology dictates its own use.

than wallowing in the moral pit where they appear to have settled, surrounded by enormous arsenals.

VI

Having described the elements of the absolutist position, we must now return to the conflict between it and utilitarianism. Even if certain types of dirty tactics become acceptable when the stakes are high enough, the most serious of the prohibited acts, like murder and torture, are not just supposed to require unusually strong justification. They are supposed *never* to be done, because no quantity of resulting benefit is thought capable of *justifying* such treatment of a person.

The fact remains that when an absolutist knows or believes that the utilitarian cost of refusing to adopt a prohibited course will be very high, he may hold to his refusal to adopt it, but he will find it difficult to feel that a moral dilemma has been satisfactorily resolved. The same may be true of someone who rejects an absolutist requirement and adopts instead the course yielding the most acceptable consequences. In either case, it is possible to feel that one has acted for reasons insufficient to justify violation of the opposing principle. In situations of deadly conflict, particularly where a weaker party is threatened with annihilation or enslavement by a stronger one, the argument for resorting to atrocities can be powerful, and the dilemma acute.

There may exist principles, not yet codified, which would enable us to resolve such dilemmas. But then again there may not. We must face the pessimistic alternative that these two forms of moral intuition are not capable of being brought together into a single, coherent moral system, and that the world can present us with situations in which there is no honorable or moral course for a man to take, no course free of guilt and responsibility for evil.[12]

The idea of a moral blind alley is a perfectly intelligible one. It is possible to get into such a situation by one's own fault, and people do it all the time. If, for example, one makes two incompatible promises or commitments—becomes engaged to two people, for example—then there is no course one can take which is not wrong, for one must break

[12] In his reply to this essay ('Rules of War and Moral Reasoning', *Philosophy & Public Affairs*, I, no. 2 (Winter, 1972), 167 [See p. 253 this volume.—Ed.]), R. M. Hare pointed out the apparent discrepancy between my acceptance of such a possibility here and my earlier claim in section IV that absolutism must be formulated so as to avoid the consequence that in certain cases nothing one could do would be morally permissible. The difference is that in those cases the moral incoherence would result from the application of a single principle, whereas the dilemmas described here result from a conflict between two fundamentally different types of principle.

one's promise to at least one of them. Making a clean breast of the whole thing will not be enough to remove one's reprehensibility. The existence of such cases is not morally disturbing, however, because we feel that the situation was not unavoidable: one had to do something wrong in the first place to get into it. But what if the world itself, or someone else's actions, could face a previously innocent person with a choice between morally abominable courses of action, and leave him no way to escape with his honor? Our intuitions rebel at the idea, for we feel that the constructibility of such a case must show a contradiction in our moral views. But it is not in itself a contradiction to say that someone can do *X* or not do *X*, and that for him to take either course would be wrong. It merely contradicts the supposition that *ought* implies *can*—since presumably one ought to refrain from what is wrong, and in such a case it is impossible to do so.[13] Given the limitations on human action, it is naïve to suppose that there is a solution to every moral problem with which the world can face us. We have always known that the world is a bad place. It appears that it may be an evil place as well.

[13] This was first pointed out to me by Christopher Boorse. The point is also made in E. J. Lemmon's 'Moral Dilemmas', *Philosophical Review*, LXXI (April, 1962), 150.

XVIII

Utilitarianism and the Rules of War

R. B. Brandt

I. Nagel's Absolutism

I take Nagel* to be defending, first, the general view that certain kinds of action are, from a moral point of view, absolutely out of bounds, no matter what the circumstances; and second, a specific prohibition that applies this principle to the area of our interest. (His first thesis makes it proper to call his view "absolutist," in the sense that some general moral prohibitions do not have prima facie force only but are binding without exception, indefeasible.) Now Nagel is tentative in his espousal of these two theses, and sometimes contends only that we have some moral intuitions of this sort and that a study of these will show "the complexity, and perhaps the incoherence" of our moral ideas. Indeed, he says he is offering only a "somewhat qualified defense of absolutism," and concedes that in extreme circumstances there may be exceptions to his absolutist principles after all. Where Nagel is committed definitely is to a criticism of utilitarianism; he speaks scathingly of "the abyss of utilitarian apologetics for large-scale murder." In view of Nagel's tentativeness, I think it fair to disassociate him from the positive view I wish to criticize, although I am *calling* it Nagel's "absolutism." This positive view is, however, the only definite proposal he puts forward, and if I am to consider critically any positive antiutilitarian view in connection with Nagel's essay, it has to be this one. At any rate, this view is one that somebody *might* hold, and is well worth discussing.

The first point I wish to make is that a rule-utilitarian may quite well agree with Nagel that certain kinds of action are morally out of bounds

*["War and Massacre," *Philosophy and Public Affairs*, Vol. 1 (1972), pp. 124–44. See p. 217 this volume.—Ed.]

absolutely and no matter what the circumstances. Take, for instance, some of the rules of warfare recognized by the United States Army:

> It is especially forbidden . . . to declare that no quarter will be given. . . . It is especially forbidden . . . to kill or wound an enemy who, having laid down his arms, or having no longer means of defense, has surrendered at discretion. . . .
>
> It is especially forbidden . . . to employ arms, projectiles, or material calculated to cause unnecessary suffering. . . .
>
> The pillage of a town or place, even when taken by assault, is prohibited. . . .
>
> A commander may not put his prisoners to death because their presence retards his movements or diminishes his power of resistance by necessitating a large guard, or by reason of their consuming supplies, or because it appears certain that they will regain their liberty through the impending success of their forces. It is likewise unlawful for a commander to kill his prisoners on grounds of self-preservation, even in the case of airborne or commando operations, although the circumstances of the operation may make necessary rigorous supervision of and restraint upon the movement of prisoners of war.[1]

A rule-utilitarian is certainly in a position to say that utilitarian considerations cannot morally justify a departure from these rules; in that sense they are absolute. But he will of course also say that the moral justification of these rules lies in the fact that their acceptance and enforcement will make an important contribution to long-range utility. The rule-utilitarian, then, may take a two-level view: that in justifying the rules, utilitarian considerations are in order and nothing else is; whereas in making decisions about what to do in concrete circumstances, the rules are absolutely binding. In the rule-utilitarian view, immediate expediency is not a moral justification for infringing the rules.[2]

---

[1] Department of the Army Field Manual PM 27-10, *The Law of Land Warfare* (Department of the Army, July 1956), pp. 17, 18, 21, 35. The Manual specifically states that the rules of war may not be disregarded on grounds of "military necessity" (p. 4), since considerations of military necessity were fully taken into account in framing the rules. (All page numbers in the text refer to this publication, hereafter called the Army Manual.)

Other valuable discussions of contemporary rules of warfare are to be found in L. Oppenheim, *International Law*, ed. H. Lauterpacht, 7th edn. (New York, 1952) and in Marjorie M. Whiteman, *Digest of International Law*, esp. Vol. X (U.S. Department of State, 1963).

[2] It is conceivable that ideal rules of war would include one rule to the effect that anything is allowable, if necessary to prevent absolute catastrophe. As Oppenheim remarks, it may be that if the basic values of society are threatened nations are possibly released from all the restrictions in order to do what "they deem to be decisive for the ultimate vindication of the law of nations" (*International Law*, p. 351).

It is not clear that Nagel recognizes this sort of absolutism about "ideal" rules of war as a possible utilitarian view, but he seems to disagree with it when he claims that some moral prohibitions are entirely independent of utilitarian considerations.

What absolute rule, then, does Nagel propose? I shall formulate and criticize his proposal in a moment. But first we should note that his rule is intended to be restricted in scope; it applies only to what we "deliberately do to people." This is an important restriction. Suppose bombers are dispatched to destroy a munitions factory—surely a legitimate military target in a night raid; in fact and predictably, and from a military point of view incidentally, the bombs kill five thousand people. Is this a case of "deliberately doing" something to these people? Nagel's view here seems obscure. He rejects the law of double effect and says he prefers to "stay with the original, unanalyzed distinction between what one does to people and what merely happens to them as a result of what one does." He concedes that this distinction "needs clarification." Indeed it does. Without more clarification, Nagel is hardly giving an explicit theory. I note that the U.S. Army Manual appears to reject this distinction, and in a paragraph declaring the limitations on strategic bombing states that "loss of life and damage to property must not be out of proportion to the military advantage to be gained" (p. 19).

The absolutist principle that Nagel espouses as the basic restriction on legitimate targets and weapons is this: "hostility or aggression should be directed at its true object. This means both that it should be directed at the person or persons who provoke it and that it should aim more specifically at what is provocative about them. The second condition will determine what form the hostility may appropriately take." Now, while I find this principle reasonably clear in its application to simple two-person cases discussed by him, I find it difficult to apply in the identification of morally acceptable military operations. With some trepidation I suggest that Nagel intends it to be construed to assert something like the following for the case of military operations: "Persons may be attacked 'deliberately' only if their presence or their position prevents overpowering the military forces of the enemy in some way; and they may be attacked only in a manner that is reasonably related to the objective of disarming or disabling them." If this is what he has in mind it is still rather vague, since it does not make clear whether attacks on munitions factories are legitimate, or whether attacks on persons involved in supporting services, say, the provisioning of the army, are acceptable.

It is worth noting that a principle resembling this one might have a utilitarian justification of the kind alluded to above. But the principle standing by itself does not seem to me self-evident; nor does another principle Nagel asserts, that "the maintenance of a direct interpersonal response to the people one deals with is a requirement which no advantages can justify one in abandoning."

II. Morally Justifiable Rules as Rules Impartially Preferable

I shall now proceed to a positive account of the rules of war and of their justification. We shall have to consider several distinct questions, but the central question will be: Which of the possible rules of war are morally justifiable?

But first, what do I mean by "rules of war" or by talk of the "authoritative status" of rules of war? What I have in mind is, roughly, rules with the status that the articles of the Hague and Geneva Conventions have or have had. That is, certain rules pertaining to war are stated in formal treaties. These rules are seriously taught, as being legally binding, to officers and to some extent to enlisted men; they are recognized as legally binding restrictions on the decisions of the general staff; members of the army know that actions forbidden by these rules are contrary both to international law and to their own army's manual of rules for proper conduct; these rules are enforced seriously by the courts, either military or international; and so on. Proscriptions or prescriptions with this status I call "rules of war"; and in speaking of a rule having "authoritative status" I have this kind of force in mind. The U.S. Army Manual lists such rules; and digests of international law such as those by Whiteman and Oppenheim contain information on what such rules are and have been.

I have said that I shall offer a utilitarian answer to the question which rules of war (in the above sense) are morally justifiable. But I have also said that I shall be offering what I (following Rawls) call a *contractual* utilitarian answer. What I mean by that (the term "contractual" may be a bit misleading) is this. I accept the utilitarian answer to the question which rules of war are morally justifiable because utilitarian rules of war are the ones *rational, impartial persons would choose* (the ones they would be willing to put themselves under a contract to obey). The more basic question is, then: Which rules of war would people universally prefer to have accorded authoritative status among nations if the people deciding were rational, believed they might be involved in a war at some time, and were impartial in the sense that they were choosing behind a veil of ignorance? (It is understood that their ignorance is to be such as to prevent them from making a choice that would give them or their nation a special advantage; it would, for instance, prevent them from knowing what weaponry their country would possess were it to be at war, and from knowing whether, were war to occur, they would be on the front lines, in a factory, or in the general staff office.) In other words, the more fundamental question is: What rules would rational, impartial people, who expected their country at some time to be at war, want to have as the authoritative rules of war—particularly with respect to the permitted targets and method of attack? I suggest that the rules of war which rational, impartial persons would choose are the rules that would maximize long-range expectable utility for nations at war. In saying this I am offering a contractual utilitarian answer to the question what rules of war are morally justifiable. I am saying, then: (1) that rational, impartial persons would choose certain rules of war; (2) that I take as a basic premise ("analytic" in some sense, if you like) that a rule of war is morally justified if and only if it would be chosen by rational, impartial persons; and (3) that the rules rational, impartial persons would choose are ones which will maximize expectable long-range utility for nations at war.[3]

Nagel objects to utilitarianism and hence presumably would object to (3), but he might be agreeable to both (1) and (2). At least he seems close to these principles, since he seems to hold that an action is justified if one can justify to its victim what is being done to him. For instance, he implies that if you were to say to a prisoner, "You understand, I have to pull out your fingernails because it is absolutely essential that we have the name of your confederates" and the prisoner agreed to this as following from principles he accepts, then the torture would be justified. Nagel rather assumes that the prisoner would not agree, in an appropriate sense. In this connection we must be clearly aware of an important distinction. A judge who sentences a criminal might also be unable to persuade the criminal to want the sentence to be carried out; and if persuading him to want this were necessary for a moral justification of the criminal law, then the system of criminal justice would also be morally objectionable. We must distinguish between persuading a person to whom something horrible is about to be done to want that thing to happen or to consent to its happening at that very time and something quite different—getting him to accept, when he is rational and choosing in ignorance of his own future prospects, some general principles from which it would follow that this horrible thing should or might be done to a person in his present circumstances. I think Nagel must mean, or ought to mean, that a set of rules of war must be such as to command the assent of rational people choosing behind a veil of ignorance, *not* that a person must be got to assent at the time to his fingernails being pulled out in order to

[3] This summary statement needs much explanation, e.g., regarding the meaning of "rational." It is only a close approximation to the view I would defend, since I think it is better to substitute a more complex notion for that of impartiality or a veil of ignorance.

get information, if that act is to be justified. It may be, however, that Nagel does not agree with this distinction, since he hints at the end of his discussion that something more may be required for moral justification than I have suggested, without indicating what the addition might be. . . .

III. The Rational, Impartial Choice: Utilitarian Rules

I wish now to explain in a few words why I think rational, impartial persons would choose rules of war that would maximize expectable utility. Then—and this will occupy almost all of the present section—I shall classify the rules of war into several types, and try to show that representative rules of each type would be utility-maximizing and therefore chosen. I shall hope (although I shall not say anything explicitly about this) that the ideal rules of war, identified in this way, will coincide with the reflective intuitions of the reader. If so, I assume that this fact will commend to him the whole of what I am arguing.

I have suggested that rational persons, choosing behind a veil of ignorance but believing that their country may well be involved in a war at some time, would prefer rules of war that would maximize expectable utility, *in the circumstance that two nations are at war.* Why would they prefer such rules? About this I shall say only that if they are self-interested they will choose rules which will maximize expectable utility generally, for then their chance of coming out best will be greatest (and they do not know how especially to favor themselves); and that if they are altruistic they will again choose that set of rules, for they will want to choose rules which will maximize expectable utility generally. The rules of war, then, subject to the restriction that the rules of war may not prevent a belligerent from using all the power necessary to overcome the enemy, will be ones whose authorization will serve to maximize welfare. . . .

Which rules, then, would maximize expectable utility for nations at war? (I shall later discuss briefly whether the ideal rules would altogether forbid war as an instrument of national policy.)

First, however, we must understand why the above-mentioned restriction, guaranteeing that the rules of war will not prevent a belligerent from using all the force necessary to overcome the enemy, must be placed on the utility-maximizing rules of war. The reason for this restriction is to be found in the nature of a serious war. There are, of course, many different kinds of war. Wars differ in magnitude, in the technologies they employ, in the degree to which they mobilize resources, in the type of issue the belligerents believe to be at stake, and in many other ways as well. The difference between the Trojan War and World War II is obviously enormous. The former was a simple, small-scale affair, and the issues at stake might well have been settled by a duel between Paris and Menelaus, or Hector and Achilles, and the belligerents might not have been seriously dissatisfied with the outcome. In the case of World War II, the British thought that Hitler's Germany and its policies threatened the very basis of civilized society. The destruction of Hitler's power seemed so important to the British that they were willing to stake their existence as a nation on bringing it about. Wars have been fought for many lesser reasons: to spread a political or religious creed, to acquire territory or wealth, to obtain an outlet to the sea, or to become established as a world power. Wars may be fought with mercenaries, or primarily by the contribution of equipment and munitions; such wars make relatively little difference to the domestic life of a belligerent.

It is possible that the rules which would maximize expectable utility might vary from one type of war to another. I shall ignore this possibility for the most part, and merely note that practical difficulties are involved in equipping military handbooks with different sets of rules and establishing judicial bodies to identify the proper classification of a given war. I shall take the position of Britain in World War II as typical of that of a belligerent in a serious war.

The position of a nation in a serious war is such, then, that it considers overpowering the enemy to be absolutely vital to its interests (and possibly to those of civilized society generally)—so vital, indeed, that it is willing to risk its very existence to that end. It is doubtful that both sides can be well justified in such an appraisal of the state of affairs. But we may assume that in fact they do make this appraisal. In this situation, we must simply take as a fact that neither side will consent to or follow rules of war which seriously impair the possibility of bringing the war to a victorious conclusion. This fact accounts for the restriction within which I suggested a choice of the rules of war must take place. We may notice that the recognized rules of war do observe this limitation: they are framed in such a way as not to place any serious obstacle in the way of a nation's using any available force, if necessary, to destroy the ability of another to resist. As Oppenheim has observed, one of the assumptions underlying the recognized rules of war is that "a belligerent is justified in applying any amount and any kind of force which is necessary for . . . the overpowering of the opponent."[4] This limitation, however, leaves a good deal of room for rules of war which will maximize expectable long-range utility for all parties.

This restriction, incidentally, itself manifests utilitarian considerations, for a nation is limited to the use of means *necessary* to overcome an opponent. Clearly it is contrary to the general utility that any

---

[4] *International Law*, p. 226.

amount or manner of force be employed when it is *not* necessary for victory.

It will be convenient to divide the rules restricting military operation, especially the targets and weapons of attack, into three types. (I do not claim that these are exhaustive.)

1. *Humanitarian restrictions of no cost to military operation.* There are some things that troops may be tempted to do which are at best of negligible utility to their nation but which cause serious loss to enemy civilians, although not affecting the enemy's power to win the war. Such behavior will naturally be forbidden by rules designed to maximize expectable utility within the understood restriction. Consider, for example, rules against the murder or ill-treatment of prisoners of war. A rule forbidding wanton murder of prisoners hardly needs discussion. Such murder does not advance the war effort of the captors; indeed, news of its occurrence only stiffens resistance and invites retaliation. Moreover, there is an advantage in returning troops having been encouraged to respect the lives of others. A strict prohibition of wanton murder of prisoners therefore has the clear support of utilitarian considerations. Much the same may be said for a rule forbidding ill-treatment of prisoners. There can, of course, be disagreement about what constitutes ill-treatment—for instance, whether a prisoner is entitled to a diet of the quality to which he is accustomed if it is more expensive than that available to troops of the captor army. It is clear, however, that in a war between affluent nations prisoners can generally be well-housed and well-fed and receive adequate medical care without cost to the war effort of the captors. And if they receive such treatment, of course the captives gain. Thus a policy of good treatment of prisoners may be expected to make many nationals of both sides better off, and at a cost which in no way impairs the ability of either to wage the war.

Again, much the same may be said of the treatment of civilians and of civilian property in occupied territories. There is no military advantage, at least for an affluent nation, in the plunder of private or public property. And the rape of women or the ill-treatment of populations of occupied countries serves no military purpose. On the contrary, such behavior arouses hatred and resentment and constitutes a military liability. So utility is maximized, within our indicated basic limitations, by a strict rule calling for good treatment of the civilian population of an occupied territory. And the same can be said more generally for the condemnation of the wanton destruction of cities, towns, or villages, or devastation not justified by military necessity, set forth in the Charter of the Nuremberg Tribunal.

Obviously these rules, which the maximization of expectable utility calls for, are rules that command our intuitive assent.

2. *Humanitarian restrictions possibly costly to military victory*. Let us turn now to rules pertaining to actions in somewhat more complex situations. There are some actions which fall into neither of the classes so far discussed. They are not actions which must be permitted because they are judged necessary or sufficient for victory, and hence actions on which no party to a major war would accept restrictions. Nor are they actions which morally justified rules of war definitely prohibit, as being actions which cause injury to enemy nationals but serve no military purpose. It is this large class of actions neither clearly permitted nor definitely prohibited, for reasons already discussed, that I wish now to consider. I want to ask which rules of war are morally justified, because utility-maximizing, for actions of this kind. In what follows I shall be distinguishing several kinds of action and suggesting appropriate rules for them. The first type is this: doing something which will result in widespread destruction of civilian life and property and at the same time will add (possibly by that very destruction) to the *probability* of victory but will not definitely decide the war. Some uses of atomic weapons, and area bombing of the kind practiced at Hamburg, illustrate this sort of case.

A proper (not ideally precise) rule for such operations might be: substantial destruction of lives and property of enemy civilians is permissible only when there is good evidence that it will significantly enhance the prospect of victory. Application of the terms "good evidence" and "significantly enhance" requires judgment, but the rule could be a useful guideline all the same. For instance, we now know that the destruction of Hamburg did not significantly enhance the prospect of victory; in fact, it worked in the wrong direction, since it both outraged the population and freed workers formerly in non-war-supporting industries to be moved into industry directly contributing to the German war effort. The generals surely did not have good evidence that this bombing would significantly enhance the prospect of victory.

This rule is one which parties to a war might be expected to accept in advance, since following it could be expected to minimize the human cost of war on both sides, and since it does not involve a significant compromise of the goal of victory. The proposed rule, incidentally, has some similarities to the accepted rule cited above from the U.S. Army Manual, that "loss of life and damage to property must not be out of proportion to the military advantage to be gained."

This rule, which I am suggesting only for wars like World War II, where the stakes are very high, may become clearer if seen in the perspective of a more general rule that would also be suitable for wars in which the stakes are much lower. I pointed out above that what is at stake in a war may be no more than a tiny strip of land or national prestige. (The utility of these, may, however, be considered very great by a nation.) Now, it is clear that a risk of defeat which may properly be taken when the stakes are small may not be a proper risk when the stakes are virtually infinite; and a risk that could not properly be run when the stakes are enormous might quite properly be run when the stakes are small. So if the above-suggested rule is plausible for serious wars, in which the stakes are great, a somewhat different rule will be plausible in the case of wars of lesser importance—one that will require more in the way of "good evidence" and will require that the actions more "significantly enhance" the prospect of victory than is necessary when the stakes are much higher. These thoughts suggest the following general principle, applicable to all types of war: a military action (e.g., a bombing raid) is permissible only if the utility (broadly conceived, so that the maintenance of treaty obligations of international law could count as a utility) of victory to all concerned, multiplied by the increase in its probability if the action is executed, on the evidence (when the evidence is reasonably solid, considering the stakes), is greater than the possible disutility of the action to both sides multiplied by its probability. The rule for serious wars suggested above could then be regarded as a special case, one in which the utility of victory is virtually set at infinity—so that the only question is whether there is reasonably solid evidence that the action will increase the probability of victory. The more general rule obviously involves difficult judgments; there is a question, therefore, as to how it could be applied. It is conceivable that tough-minded civilian review boards would be beneficial, but we can hardly expect very reliable judgments even from them.[5]

These rules are at least very different from a blanket permission for anything the military thinks might conceivably improve the chances of victory, irrespective of any human cost to the enemy. In practice, it must be expected that each party to a war is likely to estimate the

---

[5] If we assume that both sides in a major struggle somehow manage to be persuaded that their cause is just, we shall have to expect that each will assign a net positive utility to its being the victor. For this reason it makes very little difference whether the more general principle uses the concept of the utility of victory by one side for everyone concerned, or the utility of that side only.

One might propose that the general restriction on rules of war, to the effect that in a serious war the use of any force necessary or sufficient for victory must be permitted, might be derived from the above principle if the utility of victory is set virtually at infinity and the probability of a certain action affecting the outcome is set near one. I believe this is correct, if we assume, as just suggested, that each side in a serious war will set a very high positive utility on *its* being the victor, despite the fact that both sides cannot possibly be correct in such an assessment. The reason for this principle as stated in the text, however, seems to me more realistic and simple. There is no reason, as far as I can see, why *both* lines of reasoning may not be used in support of the claim that the principle (or restriction) in question is a part of a morally justifiable system of rules of war.

stakes of victory quite high, so that the rule which has the best chance of being respected is probably the first one mentioned, and not any modification of it that would be suggested to an impartial observer by the second, more general principle.

The reader may have been struck by the fact that these suggested rules are essentially institutionalized applications of a kind of act-utilitarian principle for certain contexts. This may seem inconsistent with the notion of a system of absolute rules themselves justified by long-range utilitarian considerations. But there is nothing inconsistent in the suggestion that some of the "absolute" rules should require that in certain situations an action be undertaken if and only if it will maximize expectable utility.

It may be objected that the rules suggested are far too imprecise to be of practical utility. To this I would reply that there is no reason why judgment may not be required in staff decisions about major operations. Furthermore, the U.S. Army Manual already contains several rules the application of which requires judgment. For example:

> Absolute good faith with the enemy must be observed as a rule of conduct. . . . In general, a belligerent may resort to those measures for mystifying or misleading the enemy against which the enemy ought to take measures to protect himself.
>
> The measure of permissible devastation is found in the strict necessities of war. Devastation as an end in itself or as a separate measure of war is not sanctioned by the law of war. There must be some reasonably close connection between the destruction of property and the overcoming of the enemy's army. . . .
>
> The punishment imposed for a violation of the law of war must be proportionate to the gravity of the offense. The death penalty may be imposed for grave breaches of the law. . . . Punishments should be deterrent. . . . (pp. 22, 23–24, 182)

It has sometimes been argued, for instance by Winston Churchill, that obliteration bombing is justified as retaliation. It has been said that since the Germans destroyed Amsterdam and Coventry, the British had a right to destroy Hamburg. And it is true that the Hague Conventions are sometimes regarded as a contract, breach of which by one side releases the other from its obligations. It is also true that a government which has itself ordered obliteration bombing is hardly in a position to complain if the same tactic is employed by the enemy. But maximizing utility permits obliteration bombing only as a measure of deterrence or deterrent reprisal. This rule, incidentally, is recognized by the Army Manual as a principle governing all reprisals: "Reprisals are acts of retaliation . . . for the purpose of enforcing future compliance with the recognized rules of civilized warfare. . . . Other means of securing compliance with the law of war should normally be exhausted before resort is had to reprisals. . . . Even when appeal to the enemy for redress has failed, it may be a matter of policy to consider, before resorting to reprisals, whether the opposing forces are not more likely to be influenced by a steady adherence to the law of war on the part of the adversary" (p. 177). Purposes of retaliation, then, do not permit bombing in contravention of the suggested general principles.

Special notice should be taken that widespread civilian bombing might be defended by arguing that a significant deterioration in civilian morale could bring an end to a war by producing internal revolution. Our principle does not exclude the possibility of such reasoning, in the presence of serious evidence about civilian morale, when the stakes of victory are high. But we know enough about how bombing affects civilian morale to know that such bombing could be justified only rarely, if at all. The U.S. Army seems to go further than this; its rule asserts that any attack on civilians "for the sole purpose of terrorizing the civilian population is also forbidden."[6] It may be, however, that in actual practice this rule is interpreted in such a way that it is identical with the less stringent rule which is as much as utilitarian considerations can justify; if not, I fear we have to say that at this point the Army's theory has gone somewhat too far.

3. *Acceptance of military losses for humanitarian reasons.* Let us now turn to some rules which have to do with what we might call the *economics* of warfare, when the ultimate outcome is not involved, either because the outcome is already clear or because the action is fairly local and its outcome will not have significant repercussions. What damage may one inflict on the enemy in order to cut one's own losses? For instance, may one destroy a city in order to relieve a besieged platoon, or in order to avoid prolonging a war with consequent casualties? (The use of atom bombs in Japan may be an instance of this type of situation.) It is convenient to deal with two types of cases separately.

First, when may one inflict large losses on the enemy in order to avoid smaller losses for oneself, given that the issue of the war is not in doubt? A complicating fact is that when the issue is no longer in doubt it would seem that the enemy ought to concede, thereby avoiding losses to both sides. Why fight on when victory is impossible? (Perhaps to get better terms of peace.) But suppose the prospective loser is recalcitrant. May the prospective victor then unleash any horrors whatever in order to terminate the war quickly or reduce his losses? It is clear that the superior power should show utmost patience and not make the terms of peace so severe as to encourage further resistance.

[6] Whiteman, *Digest of International Law*, X, 135.

On the other hand, long-range utility is not served if the rules of war are framed in such a way as to provide an umbrella for the indefinite continuation of a struggle by an inferior power. So it must be possible to inflict losses heavy enough to produce capitulation but not so heavy as to be out of proportion to the estimated cost of further struggle to both sides. This condition is especially important in view of the fact that in practice there will almost always be other pressures that can be brought to bear. The application of such a rule requires difficult judgments, but some such rule appears called for by long-range utilitarian considerations.

The second question is: Should there be restrictions on the treatment of an enemy in the case of local actions which could hardly affect the outcome of the war, when these may cause significant losses? Rules of this sort are in fact already in force. For instance, as mentioned above, the Army Manual forbids killing of prisoners when their presence retards one's movements, reduces the number of men available for combat, uses up the food supply, and in general is inimical to the integrity of one's troops. Again, the Second Hague Convention forbids forcing civilians in occupied territory to give information about the enemy, and it forbids reprisals against the general civilian population "on account of the acts of individuals for which they cannot be regarded as jointly and severally responsible."[7] The taking of hostages is prohibited (Army Manual, p. 107).

All these rules prescribe that a belligerent be prepared to accept certain military disadvantages for the sake of the lives and welfare of civilians and prisoners. The disadvantages in question are not, however, losses that could be so serious as to affect the outcome of a war. Furthermore, the military gains and losses are ones which are likely to be evenly distributed, so that neither side stands to gain a long-term advantage if the rules are observed by both. So, without affecting the outcome of the war and without giving either side an unfair advantage, a considerable benefit can come to both belligerents in the form of the welfare of their imprisoned and occupied populations. Thus the long-run advantage of both parties is most probably served if they accept forms of self-restraint which can work out to be costly in occasional instances. Such rules will naturally be accepted by rational, impartial people in view of their long-range benefits.

IV. Rules of War and Morality

I have been arguing that there is a set of rules governing the conduct of warfare which rational, impartial persons who believed that their

---

[7] Article L.

country might from time to time be engaged in a war would prefer to any alternative sets of rules and to the absence of rules. I have also suggested, although without argument, that it is proper to say of such a set of rules that it is morally justified (and of course I think that such a set ought to be formally recognized and given authoritative status). There is thus a fairly close parallel with the prohibitions (and justifications and recognized excuses) of the criminal law: certain of these would be preferred to alternative sets and to an absence of legal prohibitions by rational, impartial persons; the prohibitions that would be so preferred may (I think) be said to be morally justified; and such rules ought to be adopted as the law of the land. I do not say the parallel is exact.

It may be suggested that there will be a considerable discrepancy between what is permitted by such "morally justifiable" rules of war and what it is morally permissible for a person to do in time of war. (Nagel mentions dropping the bomb on Hiroshima, attacks on trucks bringing up food, and the use of flamethrowers in any situation whatever as examples of actions not morally permissible; but it is not clear that he would say these would be permitted by morally justifiable rules of war, or even that he recognizes a distinction between what is morally permissible and what is permitted by morally justifiable rules of war.) Moreover, it might be thought that such "morally justifiable" rules of war could not be derived from justified moral principles. It might be asked, too, what the moral standing of these "morally justified" rules of war is, in view of the fact that the rules of war actually accepted and in force may, at least in some particulars, be rather different. These are difficult questions, about which I wish to say something.

It is obvious that there may well be discrepancies between what a person morally may do in wartime and what is permitted by morally justified rules of war, just as there are discrepancies between what is morally permitted and what is permitted by morally justifiable rules of the criminal law. For one thing, the rules of war, like the criminal law, must be formulated in such a way that it is decidable whether a person has violated them; it must be possible to produce evidence that determines the question and removes it from the realm of speculation. More important, just as there are subtle interpersonal relations—such as justice and self-restraint in a family—which it is undesirable for the criminal law to attempt to regulate but which may be matters of obligation, so there may well be moral obligations controlling relations between members of belligerent armies which the rules of war cannot reach. For instance, one might be morally obligated to go to some trouble or even take a certain risk in order to give aid to a wounded enemy, but the rules of war could hardly prescribe doing so. I am unable to think of a case in which moral principles require a person to do what is forbidden by morally justifiable rules of war; I suppose this is possible. But it is easy to think of cases in which moral principles forbid a person to injure an enemy, or require him to aid an enemy, when morally justifiable rules of war do not prescribe accordingly and when the military law even forbids the morally required behavior. (Consider, for instance, the fact that, according to the Manual, the U.S. Army permits severe punishment for anyone who "without proper authority, knowingly harbors or protects or gives intelligence to, or communicates or corresponds with or holds any intercourse with the enemy, either directly or indirectly . . ." [p. 33].)

The possible contrast between morally justifiable rules of war and what is morally permitted will seem quite clear to persons with firm moral intuitions. It may be helpful, however, to draw the contrast by indicating what it would be, at least for one kind of rule-utilitarian theory of moral principles. A rule-utilitarian theory of morality might say that what is morally permissible is any action that would not be forbidden by the kind of conscience which would maximize long-range expectable utility were it built into people as an internal regulator of their relations with other sentient beings, as contrasted with other kinds of conscience or not having a conscience at all. Then justifiable rules of war (with the standing described above) would be one thing; what is morally permissible, in view of ideal rules of conscience, might be another. Rational, impartial persons, understanding that their country may be involved in a war, might want one set of rules as rules of war, whereas rational, impartial persons choosing among types of conscience might want a different and discrepant set of rules as rules of conscience. In the same way there may be a discrepancy between a morally justified system of criminal law and morally justified rules of conscience. And just as, consequently, there may occasionally be a situation in which it is one's moral duty to violate the criminal law, so there may occasionally be a situation in which it is one's moral duty to violate morally justifiable rules of war.

It might be asked whether a person who subscribed to sound moral principles would, if given the choice, opt for a system of rules of war; and if so, whether he would opt for a set that would maximize expectable utility for the situation of nations at war. I suggest that he would do so; that such a person would realize that international law, like the criminal law, has its place in human society, that not all decisions can simply be left to the moral intuitions of the agent, and that the rules of war and military justice are bound to be somewhat crude. He would opt for that type of system which will do the most good, given that nations will sometimes go to war. I am, however, only *suggesting* that he would; in order to show that he would one would have to identify the sound moral principles which would be relevant to such a decision.

Another question that might be raised is whether a person should follow the actual military rules of his country or the morally justifiable ones (in the sense explained above). This question can obviously be taken in either of two ways. If the question is which rules are legally binding, of course the actual rules of war recognized at present are legally binding on him. But the question might be: Is a person morally bound to follow the "ideal" rules of war, as compared with the actual ones (or the legal orders of his officer), if they come into conflict? Here two possible situations must be distinguished. It is logically possible that a morally justifiable set of rules of war would permit damage to the enemy more severe than would the actual rules of war; in that case, assuming the actual rules of war have the status of an obligation fixed by a treaty, the moral obligation would seem to be to follow the provisions of the treaty (subject to the usual difficulties about older treaties not contemplating contemporary situations). Suppose, however, that a superior officer commands one to do something that is permitted by the actual rules of war (that is, not explicitly forbidden) but which clearly would be forbidden by morally justifiable rules of war. The question is then whether a moral person would refuse to do what is permitted by an unjust institution but would be forbidden by a just one. It would have to be argued in detail that sound moral principles would not permit a person to do what would be permitted only by an unjust institution. I shall not attempt to argue the matter, but only suggest that sound moral principles would *not* permit obedience to an order forbidden by morally justifiable rules of war. It is quite possible, incidentally, contrary to what I have just said about the legal issues, that a court-martial would not succeed in convicting a person who refused an order of this sort and defended his action along these lines.

There is space only to avert to the larger issue of the moral justification for nations being belligerents at all. Presumably, just as there are morally justified rules of war, in the sense of rules which rational, impartial persons would choose on the assumption their country might be involved in a war, so there are morally justified rules about engaging in a war at all, in the sense of rules governing the behavior of nations which rational, impartial persons would subscribe to if they believed that they would live in a world in which the chosen rules might obtain. Not only are there such morally justified rules regarding belligerency, but almost every nation is in fact signatory to a treaty abjuring war as an instrument of policy. Moreover, it has been declared criminal by the Treaty of London for a person to plan, prepare, initiate, or wage a war of aggression or a war in violation of international treaties, agreements, or assurances. So there is basis both in morally justified principles of international law and in actual international law for questioning the position of a belligerent. Presumably the relation between these and the moral obligations of citizens and government officials is complex, rather parallel to that just described for the case of rules of war.

XIX

Rules of War and Moral Reasoning

R. M. Hare

I have the same difficulty as Brandt* evidently had in believing that Nagel† is really wedded to the "absolutism" that he expounds in his article; but since it is a kind of position which undoubtedly has adherents, and indeed has superficial attractions, it is worthwhile trying to be clear what is wrong with it. For brevity, I shall be referring to the "absolutist" whose views are set out in Nagel's paper as "Nagel." But before I start doing this, some remarks about what I take to be the predicament of the real Nagel may be in place.

This real person seems to be torn between two ways of moral thinking which he dubs "utilitarian" and "absolutist." That is to say, he wants sometimes to use utilitarian arguments, with all their consideration of the consequences for good or ill of alternative courses of action; but sometimes he wants to override such considerations with an absolute ban, founded upon simple general rules, on certain kinds of actions. We must note that Brandt also wishes to operate both with simple general rules and with calculations about consequences; both the real Nagel and he, therefore, have on their hands the problem of reconciling the two ways of thinking (which might, it seems, come into conflict). My verdict will be that, whereas Brandt has a way of dealing with this problem, the real Nagel has conspicuously failed to provide one. That is why, although halfway through his paper, when flirting with the law of double effect, he claims it as a merit of that device that it avoids the problem that in certain cases "nothing one could do would be morally permissible," at the end of the paper he admits that his

* ["Utilitarianism and the Rules of War," *Philosophy and Public Affairs*, Vol. 1 (1971–72), pp. 146–165. See pp. 237ff. this volume.—Ed.]

† [See pp. 217ff. this volume.—Ed.]

own position has this same consequence. Absolutism, or an impure absolutism which tries to incorporate utilitarian elements without coherently relating them to its own absolutist structure, is bound to have this trouble.

It may help to clarify these obscure remarks if I start by summarizing five theories about the basis of moral thought which have been current recently, one of which I have advocated myself. I shall argue that *for practical purposes* there is no important difference between these theories as regards the method of moral thinking which they generate—that they are, if I may be allowed to use a deplorably vague expression, practically equivalent. If, as I think, the version which I have advocated can be shown to have a basis in the logic of the moral concepts themselves,[1] and if this basis needs the addition of no substantial *moral* assumptions, this will provide equally strong support for all the other versions, since they do not differ from it in any respect which would deprive them of this support. I hope to show that the conclusions which Brandt has reached could be that much more firmly based if they were to rest on this foundation.

I shall call the five positions: (1) the ideal observer theory; (2) the rational contractor theory; (3) specific rule-utilitarianism; (4) universalistic act-utilitarianism; (5) universal prescriptivism. My bald summaries of these positions will be far from representing accurately the views of any particular thinkers (even Brandt's and my own). (1), (2), and (3), as I shall summarize them, bear a certain relation (which is not one of identity) to theories which Brandt has advocated in the past, and (4) is, as I have argued elsewhere, and as Professor David Lyons has argued more rigorously, equivalent to (3). Mr. David Richards has expounded a theory of type (2), and he, in turn, is heavily influenced by Professor Rawls's views.[2] Many other writers both in the past and recently have put forward theories which approximate to one or another of these types. A clear display of their practical equivalence would therefore be of some significance for moral philosophy, and have practical moral implications far beyond the issue of war and massacre raised by Nagel.

The ideal observer theory (as I shall summarize it) holds that in considering what we ought to do, we have to conform our thought to what would be said by a person who had access to complete knowledge

---

[1] See my *Freedom and Reason* (Oxford, 1963), chaps. 6ff.

[2] R. B. Brandt, "The Definition of an 'Ideal Observer' Theory in Ethics," *Philosophy and Phenomenological Research* 15, no. 3 (1955): 407–413, and *Ethical Theory* (Englewood Cliffs, N.J., 1959); David Lyons, *Forms and Limits of Utilitarianism* (Oxford, 1965), chaps. 3–4; D.A.J. Richards, *A Theory of Reasons for Action* (Oxford, 1971); John Rawls, *A Theory of Justice* (Cambridge, Mass., 1971).

of all the facts, was absolutely clear in his thinking, was impartial between all the parties affected by the action, and yet equally benevolent to them all. That is to say, we are to think like a person who gives equal, and positive, weight to the interests of all the parties and to nothing else, and in serving these makes no factual or conceptual errors.

The rational contractor theory (in the version I shall discuss) holds that what we ought to do is to follow those principles which would be adopted by a set of rational people, each prudently considering his own interest, who were seeking agreement with each other on the principles which should govern their conduct in a society of which they were to be members; these rational contractors are presumed to have complete knowledge of all facts about the society and the environment in which they are to live, *except* the particular role which is to be played by each individual one of them.

It is easy to see that these two theories are practically equivalent. For, firstly, the requirement of knowledge of the facts is common to both theories. The ideal observer, it is true, has access to one sort of fact of which the rational contractors have to be ignorant—namely the role which each individual plays. But this will make no difference, because the ideal observer, being required to be impartial between individuals, can make no use of this extra piece of knowledge in his moral thinking. Secondly, we may presume that the rational contractors, being rational, will, like the ideal observer, make no conceptual errors. Thirdly, the requirement that the ideal observer be impartial between individuals is exactly matched by the requirement that the rational contractors be ignorant of the individual roles which they are to play. For to be impartial (in the sense in which I shall be using the term) is to take no account of individuals qua those individuals; and it makes no difference whether this is done because of a direct requirement that no account be taken, or because no account *can* be taken owing to ignorance of which individual is to play which role. And lastly, the requirement that the ideal observer be benevolent is matched by the requirement that the rational contractors be prudent. We have already seen that both will give equal weight to the interests of all parties; that this equal weight will be positive is guaranteed in the one case by express stipulation, and in the other by the requirement that the rational contractors be prudent, i.e., consider their own interests. This, in conjunction with equality of weight, entails impartial *benevolence*.

It might be objected that the rational contractor theory introduces the notion of *principles* to be followed, whereas the ideal observer theory does not. But it does by implication. If no account is to be taken of individual (as opposed to qualitative) differences, the ideal observer will have to make his moral judgments in the form of principles expressed in purely universal terms; any individual name that occurred in them would have to be excluded as an irrelevancy. We see here how the feature of moral judgments which position (5) makes explicit, namely universalizability, is implicitly, but essentially, a feature of (1) and (2). As we shall see in a moment, it is also a feature of (3) and (4), which we must consider next.

I mean by *specific* rule-utilitarianism a type of rule-utilitarianism whose rules (or principles, as I prefer to call them) are allowed to be of unlimited specificity provided that they do not cease to be universal.[3] It is thus the practical equivalent of (4), namely an act-utilitarianism which accepts the meta-ethical view that moral judgments are universalizable. Positions (3) and (4) are practically equivalent, because (4), in accepting universalizability, admits that moral judgments made (on a utilitarian basis) about individual acts commit their maker also to principles applying to all precisely similar acts; and this is tantamount to accepting *specific* rule-utilitarianism. I shall therefore not deal with (4) separately. (3) holds that we ought on any occasion to do that act which is required by the set of principles whose universal observance would best serve the interests of all. For reasons given by Lyons, it will be possible for an act-utilitarian to force such a rule-utilitarian, since his principles *can* be as specific as he pleases, to *make* them specific enough to suit the particularities of each individual case; thus, again, (3) collapses into (4), as well as vice versa.

It now looks plausible to say that (3) and (4) come for practical purposes to the same thing as (1) and (2). I think that this is so, although the problem of distributive justice, to be mentioned shortly, might make me qualify this claim. The similarities, in any case, are obvious. The requirements of factual knowledge and of conceptual clarity are there as before; for one cannot successfully undertake utilitarian calculations without both of these. This is not to say that it is no use *trying* to do them unless one is perfect in these respects; here, as in the case of the first two theories, we are told what moral thought would be if done correctly, and enjoined to aim at this (though, as we shall see, a big practical qualification is needed here). The requirement of impartiality has been a part of utilitarianism at least since Bentham's "Everybody to count as one and nobody as more than one"; and these varieties are no exception, since impartiality is guaranteed by the stipulation that the principles must be universal. They cannot even mention individuals. The requirement of benevolence is secured by the reference to serving the interests of all.

---

[3] For the distinction between generality (the opposite of specificity) and universality, see *Freedom and Reason*, pp. 38f., and my paper "Reasons of State" in my *Applications of Moral Philosophy* (London: Macmillan, 1972).

Coming now to the universal prescriptivist theory, we can see that it exhibits, in perhaps the clearest form of all, the essential features of the other four theories. It holds, on the basis of its analysis of the moral concepts, that when I am making up my mind what I ought to do, I am making up my mind what to prescribe for all cases exactly like this one in their universal properties. It should be evident that if this is what I am doing, I shall have to find out, first of all, just what I *am*, in effect, prescribing. This entails arming myself with the factual knowledge of what I should be bringing about if I acted upon one or another of the prescriptions between which I am deciding. It is part of this theory, too, that conceptual clarity is a necessary condition of rational moral thought.[4] Impartiality is guaranteed by the fact that my prescription has to apply to all cases resembling this one in their universal properties; since these will include cases (hypothetical or actual) in which I myself play the roles of each of the other parties affected, I am put by this theory in exactly the same position as the rational contractors. And benevolence is secured by the element of prescriptivity. Since I am prescribing actions which will affect the interests of myself and of others, and am bound to treat the interests of others as of equal weight to my own, we may presume that this weight will be at least positive. I shall not inquire here whether this last presumption could be defended a priori.

This is hardly the place to elaborate and defend the five theories that I have been trying to merge with one another. Nor shall I even ask what other theories might also be merged with them, though it is obviously tempting to suggest that by making God the ideal observer (as in effect Butler does) some varieties of theological ethics could be brought in. It is worth mentioning, however, that there are at least four difficulties which all five of these theories have to face, and that this lends some support to my proposed merger. Three of these difficulties I shall simply list; but I shall deal at greater length with the fourth, since it has a close bearing on the dispute between Brandt and Nagel.

The first difficulty is that presented by the problem of distributive justice. So far, we do not know what the ideal observer, or the rational contractors, or I when I am universally prescribing will do when we are faced with a choice between maximizing benefits and distributing them in other ways which, though reducing their total, might be thought preferable for other reasons (for example, on grounds of fairness). Various such ways have been suggested—e.g., equality, the Pareto principle, and the maximin principle. Mr. Richards has not convinced me that there is a unique answer to the question of what the

[4] See *Freedom and Reason*, esp. p. 185.

rational contractors would do when faced with such a choice (it might depend on how much gambling instinct they had); and the ideal observer is in the same trouble, as is the universal prescriber.[5]

It has been traditional among utilitarians to say that benefits should be maximized whatever their distribution; and this puts them at variance not only with common opinion, but with some exponents of the other kinds of theory—(1), (2), and (5)—that I have been summarizing. It might therefore be objected to my proposed merger that the five theories are not even practically equivalent, since (3) and (4)—the utilitarian theories—are committed to a particular answer to the question about distributive justice, whereas for the other theories the question at least remains open. My own tentative view is that it will not remain open once the implications of the three nonutilitarian theories have been fully understood, but that they too will be bound to accept the answer which requires maximization of benefits, though this answer will be qualified, and at the same time brought more into accord with received opinion, by the moves which I shall shortly make in discussing the fourth difficulty. I shall not try to defend this view here.

The second difficulty is that of justifying the enterprise of moral thought in the first place: What are we to say to the amoralist who just will not use the language whose logic requires him to reason in this way? The third difficulty is that presented by the fanatic who is prepared to prescribe universally that some particular ideal or goal of his should be realized at the expense of all other interests of himself and others. Both these difficulties affect all five theories—the second difficulty obviously, the third less obviously. But we can see that the third does affect the other four as much as it affects universal prescriptivism, if we consider that to have a fanatical ideal is to have an interest in its realization. If the fanatic's interest in the realization of his ideal is great enough to trouble the universal prescriptivist, it will be great enough to claim a preponderant weight in the calculations of all the other four theories. All five theories will have to be content to say that fanatics of such heroic stature are unlikely ever to be encountered.[6] But I shall not pursue this argument here.

The fourth difficulty, however, is one which must be dealt with at greater length, although an adequate treatment of it will have to wait for another occasion. All these theories, unless they take precautions, will appear to have consequences which run counter to the intuitions of the ordinary man. Nagel is the latest of many thinkers to try to take

---

[5] See *Freedom and Reason*, pp. 121f.

[6] See the end of my paper in *Jowett Papers*, 1968–1969, ed. B. Y. Khanbhai et al. (Oxford, 1970), pp. 44–52.

advantage of this apparent weakness in utilitarianism and related theories. It is easy for him to think up cases in which a utilitarian calculation would seem to justify actions contrary to principles which most of us, at least when we are not philosophizing, hold sacred. On careful inspection it will turn out that these cases are either fictitious or at least highly unusual, or else that the utilitarian calculations are very sketchily done, leaving out considerations which in practice would be most important. Nagel himself refers to "the abyss of utilitarian apologetics," and a utilitarian can readily admit that it is possible by a too superficial or facile application of utilitarian arguments to justify courses of action which a more thoroughgoing utilitarianism would condemn. But all the same, many have been put off utilitarianism by this move, which takes a good deal of methodological sophistication to counter.

Brandt, with his "two-level" approach, has given a clear indication of the way in which a utilitarian can defend himself against this attack. I wish, however, to set this defense within a more general framework of ethical theory, without claiming that Brandt would agree with all that I say. The "sacred principles" of the ordinary man, and the rules of war which are a crude attempt to apply them to a particular practical sphere, have an established place in any complete utilitarian theory; unfortunately utilitarians have not sufficiently emphasized this, and therefore "absolutists" have some excuse for ignoring it. Confusion has resulted on both sides from a failure to make clear what this established place is. The best *name* for it is that chosen by the deontologist Ross: "prima facie." Indeed, it would have been better for Nagel to use, to describe the view which he expounds, the old name "deontologist," instead of adopting the term "absolutist," which invites confusion with the kind of absolutist who is the opponent of relativism (whatever that may be). I trust that Nagel does not think that his utilitarian opponents are relativists. But although "prima facie" is a good name for these principles, it does not do much to explain their nature.

The defect in most deontological theories (and this would seem to apply to Ross, Anscombe, and Nagel) is that they have no coherent rational account to give of any level of moral thought above that of the man who knows some good simple moral principles and sticks to them. He is a very admirable person; and to question his principles (at any rate in situations of stress and temptation) is indeed to "show a corrupt mind."[7] But if philosophers do no more thinking than he is capable of, they will be able to give no account, either of how we are to come by these admirable principles, or of what we are to do when they conflict.

---

[7] This phrase is used in a slightly different context by Professor G.E.M. Anscombe, "Modern Moral Philosophy," *Philosophy* 33, no. 124 (1958): 17 (reprinted in *The Is/Ought Question*, ed. W. D. Hudson [New York, 1970], p. 192).

To achieve such an account, we have to adopt a "two-level" approach.[8] We have, that is to say, to recognize that the simple principles of the deontologist, important as they are, have their place at the level of character-formation (moral education and self-education). They are what we should be trying to inculcate into ourselves and our children if we want to stand the best chance, amid the stresses and temptations of the moral life, of doing what is for the best. Moore (who was a utilitarian) perhaps exaggerates when he says that we should *never* break principles which we know to be in general sound;[9] but a utilitarian who takes his utilitarianism seriously is likely to recommend that we form in ourselves, and continue in all our actions to foster, a firm disposition to abide by the principles whose general inculcation will have, all in all, the best consequences.

The inculcation of these general principles has always been a prime concern of churches and other moral "authorities"; but in the present context it is more relevant to point out that this is equally true of armies. In the case of the typical military virtues this is obvious. Courage in attack and stubbornness in defense are strenuously cultivated; and the duty to obey orders and not to run away in battle is the center of all military training. These are not moral duties in the narrow sense (though their cultivation is instrumental to the performance of our moral duty when we are fighting in just wars, if any). If armies were to say to soldiers when training them, "On the battlefield, always do what is most conducive to the general good of mankind," or even "of your countrymen," nearly all the soldiers would easily convince themselves (battles being what they are) that the course most conducive to these desirable ends was headlong flight. Instead they say, "Leave those calculations to your superiors; they are probably in some bunker somewhere out of immediate personal danger, and therefore can consider more rationally and dispassionately, and with better information than you have, the question of whether to withdraw. Your job is to get on with the fighting." Only in this way can wars be won; and *if* the wars are just, the training was for the best. It is beyond the scope of this paper to discuss whether there are any just wars; I am inclined to think that there have been such in the past, though whether there could be just wars under modern conditions (except perhaps minor ones) is a hard question into which I shall not enter.[10]

The same is true of the more narrowly moral virtues. Let us assume for the sake of argument that it is for the greatest good that marital fidelity should be generally practiced. I could produce good arguments, concerned especially with the welfare of children, to show that this is

---

[8] See *Freedom and Reason*, pp. 42–44.

[9] *Principia Ethica* (Cambridge, Eng., 1903), pp. 162ff.

[10] See my lecture "Peace," in *Applications of Moral Philosophy*.

so; but this is not the place for them. To say this is consistent with admitting that there may be cases in which adultery would be for the greatest good—for I said "generally" and not "universally." But fidelity will not be even generally practiced if people who are contemplating adultery ask themselves on each occasion whether their own might not be one of these cases; they will persuade themselves all too often that it is, when it is not. It is for the greatest good that statesmen should in general not tell lies in their public utterances—we have recently had an example of the troubles that ensue when they do, and Suez was another. It is true, admittedly, that situations can arise (say, when a currency is in trouble) in which it is quite obvious to a statesman that he ought to tell a lie; and this sort of thing can happen in private life too (which is why the ordinary man does not, for the most part, accept the duty of truthtelling as one without exceptions). But if statesmen and other men too do not cultivate the firm disposition to tell the truth and to hate lying, they will, both in this failure itself and in their particular acts, be most probably not acting for the best.

For the same reasons, as Brandt has indicated, military training should (and in all civilized armies does) include instruction in the laws and usages of war; and this training should be backed up by legal enforcement where possible. It looks as if the failure adequately to do this, and not any particular massacres and atrocities, ought to be the main target of critics of the United States Army in the present war* (though it must be said in fairness that wars against guerrillas present peculiarly difficult problems). Even when armies are fighting wars which can be morally justified (if any), the individual soldier ought to be enabled to have as clear an idea of what he can legitimately do to the enemy as he has of when he can legitimately turn his back on the enemy. Neither kind of instruction is easy, but both are possible.

The crucial question remains of what principles are to be the basis of this training. Brandt has sketched in a most illuminating way the kind of method by which this can be rationally determined; it amounts to an application of the five methods of moral reasoning which I was trying to merge at the beginning of this paper. He has also reached some provisional conclusions by this method; with these in the main I agree, though much more discussion is obviously needed.

A stumbling block to the understanding of the method may possibly be removed if I point out that there are in play here, in different parts of the reasoning, two quite distinct things which might both be called rule-utilitarianism. The failure to distinguish between them, and to see that they are quite compatible with each other provided that their spheres are kept separate, has caused havoc in this part of moral

* [Reference is to the Vietnam War.—Ed.]

philosophy. There is first of all what may be called *general* rule-utilitarianism. This is the doctrine, supported in the last section, which says that we ought to inculcate and foster in ourselves and others, and in our actions cleave to, general principles whose cultivation is for the greatest good. In terms of a distinction which has been used in discussions of this subject, the utility appealed to by general rule-utilitarianism is an *acceptance*-utility—i.e., the utility of the general acceptance of certain principles, even if it falls short of universal observance. Such an insistence on having good general, fairly simple, teachable principles is essential to any view which takes the task of moral education (including self-education) seriously.

Secondly, there is what I have called *specific* rule-utilitarianism, one of the five mergeable theories which I listed at the beginning. This provides a kind of microscope wherewith we can, when we are in doubt about the general principles, examine particular cases in as minute specificity as we require, though always ending up with universal judgments, however specific. When using specific rule-utilitarianism we judge the morality of a particular act by assessing the utility of universal *observance* of the highly specific principle which requires acts of just this sort in just this sort of circumstances. By thus assessing particular acts in terms of the *observance*-utility of the highly specific universal principles enjoining them, we can assess the *acceptance*-utility of the general principles to be used in moral education. Once general principles are questioned, they can only be examined thus in the light of the particular results of their general adoption (of whether the policy of inculcating these principles is conducive *in general* to actions which can be thus minutely justified). Specific rule-utilitarianism thus has its place in higher-level discussions as to what the "good general principles" ought to be, and what should be done in cases where they conflict, or where there is a strong indication that the situation is so peculiar that the application of the general principle is unlikely to be for the best.

How are we to decide which cases these are? This is a matter for practical judgment rather than for theoretical reasoning (for the question is "Ought we to reason theoretically? Have we time? Are we likely to indulge in special pleading if we do?"). It might be objected to what I have said that although I have in theory allotted separate spheres to these two kinds of utilitarian reasoning, so that in principle they do not conflict, I have failed to say how we are to determine into which sphere any particular piece of reasoning is to fall. But the objection is not a real one. When faced with a choice between sticking to one of the simple general principles we have learnt and engaging in more specific reasoning, we have to ask ourselves which procedure is likely to approximate to the result which would be achieved by a reasoner not hampered by our human frailties. On the one side, there is the danger that a too rigid adherence to the standard general principles will lead us to disregard special features of the situation which ought to make a difference to our appraisal of it. On the other side, there is the danger that, if we once allow ourselves to question the general principle, our lack of knowledge and our partiality to our own interests may distort our reasoning. Which of these dangers is likely to be greater in a particular case for a particular person is not a philosophical question, and it is therefore no objection to a philosophical position that it does not answer it. My own inclination, in the light of my assessment of my own limitations, is to think that the occasions on which I should be safe in departing from my firm general principles (which are not of *extreme* generality) are very rare.

It is worth pointing out that when, by the employment of specific rule-utilitarianism at the higher level, we are seeking to select the best general principles for our general rule-utilitarianism of the lower level, we ought to consider those cases which are likely to occur. The use of hypothetical examples in philosophy, even fanciful ones, is perfectly legitimate; but in this particular field it can lead us astray. For we are seeking to discover principles which will be the most reliable in cases which are likely to preponderate in our actual experience; it would be out of place, therefore, to base our selection of the principles on a consideration of fanciful cases.

My aim has been to convince the reader that a sound theoretical foundation can in principle be provided for moral thinking about war, and that this foundation is available to Brandt and to those who seek to put his conclusions into practice. They are much more likely on this basis than on an "absolutist" one to secure an improvement in our present customs, either by new international conventions or simply by the preservation and spread of right attitudes in soldiers and their commanders and governments. A great deal has been achieved in the past along these lines (do Nagel and those who write like him about the present war ever read what the wars of earlier centuries were like?). Although the invention of new weapons brings with it new temptations, which are often succumbed to, especially by those who have a temporary monopoly of these weapons, it is not impossible to bring their use under control, provided that their potential users are willing to adopt rational procedures in discussing the matter with one another. This is asking a lot; but the history of such negotiations is not exclusively a history of failure. In World War II poison gas was not, after all, used, though many expected that it would be. In both the world wars the Red Cross was for the most part respected. Without some background of written or unwritten international convention, neither of these restraints might have been exercised; and the conventions owed more to rational thought than to emotion, even if the reasoning had more of prudence in it than of morality.

Against these modest gains, I do not think that Nagel has much to offer. He is trying to justify the very same kind of rules as Brandt has, in my view, succeeded in justifying. But whereas Brandt is able to fit these rules into a rational system which also provides means for their selection and justification, Nagel, who is confined to one level of moral thinking, predictably finds himself torn between utilitarian arguments and absolutist ones, and thinks that in difficult cases he may be in "a moral blind alley," in which "there is no honorable or moral course for a man to take, no course free of guilt and responsibility for evil." It is dangerous to talk like this, because many people will think that, if there is no way of escaping guilt, only the neurotic will worry about it.

Is "guilt," in any case, the most appropriate concept in terms of which to discuss these problems? A man with good moral principles will be very likely to *feel* guilty whatever he does in cases such as Nagel is speaking of. If he did not, he would not be such a good man. For a person, on the other hand, who is mainly concerned to avoid feelings of guilt, the best advice is to grow a thick skin. If he finds this impossible, a *pis aller* would be to get himself a set of not too exacting principles of an absolutist sort, and think that he has done all that is required of him if he has not broken any of them—no matter how disastrous the consequences of his actions for other people. Though Nagel is perfectly right in saying that it is incoherent to suggest that one might "sacrifice one's moral integrity justifiably, in the service of a sufficiently worthy end," it is not incoherent to suggest that one might so sacrifice one's peace of mind. And moral integrity and peace of mind are easily confused if one equates having sinned with having a sense of having sinned. If, say, we are theists and can convince ourselves that God has laid down some relatively simple rules and that by observing these we can keep ourselves unspotted and safe from hellfire, this may seem a good way of avoiding the agony of mind which comes, in difficult cases, from calculation of the consequences of alternative actions. This may explain the undoubted attractions of absolutism.

The real Nagel, to his credit, avoids this kind of pharisaism; for he remains enough of a utilitarian to see that the implications of consistent absolutism are unacceptable. That is how he gets into his "moral blind alley"; but there is an obvious way out of it: to treat the general principles of the absolutist as indispensable practical guides, but not as epistemologically sacrosanct, and to admit a level of thought at which they can be criticized, justified, or even on occasion rejected in their particular applications when conflicts arise or when a case is sufficiently out of the ordinary to call for special consideration.

But even if there were not this defect in Nagel's absolutism—that of trying to give his principles a higher status than they can have, and thus locking them in irresoluble conflict, on the same level, with the utilitarian principle in which he also believes—it would be defective for another reason: indeterminacy. He attempts to systematize and justify his intuitions by subsuming them under a more general principle: "whatever one does to another person intentionally must be aimed at him as a subject, with the intention that he receive it as a subject. It should manifest an attitude to *him* rather than just to the situation, and he should be able to recognize it and identify himself as its object." It is difficult to think that a principle as vague and obscure as this could be of much use in practical dilemmas. One would be likely to find rival parties justifying opposite courses of action on the basis of this same principle. We have grown accustomed to moral philosophers telling us that we can ascertain our duties to other people by appeal to an a priori principle that we ought to treat people as people.[11] But Nagel's is an unexpected use of the method, which displays how accommodating it can be. He has done nothing to show that one could not treat people as people just as well by hating them as by loving them. The simplest way, in dealing with the enemy and his friends and relations, of "manifesting an attitude to *them*," would be to learn to hate them. Then we can manifest this attitude by any barbarity that takes our fancy, in the assurance that we are not doing what Nagel's principle forbids. This would seem as good a way as any of avoiding being "bureaucratic," and of securing the "maintenance of a direct interpersonal response to the people one deals with."

In the days before wars became even as humane as they *sometimes* are now, this was an almost universal attitude. Anyone who reads the Bible, or Herodotus and Thucydides, can find massacres of *already defeated* peoples accepted as normal; and Priam in the *Iliad*, when he describes the horrors that await him at the "kill," when Troy is sacked, does not imply that the actions of the victors will be wicked—only unpleasant.[12]

I have probably got Nagel all wrong. Brandt interprets him more charitably; and maybe all he is saying is that moral judgments have to be universalizable. That is to say, we are to think of those affected by our actions, including the enemy, as people like ourselves, and do to them only what is permitted by a set of universal principles that we are prepared to see adopted for cases in which we are at the receiving end.[13] If this is what he is saying, his position is not so very different from my own. The difference is that I would include more people in

---

[11] See *Freedom and Reason*, pp. 211–213.

[12] *Iliad* 22. 60ff.

[13] See *Freedom and Reason*, esp. chap. 6.

the class of those whose sufferings are relevant to our moral decisions (for example, in the Hiroshima case, those that will die if the war is not ended quickly, as well as those actually killed by the bombing). I cannot find in Nagel's argument any justification for leaving the former class out; but if they are included, this version of the method he advocates will join the list of mergeable positions set out at the beginning of this paper. Only further clarification will reveal whether our views can be reconciled in this way.

Selected Bibliography

Anscombe, Elizabeth. "Modern Moral Philosophy." *Philosophy* 33 (1958), 1–19. Reprinted in Anscombe's *Ethics, Religion and Politics: Collected Philosophical Papers, Vol. III*. Minneapolis: University of Minnesota Press, 1981.

———. "Mr. Truman's Degree" (Oxford, 1957).

Bennett, Jonathan. "Morality and Consequences." In vol. 2 of *The Tanner Lectures*, edited by Sterling McMurrin, 47–115. Salt Lake City: University of Utah Press, 1981.

———. "Positive and Negative Relevance." *American Philosophical Quarterly* Vol. 20, No. 2 (April 1983), 185–94.

Boyle, Joseph M., Jr. "Double-Effect and a Certain Type of Embryotomy." *The Irish Theological Quarterly* 44 (1977), 303–18.

Curran, Charles, and Richard McCormick, eds. *Readings in Moral Theology*, No. 1. New York: Paulist Press, 1979.

Devine, Philip E. "Acting and Refraining/Intention and Foresight." *Dialogue* XXVI (1987), 87–94.

———. *The Ethics of Homicide*. Notre Dame, Ind.: University of Notre Dame Press, 1990.

Donagan, Alan. *The Theory of Morality*. Chicago: University of Chicago Press, 1977.

Duff, R. A. "Intentionally Killing the Innocent." *Analysis* 34 (1973), 16–19.

Finnis, John. *Fundamentals of Ethics*. Washington, D.C.: Georgetown University Press, 1983.

Fischer, John M. and Mark Ravizza, eds. *Moral Problems and Principles*. New York: Holt, Rinehart and Winston, 1992.

Fletcher, Joseph. *Situation Ethics: The New Morality*. Philadelphia, Pa.: Westminster Press, 1966.

Foot, Philippa. "Utilitarianism and the Virtues." *Mind* 94 (1985), 196–209. Reprinted in Samuel Scheffler, ed., *Consequentialism and Its Critics*. Oxford: Oxford University Press, 1988.

———. "Morality, Action and Outcome." In *Morality and Objectivity*, edited by Ted Hondreich, 23–38. London: Routledge and Kegan Paul, 1985.

Fried, Charles. *Right and Wrong*. Cambridge: Harvard University Press, 1978.

Garcia, J. L. A. "Love and Absolutes." In *Christian Philosophy*, edited by Thomas Flint. Notre Dame, Ind.: University of Notre Dame Press, 1990.

———. "Moral Absolutes." In *Encyclopedia of Ethics*.

Geach, Peter. *God and the Soul*. London: Routledge and Kegan Paul, 1969.

Gewirth, Alan. *Reason and Morality*. Chicago: University of Chicago Press, 1978.

Glover, Jonathan. "It Makes No Difference Whether or Not I Do It." *Proceedings of the Aristotelian Society* 49 (1975), 171–90.

———. *Causing Deaths and Saving Lives*. New York: Penguin, 1977.

Grisez, Germain, and Russell Shaw. *Beyond the New Morality: The Responsibilities of Freedom*. 3rd Edition. Notre Dame, Ind.: University of Notre Dame Press, 1988.

Haber, Joram Graf. "The Value of Human Life: An Absolutist Strategy for Attacking Consequentialism." In *Explorations of Value*, edited by Thomas Magnell. Rodopi Press: The Netherlands, forthcoming.

Hampshire, Stuart. *Morality and Pessimism*. Cambridge: Cambridge University Press, 1972.

Hoose, Bernard. *Proportionalism*. Washington, D.C.: Georgetown University Press, 1987.

Kagan, Shelly. *The Limits of Morality*. Oxford: Oxford University Press, 1989.

Kant, Immanuel. *Grounding of the Metaphysics of Morals*, translated by James Ellington. Indianapolis, Ind.: Hackett, 1981.

———. *On the Old Saw: That May Be Right in Theory but It Won't Work in Practice*, translated by E. B. Ashton. Philadelphia: University of Pennsylvania Press, 1974.

Kamm, Frances M. "The Doctrine of Double Effect: Reflections on Theoretical and Practical Issues." *The Journal of Medicine and Philosophy*, Vol. 16 (1991): 571–585.

Lee, Steven. "Omissions." *Southern Journal of Philosophy* 16 (1978), 339–54.

Levine, Susan. "Does the 'Counterfactual Test' Work for Distinguishing a Means from a Foreseen Concomitant?" *Journal of Value Inquiry* 18 (1984), 155–57.

McCormick, Richard, and Paul Ramsey, eds. *Doing Evil to Achieve Good*. Chicago: Loyola University Press, 1978.

Nagel, Thomas. *The View From Nowhere*. Oxford: Oxford University Press, 1986.

Neumann, Michael. "Side-Constraint Morality." *Canadian Journal of Philosophy* 12 (1982), 131–43.

Nielsen, Kai. *Ethics Without God*. Buffalo: Prometheus Books, 1990.

Nozick, Robert. *Anarchy, State, and Utopia*. New York: Basic Books, 1974.

Outka, Gene. "The Protestant Tradition and Exceptionless Moral Norms." In *Moral Theology Today*. Braintree, Mass.: The Pope John Center, 1984.

Pascal, Blaise. *The Provincial Letters*, translated by A. J. Krailsheimer. Baltimore: Penguin, 1967.

Quinn, Warren. "Actions, Intentions, and Consequences: The Doctrine of Doing and Allowing." *The Philosophical Review* Vol. XCVIII, No. 3 (July 1989), 287–312.

Russell, Bruce. "On the Relative Strictness of Negative and Positive Duties." *American Philosophical Quarterly* 14 (1977), 87–98.

Scheffler, Samuel. *The Rejection of Consequentialism*. Oxford: Oxford University Press, 1982.

———. "Agent-Centered Restrictions, Rationality, and the Virtues." *Mind* 94 (1985), 409–19.

———. *Consequentialism and Its Critics*. Oxford: Oxford University Press, 1988.

Shaw, William H. "Elementary Lifesaving." *Southern Journal of Philosophy* XVIII, No. 1 (Spring 1980), 87–97.

Taurek, John. "Should the Numbers Count?" *Philosophy and Public Affairs* 6, no. 4, 293–310 (Summer 1977). Reprinted in Joram Graf Haber, ed., *Doing and Being: Selected Readings in Moral Philosophy*. New York: Macmillan, 1993.

Thomson, Judith Jarvis. "Killing, Letting Die, and the Trolley Problem." *The Monist* 59 (1976): 204–17.

Williams, Bernard. *A Critique of Utilitarianism*. In *Utilitarianism: For and Against*, by J. J. C. Smart and Bernard Williams. Cambridge: Cambridge University Press, 1977.

———. *The Limits of Morality*.

Acknowledgments

I am grateful for the following permissions to use copyright material: (1) Immanuel Kant, "On a Supposed Right to Lie from Altruistic Motives," in *Critique of Practical Reason*, edited by Lewis White Beck (Chicago); © 1949 Lewis White Beck. (2) Germain Grisez and Russell Shaw, *Beyond the New Morality: The Responsibilities of Freedom*, 3rd ed., pp. 129–38; © 1980 University of Notre Dame Press. (3) Elizabeth Anscombe, "War and Murder," from Walter Stein (ed.), *Nuclear Weapons: A Catholic Response* (London and New York); © 1961 Elizabeth Anscombe. (4) Alan Donagan, *The Theory of Morality*, pp. 172–90, 192, 206–9; © 1977 The University of Chicago. (5) Peter Geach, *God and the Soul*; © 1969 Routledge and Kegan Paul. (6) Charles Fried, *Right and Wrong*, pp. 7–29, Cambridge, Mass.: Harvard University Press; Copyright © 1978 by the President and Fellows of Harvard College. (7) Bernard Williams, *Utilitarianism: For and Against*, pp. 82–104; © 1973 Cambridge University Press, reprinted with the permission of the author and Cambridge University Press. (8) R. G. Frey, "What a Good Man Can Bring Himself to Do," *Journal of Value Inquiry* 12 (1978):134–41; © 1978 Kluwer Academic Publishers. (9) Stuart Hampshire, *Morality and Pessimism*, pp. 11–31; © 1972 Cambridge University Press, reprinted with permission of the author and Cambridge University Press. (10) Alan Gewirth, "Are There Any Natural Rights?", *Philosophical Quarterly* 31 (1981): 1–16; © 1981 Blackwell Publishers. (11) Philippa Foot, "The Problem of Abortion and the Doctrine of the Double Effect," *Oxford Review*, No. 5, 1967; © 1967 Philippa Foot. (12) Elizabeth Anscombe's "Who is Wronged?", *Oxford Review* 5 (1967):16–17; © 1967 Elizabeth Anscombe. (13) Kai Nielsen, "Against Moral Conservatism," *Ethics* 82 (1972):219–31; © 1972 The University of Chicago. (14) Jonathan Bennett, "Whatever the Consequences," *Analysis* 26 (1965–66):82–102; © 1966 Jonathan Bennett. (15) Elizabeth Anscombe, "A Note on Mr. Bennett," *Analysis* 27 (1966); © 1966 Elizabeth Anscombe. (16) James

Rachels, "On Moral Absolutism," *Australasian Journal of Philosophy*, Vol. 48, No. 3 (Dec. 1970):338–53; © 1970 Australasian Journal of Philosophy. (17) Thomas Nagel, "War and Massacre," *Philosophy and Public Affairs*, 1 (1971–72):124–44; Copyright © 1972 Princeton University Press, reprinted by permission of Princeton University Press. (18) R. B. Brandt, "Utilitarianism and the Rules of War," *Philosophy and Public Affairs*, 1 (1971–72):145–65; Copyright © 1972 Princeton University Press, reprinted by permission of Princeton University Press. (19) R. M. Hare, "Rules of War and Moral Reasoning," *Philosophy and Public Affairs* 1 (1971–72):166–81; Copyright © Princeton University Press, reprinted by permission of Princeton University Press.

Index of Names

About the Editor

JORAM GRAF HABER is professor of philosophy at Bergen Community College. He is the author of *Forgiveness: A Philosophical Study* (Rowman & Littlefield, 1991) and editor of *Doing and Being: Selected Issues in Moral Philosophy* (Macmillan, 1993). He is also the co-editor, with Steven M. Cahn, of *Twentieth Century Ethical Theory* (Macmillan, 1995) and translator/editor, with Andrew Kelley, of Josef Popper-Lynkeus' *The Individual and the Value of Human Life* (Rowman & Littlefield, 1995). In addition, he is the author/editor of *Ethics in the 90s*, a text and video series to be published by Jones & Bartlett in 1996.

About the Contributors

G. E. M. ANSCOMBE is professor of philosophy at Cambridge University.

JONATHAN BENNETT is professor of philosophy at Syracuse University.

R. B. BRANDT is professor of philosophy at the University of Michigan.

ALAN DONAGAN was professor of philosophy at the California Institute of Technology.

PHILIPPA FOOT is Griffin professor emeritus of philosophy at the University of California, Los Angeles.

R. G. FREY is professor of philosophy at Bowling Green State University.

CHARLES FRIED is professor of law at Harvard Law School.

PETER GEACH is professor of logic at the University of Leeds.

ALAN GEWIRTH is professor of philosophy at the University of Chicago.

GERMAIN GRISEZ holds the Flynn Chair in Christian ethics at Mount Saint Mary's College, Emmitsburg.

STUART HAMPSHIRE is professor of philosophy at Stanford University.

R. M. HARE is graduate research professor of philosophy at the University of Florida.

IMMANUEL KANT (1724–1804) is a historically great philosopher who made major contributions to most of the central areas of philosophy.

THOMAS NAGEL is professor of philosophy at New York University.

KAI NIELSEN is professor of philosophy at the University of Calgary.

JAMES RACHELS is professor of philosophy at the University of Alabama at Birmingham.

RUSSELL SHAW is director of public information and publications for the Knights of Columbus.

BERNARD WILLIAMS is professor of philosophy at the University of California, Berkeley.